Venezia Kingi

The Children of Women in Prison

D1823325

Venezia Kingi

The Children of Women in Prison

The Effects of Imprisonment on Women and their Children

VDM Verlag Dr. Müller

Impressum/Imprint (nur für Deutschland/ only for Germany)

Bibliografische Information der Deutschen Nationalbibliothek: Die Deutsche Nationalbibliothek verzeichnet diese Publikation in der Deutschen Nationalbibliografie; detaillierte bibliografische Daten sind im Internet über http://dnb.d-nb.de abrufbar.

Alle in diesem Buch genannten Marken und Produktnamen unterliegen warenzeichen-, marken- oder patentrechtlichem Schutz bzw. sind Warenzeichen oder eingetragene Warenzeichen der jeweiligen Inhaber. Die Wiedergabe von Marken, Produktnamen, Gebrauchsnamen, Handelsnamen, Warenbezeichnungen u.s.w. in diesem Werk berechtigt auch ohne besondere Kennzeichnung nicht zu der Annahme, dass solche Namen im Sinne der Warenzeichen- und Markenschutzgesetzgebung als frei zu betrachten wären und daher von jedermann benutzt werden dürften.

Coverbild: www.ingimage.com

Verlag: VDM Verlag Dr. Müller GmbH & Co. KG
Dudweiler Landstr. 99, 66123 Saarbrücken, Deutschland
Telefon +49 681 9100-698, Telefax +49 681 9100-988
Email: info@vdm-verlag.de
Zugl.: Wellington, Victoria University of Wellington, Diss, 2000

Herstellung in Deutschland:
Schaltungsdienst Lange o.H.G., Berlin
Books on Demand GmbH, Norderstedt
Reha GmbH, Saarbrücken
Amazon Distribution GmbH, Leipzig
ISBN: 978-3-639-04742-4

Imprint (only for USA, GB)

Bibliographic information published by the Deutsche Nationalbibliothek: The Deutsche Nationalbibliothek lists this publication in the Deutsche Nationalbibliografie; detailed bibliographic data are available in the Internet at http://dnb.d-nb.de.

Any brand names and product names mentioned in this book are subject to trademark, brand or patent protection and are trademarks or registered trademarks of their respective holders. The use of brand names, product names, common names, trade names, product descriptions etc. even without a particular marking in this works is in no way to be construed to mean that such names may be regarded as unrestricted in respect of trademark and brand protection legislation and could thus be used by anyone.

Cover image: www.ingimage.com

Publisher: VDM Verlag Dr. Müller GmbH & Co. KG
Dudweiler Landstr. 99, 66123 Saarbrücken, Germany
Phone +49 681 9100-698, Fax +49 681 9100-988
Email: info@vdm-publishing.com

Printed in the U.S.A.
Printed in the U.K. by (see last page)
ISBN: 978-3-639-04742-4

Copyright © 2011 by the author and VDM Verlag Dr. Müller GmbH & Co. KG and licensors
All rights reserved. Saarbrücken 2011

CONTENTS

Chapter 4   Mothers, children and their caregivers   45

Chapter 5   Still behind bars   73

Acknowledgements

This work would never have been completed without the support and encouragement of many people. First and foremost, I would like to thank the women and the caregivers for sharing their concerns with me by allowing me into their lives for a short time and, in many cases, for inviting me into their homes. I hope that I have justified their trust in me and managed in some small way to give them a voice.

I would also like to thank the Department of Justice, the Social Policy Unit and the Crime Prevention Unit for providing me with funding, without which this research would not have been viable. In addition, I would like to express my appreciation to the Department of Corrections for being allowed access to the women's prisons and to say a special thanks to the women who were managing these at the time I conducted my research: Dorothy Coster at Mount Eden Women's Division, Fleur Grenfell at Arohata and Ces Lashlie at Christchurch Women's Prison.

A huge vote of thanks is due to Allison Morris who helped me to form some order out of a huge amorphous mass of data and who wisely told me that I did not have to include everything I had ever thought or everything that I had ever read. Thanks is also due to Jan Jordan who helped me to fine tune the final version of the work at a stage when I was definitely flagging.

I would also like to thank Sandy Taylor at the Institute of Criminology who was always available to advise on curly formatting problems and who in addition to my colleagues, Trevor Bradley and Anna Duncan, was always a source of encouragement and support.

Finally, I would like to thank all those special people in my life; particularly my family who have coped with me on a daily basis for the time it has taken me to undertake this course of study. I can now answer in the affirmative the question that was continually asked,: Yes, I have finished!

Venezia Kingi
Wellington, 2008

CHAPTER 1   INTRODUCTION

The rationale for this study is that prisoners, particularly mothers, and their children are a vulnerable population. Although this notion is largely inferred, the reasoning draws on knowledge and understanding of the factors that contribute to family cycles of violence, abuse and criminal offending,[1] the chaotic lifestyle and ineffective parenting patterns associated with addictions,[2] and the data we have on prison populations (Lash, 1998).[3]

Before embarking on this project, I had carried out a piece of research to ascertain the needs of mothers in prison. I had assumed that information on the children that the women had left behind when they went to prison would be readily obtained from prison records. I had assumed I would be able to find out how many children there were, their ages, who was caring for them and where they were living. I was mistaken; this information was not routinely collected. This led me to question how the prison system could address the individual needs of these women and meet the stated goal of the Department of Corrections in New Zealand[4] - "reducing re-offending" - if this crucial information was lacking. I decided, therefore, to ask these questions of the imprisoned women themselves in this research.

During the course of this research, I interviewed 56 imprisoned mothers, as well as the caregivers of the children of 11 of these women. At a later date, I re-interviewed 37 of the women who were either still in prison or at home in the community. This chapter attempts to place the data I have collected in context by first briefly describing the sentencing principles which guide judges when mothers and pregnant women come before the courts. The number and characteristics of imprisoned women (and men) in New Zealand are then discussed, including the crimes they have committed and the length of the sentences they are given. I

---

[1]   For example, research carried out by Widom (1989) found that being abused as a child significantly increased the individual's risk of having an adult criminal record. Farrington (1988, 1989, 1995), Fergusson et al (1992, 1993, 1994) and Henry et al (1993) all describe the relationship between family related demographic variables, ineffective parenting and crime. Dutton & Hart (1992) also discuss risk markers for the perpetration of family violence in the male prison population and produce findings that coincide with those of Widom (1989). There appears to be growing recognition that the children of incarcerated parents may be at greater risk of future involvement with the criminal justice system than their peers (Jose-Kampfner, 1991; Kempner & Rivara, 1993; Koban, 1983; McPeek & Tse, 1988, cited in Harris, 1996; Michigan Women's Commission, 1993; Moses, 1995).

[2]   See Kumpfer (1995) for a comprehensive discussion on the negative impacts of maternal substance abuse on children and the importance of strengthening families and parenting skills as an intervention to counteract these. Bekir et al (1993) provides an insight into the role reversals that often occur in the families of substance abusers where adult roles are often taken over by children (the "parentified child") and the transgenerational nature of this phenomenon.

[3]   The 1987 New Zealand Prison Census stated that of the 120 women in prison at the time of the census, 43% had problems with alcohol and 42% had problems with drugs (Braybrook & O'Neill, 1988). More recently, a Department of Justice study to survey the substance abuse treatment needs of prisoners identified more than two-thirds (69%) of the 143 women in prison (on 17 October, 1990) as having a substance abuse problem (Whitney, 1992). The comparable figure for the 3,281 men in prison was estimated at almost half (49%). Overseas research has also noted that many women prisoners have substance abuse problems (Austin et al, 1992; Hampton, 1993; Moon et al, 1993; Prison Reform Trust 1996; Snell & Morton, 1994, cited in Chesney-Lind, 1997; Task Force on the Female Offender, 1990).

[4]   The Department of Corrections was established on 1 October, 1995. While many of the policies under discussion in this research were established by the Department of Justice, the Department of Corrections now had responsibility for these policies at the time this research was undertaken.

will then set the scene for the presentation of my data by describing the three women's prisons in New Zealand and discuss the Department of Corrections policy for women in prison, focussing in particular on the special problems faced by mothers in New Zealand prisons.

The sentencing process

The general sentencing principles which judges are required to consider in sentencing offenders are set out in Part 1 of the Criminal Justice Act 1985; these do not distinguish between those offenders who have dependent children and those who do not. The Act emphasises the protection of the public in that those who have committed violent offences are required by statute to be imprisoned, unless there are exceptional circumstances surrounding the offence. Conversely, persons convicted of property offences punishable by terms of imprisonment of seven years or less should not be imprisoned unless the court is satisfied that any other sentence would not be appropriate. The Act also states that imprisonment is a sentence to be imposed as a last resort in the majority of cases that do not involve violence.

Parents of dependent children

Hall (1987) notes that distress and hardships suffered by the families and dependents of offenders are one of the inevitable consequences of crime. Therefore, male and female offenders cannot generally seek to escape a term of imprisonment through having the responsibility of young children. Nevertheless, it appears that these are factors which may be considered by the court though they are unlikely to be given much weight in cases of serious or premeditated offending.

One mitigating factor in determining the appropriate sentence for an offender, which may be taken into account by the court, is the effect that sentences will have on the offender's family (Hesketh & Young, 1994). In *Beere* (CA 301/82), a sentence of 2 years' imprisonment was reduced on appeal to 6 months imprisonment, thus enabling the appellant's immediate release. Part of the rationale behind this decision was the fact that she had a young baby who had become unsettled since her sentence and there was some uncertainty as to the stability of the current care arrangements. In *Henry* (CA 187/78), the Court of Appeal reduced a prison sentence for infanticide to allow the immediate release of an imprisoned mother where there was the likelihood of grave emotional damage to her children and husband unless the family was reunited (Hall, 1987). Her 2 year sentence was reduced to 6 months imprisonment. Also, in a recent decision (*Sing v* ARCIA, HC Auckland JP66R95 13/4/95), the judge allowed an appeal against a 5 month prison sentence by a women with a 5 month old baby which was still breastfeeding. The baby was being cared for by the woman's elderly mother and was being taken to the prison twice a day to be fed. A medical report referred to the effects on the child of separation from its mother and the judge substituted a sentence of 200 hours community service and reparation (cited in Williams, 1996).

However, there are no hard and fast rules in this respect. The fact that an offender has the care of young children does not necessarily justify a reduction in sentence: this depends upon the nature of the offence, the particular circumstances and the availability of alternative care arrangements. For example, in *Rackley* (CA 206/81) the fact that the mother's imprisonment was having negative consequences on her 5 year old daughter did not result in a reduction of sentence on appeal (Hesketh & Young, 1994). The Court stated that if any serious problems arose relating to the child, the appropriate course for the prisoner to take was to apply under the provisions of the Criminal Justice Act 1985 for a discharge from imprisonment on parole. Again, in *Brand* (CA 8/87), an appeal against a 6 year sentence, imposed on a woman in respect of a charge of importing heroin, was declined by the Court of Appeal. This was despite the fact that the woman was responsible for the care of a young child who suffered from multi-handicapped congenital conditions which affected both his mental and physical ability. In *Beere* (CA 308/93 and 393/93), the Court of Appeal upheld a Crown appeal and imposed 9 month's imprisonment on a woman for social welfare fraud. Although the woman had four children aged 2, 3, 5 and 8 in her care, she had previously received leniency on this ground and therefore the interests of the public now had to take precedence.

Pregnancy

Hesketh & Young (1994) state that an offender's pregnancy may be taken into account in determining the length of a prison sentence. However, they also note that the courts must take heed of the fact that, if a woman wishes to retain a child she has given birth to in prison, then it is the policy of the Department of Corrections to recommend to the Minister of Justice that the prisoner be released from prison pursuant to s 94 (1) (a) of the Criminal Justice Act 1985, and that she is not recalled to serve her sentence once released.[5] In the light of this policy, the Court of Appeal in *Maney* (CA 12/88) held that pregnancy should not prevent the imposition of a custodial sentence which might be warranted by the offence (ibid, P 61):

> *The responsibilities of a mother to her children and the likely increase in those responsibilities in the birth of another child and the undesirability in general of keeping a mother and her new born child in prison, or rearing the child away from the mother are, of course, personal circumstances relevant to the matter of sentence even allowing for the proposition that the personal circumstances of an offender in drug cases are of much less significant than in other classes of offending. At the same time it cannot be taken as always the case that women who are pregnant are immune from punishment in prison by reason only of that fact ... Section 91[6] is specifically designed to cover the case of a woman who gives birth to a child while serving a sentence of imprisonment, and on that account it can be fairly said that the framers of the statute never intended that the pregnancy of a woman to the point where she will be delivered of the child in prison would be a bar to the imposition of a prison sentence, if that sentence were otherwise called for.*

The effect of this approach (subsequently reiterated in *Roulston* (CA 39/88), *Sylvia* (CA 316/88) and *Watts* (CA 261/91)) is that while pregnancy is relevant to the extent that it is part of the overall family circumstances of the offender, it should not, in itself, prevent the imposition of a prison term which is required to adequately denounce the offending (Hesketh & Young, 1994).

---

[5]   Each case is judged on its individual merits; not all women are eligible since security reasons are taken into account. However, the majority of women who give birth in prison and who wish to care for their babies, apply for and are granted a release under this section.

[6]   Section 91 of the Criminal Justice Act 1985 was amended as from 1 September 1996 to s 94.

The number of women in prison in New Zealand

Although New Zealand is made up of two islands which together make up a country approximately the size of the United Kingdom, it has only three prisons for women. These are Mount Eden, which can hold 54 women and is situated in Auckland at the upper end of the North Island; Arohata, which can hold 105 women and is situation in Wellington at the bottom of the North Island; and Christchurch Women's Prison, which can hold 98 and is situated in Christchurch which is towards the middle of the South Island: a total operating capacity, therefore, of 257 prison places for women.

At the most recent prison census (20 November 1997), there were 207 sentenced women in prison: a mere 4% of all sentenced prisoners (Lash, 1998).[7] This number, however, represents a 37% increase over the number of sentenced women in prison at the time of the previous prison census (23 November 1995). At that date, there were only 151 women in prison: a number which had fluctuated little since 1989. For example, at the time of the 1991 prison census (14 November 1991) there had been 139 sentenced women in prison;[8] the 1995 figure, therefore, was only a 9% increase over the 1991 number.[9] This recent increase, however, means that New Zealand has now begun to reflect the trends in women's imprisonment apparent in other western jurisdictions although the increases here have occurred somewhat later.[10]

These recent increases could be due to a number of possible reasons. First, women might be committing more serious offences. There is no recent published information which can confirm this. There has certainly been a growth in women's offending since the 1980s. For example, the rate of women's offending per 1000 population increased from 16.5 in 1986 to 24.0 in 1995 and violent offending by women increased by almost 200 percent over this period (Statistics New Zealand, 1996). However, data are not available on the seriousness of this offending. Second, there may be a trend towards more "equal" sentencing so that men and women convicted of similar offences are now receiving similar sentences. However, again there is no recently published information which can confirm that the proportion of women sent to prison has increased. The information which is available indicates that, in 1997, 14% of men and 5% of women were sentenced to imprisonment (Spier, 1998); the comparable figures in 1992 were 14% and 4% respectively (Spier & Norris, 1993). The third

---

[7]   The women's prison population in New Zealand has not always been so small. During the latter part of the 19th century, women comprised just under 20% of the New Zealand prison population. Clark (1979), Ministerial Committee of Inquiry into the Prisons System (1989) and Phillips (1992) all provide earlier descriptions of women's prisons in New Zealand.

[8]   I have used the 1991 census figure as a comparison rather than that from 1993 as Lash (1997) postulates that a decrease in the number of female sentenced inmates recorded (118) in the prison census of November 1993 might have been caused, to a large extent, by the change in the release provisions for some prisoners introduced on 1 September 1993 in the Criminal Justice Amendment Act 1993.

[9]   There was also a marked increase between 1987 and 1989; from 109 to 148 - an increase of 36%.

[10]   For example, Chesney-Lind (1996) notes that the number of women imprisoned in the United States tripled during the 1980s and 1990s. She cites federal statistics which state that during 1994 64,403 women were in state and federal prisons and that in addition the "average daily" jail population included 48,894 women. The Prison Reform Trust (1996) discusses how the female prison population in England and Wales increased by 68% between the 1992/93 period when the average number of women in prison was 1,374, and 1996 (July 26) when there were 2,313 women in prison. Furthermore, this number had risen to the highest ever recorded female prison population in England and Wales by December 1999: 3245 women and girls (Howard League, 1999a).

4

possible reason why the numbers of women in prison have increased is that there may have been recent changes in the 'type' of woman sent to prison. The following section explores this possibility further by comparing information on female prisoners provided by the two most recently published prison censuses - 1995 (Lash, 1996) and 1997 (Lash, 1998) - which suggests that this has not occurred. Fourth, women may be receiving longer prison sentences - again data from the censuses would not appear to support this. Finally, increases in the number of women in prison may merely be the result of a seasonal variation. Only time will confirm which of these explanations hold true.

Characteristics of women in New Zealand's prisons

The 1997 prison census provides the most recent published information about women in prison. Table 1.1 sets out key information on them and contrasts this with comparable information for their male counterparts from the same source. In this way, we can assess the extent to which women and men in prison present different profiles and needs. Table 1.1 also contrasts information on female prisoners from the 1995 census.

Table 1.1 Selected information on female and male prisoners from the 1997 prison census and information on female prisoners from the 1995 prison census: percentages

| | 1997 Census | | 1995 Census |
	Female Prisoners	Male Prisoners	Female Prisoners
Previous criminal history			
No previous experience of prison	71	44	58
6 or more periods of custody	3	10	5
No previous convictions	26	18	19
More than 50 previous convictions	10	12	16
Offence Type			
Property	40	20	39
Violence	34	57	36
Drugs	14	7	13
Length of Sentence			
Less than 1 year	34	20	37
1 and under 3 years	32	28	39
3 and under 5 years	18	17	7
5 years and over	7	27	7
Life	8	6	10
Age			
Under 20	13	9	9
Under 30	50	54	49
Ethnicity			
Identify as Māori	42	44	49
Identify as New Zealand European	37	38	39
Income			
Beneficiaries prior to imprisonment	69	52	82
Qualifications			
No educational qualifications	74	75	73
Dependent Children			
Living with children prior to imprisonment	58	44	53
Single parent	76	28	68

Table 1.1 indicates that the majority of women in New Zealand prisons are there for the first time. Almost three-quarters of the women in prison in 1997 had never been there before compared with just over two-fifths of the men. On the other hand, women and men in prison in 1997 had a similar number of previous convictions. Comparisons with data from the 1995

6

prison census show increases in the numbers of women going to prison for the first time and those with no prior convictions. In addition, the number of women in prison with more than 50 previous convictions has steadily decreased (from 16% in 1995 to 10% in 1997).[11]

Table 1.1 also shows that property offences were the largest category of offence committed by women in prison in 1997: two-fifths had committed these compared with only one-fifth of the men.[12] The most common offence for men in prison was violence against the person. Also the proportion of women in prison for drug offences was twice that of men. The types of offences committed by women in prison had changed little since the 1995 census (and indeed since the 1991 census).[13]

We can also see from Table 1.1 that women are serving relatively short prison sentences. Approximately a third of women in prison in 1997 were serving sentences of less than one year compared with one-fifth of men. Conversely, a greater proportion of the men were serving longer sentences, i.e. five years or more, although a greater proportion of the women were serving sentences of life imprisonment. Most of these women were in prison for killing their partners, their children or people they believed had harmed, or were going to harm, their children.[14] Moreover, the proportion of women serving longer sentences has increased in recent years: 2% of women were serving more than five years in 1989 compared with 7% in 1997.[15] There has also been an increase in the number of women serving sentences of life imprisonment: from 7 in 1987 to 17 in 1997.[16] Furthermore, at the time of the 1995 prison census a quarter of women in prison were serving sentences of three or more years (including life), whereas the number had increased to a third of women in 1997. Indeed, in 1997, the daily average number of female sentenced prisoners had increased to 187, the highest number

---

[11]   The 1991 prison census recorded 24% of female prisoners had more than 50 previous convictions.

[12]   It has long been recognised that patterns of women's offending are related to the economic marginalization of women and that research indicates that the largest numbers of women imprisoned in western countries are for predominantly property or drug related offences (Bardsley, 1987; Braybrook & O'Neill, 1988; Carlen, 1983, 1988; Chesney-Lind, 1997, Feinman, 1986; Johnston & Gabel, 1995; Mandaraka-Sheppard, 1986; Padel & Stevenson, 1988; Pollock-Byrne, 1990).

[13]   The 1991 prison census records: 40% of women serving sentences for property offences, 34% for violence and 16% for drug related offences.

[14]   Chesney-Lind (1997) cites data from recent research in the United States (Snell & Morton, 1994) which noted that when contrasting women and men imprisoned for murder, women were more likely to have killed an intimate or a relative that men (50% compared to 16.3%). In contrast, men imprisoned for murder were more likely to have killed a stranger (51% compared to 35%). Other researchers made similar comments about women who have been convicted of crimes of a violent nature, that is, the victims are most often members of their families, or those with whom they have close relationships (Crites, 1976; Immarigeon & Chesney-Lind, 1992; Morris, 1988; Simon, 1975). Crites (1976) cites a study of women's violent crimes (Ward, 1968) in which findings indicated that few of these crimes were premeditated - in fact most were the outcome of many years of frustration and abuse.

[15]   Since the 1995 census a new classification of sentence length has been used. This new system has been applied to previous census information from 1989, 1991 and 1993 to enable comparisons to be made. However, it was not possible to access the 1987 census information for such reclassification (Lash, 1998).

[16]   Lash (1998) states that such increases can partly be explained by changes in eligibility for parole. Prior to 1 August 1987, offenders sentenced to life imprisonment were eligible for parole after serving seven years of their sentence; at that date the non-parole period was extended to 10 years. Additionally the Criminal Justice Amendment Act 1993 allowed Judges to impose non-parole periods of more than 10 years in exceptional circumstances.

in the decade.[17] Lash (1996 & 1998) notes, however, that there is no clear trend in the length of sentences imposed on female prisoners over the time period 1987 to 1995 compared with a trend towards imposing longer sentences on male prisoners. In summary, women in prison generally speaking have less prior custodial experience, fewer previous convictions, a smaller proportion have been sentenced to prison for violent offences and they are serving shorter sentences than male prisoners. These differences are reflected in the fact that more than three-quarters of the women in prison in 1997 were classified as minimum security status compared with 59% of male prisoners.

Both men and women in prison are relatively young, as Table 1.1 indicates. The proportion of the women in prison aged under 30 has changed only a little since the 1995 census. In addition, Table 1.1 shows that Māori - the indigenous population of New Zealand - are over-represented in prison: more than two-fifths of the women in prison in 1997 identified as Māori, which is slightly less than the 1995 figure of almost half.[18] Māori make up only around 14% of the total population of New Zealand (Statistics New Zealand, 1997).

It would also appear that women enter prison with a range of problems. Table 1.1 shows that women tend to have been living on lower incomes prior to their imprisonment than male prisoners, that they tend to have few educational qualifications (though this is so for men in prison too) and they tend to have more child care responsibilities than men prior to their imprisonment. The actual number of children whose mothers are in custody is unknown,[19] but a much greater proportion of women than men (58% and 44% respectively)[20] had children living with them before they were imprisoned,[21] and these women were far more likely than men to be sole parents - this was so for 76% of the women compared with 28% of the men.[22]

Information from other sources indicates that women in prison also tend to have histories of drug and alcohol abuse;[23] and that they tend to have experienced high levels of

---

[17]   This was also the situation for male prisoners with the comparable figure being 4399. In fact Spier (1998) remarks that the average daily female prison numbers during 1997 were 61% greater than the number in 1988 (116).

[18]   The figures for both women and men become higher if we take into account those who indicated that they had some Māori ancestry (55% and 50% respectively). Ethnicity was recorded as unknown for 13% of female prisoners compared with 24% of male prisoners.

[19]   Any figure available is likely to be an under-estimate due to commonly expressed concerns among female prisoners about their children being taken into custody by the state whilst they are in prison.

[20]   This excludes 33 female and 1168 male prisoners where information on dependent children was not known.

[21]   Estimates as to the number of women in prison in western countries who are mothers vary due to the lack of demographic information on this population. However, overseas researchers have noted that approximately fifty to eighty per cent of women in prison are mothers (Applebome, 1992, cited in Clark, 1995; Baunach, 1979, 1982; Bloom,, 1995; Henriques, 1996; Kiser, 1991; McGowan & Blumenthal, 1976, 1978; Ross & Fabiano, 1986; Toner, 1984) and studies have produced data indicating women prisoners were more likely to have children than men prisoners, and to have lived with them prior to their imprisonment (Koban, 1983, Snell & Morton, 1994 cited in Chesney-Lind, 1997).

[22]   These data are in line with that from overseas (Austin et al, 1992; Bloom, 1995a; Datesman & Cales, 1983; Hampton, 1993; Pollock-Byrne, 1990).

[23]   Refer to Footnote 3 in this chapter for details of the number of women in New Zealand prisons with substance abuse problems (Braybrook & O'Neill, 1988; Whitney, 1992). Johnston & Gabel (1995) note that in relation to United States prison populations women prisoners tend to evidence higher rates of drug use and addictions than men in prison. Similar comments have been made by other researchers in the

victimisation.[24]   Overall, therefore, the profile of women in New Zealand prisons has not changed much in recent years and indeed does not differ greatly from the general profile of women in prison in other western countries.   What is important is that the profile does differ to some extent from that of men in prison, particularly in the case of women with children.

Women's prisons in New Zealand

As described previously, there are only three prisons for women in New Zealand. All three hold women on remand along with sentenced prisoners, and provide places for 257 women. This section provides a short history of each prison, and describes them, their location, and their accessibility.

Mount Eden Women's Division

Mount Eden Prison Women's Division is situated about 4 km from the centre of Auckland city, at the upper end of the North Island. The Women's Division is located outside the main (men's) facility.   There are places for 54 women at Mount Eden, the majority of who are serving short sentences. The prison caters for both remand and sentenced prisoners. Most women who are sentenced in the north of the North Island go to Mount Eden Women's Division to await transfer to Arohata or Christchurch. There is no public transport directly to the prison; however, it is only a short walk to the prison from adjacent bus stops.

There has been a prison on this site since 1856. The original facility was a military stockade which became Auckland's major place of confinement when the old city jail was demolished in 1865. The existing stone wall was completed in 1872, at which time the prison buildings were wooden. The present stone buildings were completed in 1917.

The women's division was formerly located within the main prison. Until 1959, women prisoners were housed in the north wing extension and in a wooden building. That year, the majority of female prisoners were moved to Dunedin prison (at the southern end of the South Island) to provide additional accommodation in Mount Eden for male prisoners. Only remand prisoners and those serving short sentences were retained at Mount Eden. In 1965, the last female prisoners moved out of the main prison into the buildings which had formerly been the superintendent's residence. The women's division had dormitory style accommodation until new cells were provided in 1988, built within and around the old two-storey facility.

One side of the Mount Eden prison is situated next to the railway line and barred doors are visible from the road which runs alongside. It is a very old stone block building with the appearance of a fortress or medieval castle. It is not obvious, when approaching the main entrance, where the women's division is situated; all that can be seen is a row of buildings on the left and the men's prison towering at the end of the driveway ahead. It is not until

---

United States (Hairston, 1991b; Owen & Bloom, 1995a, 1995b; Task Force on the Female Offender, 1990), England (Caddle & Crisp, 1997) and Australia (D'Arcy, 1994; Hampton, 1993).

[24]   The Roper Committee Report (1989) refers to claims by prison staff that 80% of female prisoners had been sexually abused. Again this profile is validated by overseas data (Comack, 1996; O'Connor, 1996; Shaw et al, 1991; Sugar & Fox, 1990). For example, research carried out by Snell & Morton (1994, cited in Chesney-Lind, 1997) indicated that about a third of the women in American prisons in 1991 had been abused either physically or sexually before they reached the age of 18, often by someone they were either closely related to or who was known to them; and by adulthood 43% had been the victim of sexual or physical violence, again often at the hands of a partner or friend.

walking past a staff training centre situated on the left hand side of the drive that a visitor realises that the women's division is in the building next door behind a large metal door with a grill in it, set in the wall. There is a bell situated in the wall next to the door which, when rung, eventually summons a staff member who provides access into a courtyard between the buildings. The courtyard wall has scenic murals painted on it by ex-prisoners. On entering the building, a visitor is immediately aware of the confined space of the administration area, doors restricting access to various areas (e.g. from reception to rooms used for general purposes and to the cell block area) are open grill type rather than solid locked doors. This is the prevailing image: confined spaces and bars.

This prison is the only women's prison with a dedicated visiting room and it is located in this part of the building, along with rooms used for education and group work. The visiting room itself is not large (approximately 4 metres square); this means that staff supervising visiting sessions and prisoners and their visitors are in fairly close proximity. Through another locked grill there is a passage which leads down to the control room (affectionately known as the fishbowl) from where custodial staff have a clear view of women coming and going from the various wings. To the left of this area are the segregation/punishment cells. The remand cells and those for sentenced prisoners are located in a series of wings which are accessed from a main corridor which runs along in front of and past the control room.

The cell blocks themselves are arranged around two sides of a square built around an open courtyard area which is covered by a steel mesh grill, through which is the only view the women have of the sky. At the far end of the L shape is a recreation area. The other two sides of the square are a solid wall and a glass wall which forms part of the main corridor and through which the women can be observed at all times. Some of the cells are situated right next to the railway line. The only deviation from this design is the minimum security block which is arranged around an enclosed yard area formed between the old part of the building and the new additions. Cells are placed around this area and open on to a veranda. The recreation and eating area for the women in this unit is situated in another building situated on the opposite side of the yard. This is probably the least enclosed part of the prison, yet there is still a real sense of being confined in a restricted area.

Arohata Women's Prison

Arohata Women's Prison is situated at Tawa, 13 km north of Wellington city, at the bottom of the North Island. Arohata has places for 105 women, and is the largest women's prison in New Zealand. The prison caters for remand prisoners, sentenced prisoners and corrective trainees.[25] Women from all over the country are sent to Arohata. At any one time, only a few of the women in residence are from the greater Wellington area. Access to the prison by public transport involves a 10 minute train ride from Wellington and a 10-15 minute walk from the closest railway station to the prison.

During World War II, the War Cabinet decided to move the Point Halswell Women's Reformatory, situated on the shores of Wellington Harbour, away from possible sea attack. Arohata was built in 1944 and originally opened as a women's borstal. The name of Arohata (meaning the bridge) given to the borstal, was chosen for the nearby Takapu Road Bridge and in the hope that the facility might provide the bridge between past failings and a future useful life.

---

[25]   Corrective training is a short sentence of imprisonment for 16 to 19 year olds.

Arohata's function changed from a borstal to a youth prison in 1981 and later to a women's prison and the national facility for female corrective trainees. At various times (e.g. from April 1992 until mid 1994) minimum security male prisoners have been housed at Arohata, in response to overcrowding at men's prisons in the area.

Arohata is situated on the side of a hill in a semi-rural setting and looks out over the valley at Tawa. Driving up to the prison, one quite often passes women prisoners working in the gardens and the environment is more like that of a hospital than a prison until you are confronted by the wire mesh fence which runs along in front of the cell blocks. Women who have been transferred to Arohata from Mount Eden often talk about how wonderful it is to be able to go outside and touch the grass again. There is a large two storey building which houses the administration block, the chapel, interview rooms and the control room. From the control room, which is at the far left hand corner of the administration building, staff have a view directly ahead down the main corridor from which the cell blocks, or wings, are accessed.

The wings themselves are all accessed from the right-hand side of the main corridor, which runs at right angles to the administration building. Again, there is the feeling of an institutional setting, but that of a hospital with its long corridors. However, instead of wards running off that corridor, there are all the amenities for the prisoners (for example, the library, kitchen, laundry and sewing room) and the cell blocks through locked doors. Each wing is roughly of the same design. Just inside the door is a guard room with a recreation/day room next door and an ablutions block opposite. The cells themselves are located on both sides of a corridor which runs directly ahead of the entrance door. The women have access to an outside exercise area which runs the length of the wing and which is boarded in at the far end obscuring the view. At one time, this fence was not in place and the women could look out across the valley through the wire fencing.

At the far end of the main corridor past the gymnasium, where visits are conducted, the minimum security/work release wing - Te Araroa - is situated. This wing is practically self contained and has its own kitchen, interview rooms and a large pleasant day room with windows all around. This wing is not within the fenced-in area of the prison and has a separate main access door. The cells are located around the perimeter of an exercise yard which is accessed through doors at the rear of the day room. There is also a swimming pool in the grounds, which is used mainly by the corrective trainees.

Christchurch Women's Prison

Christchurch Women's Prison is in Paparua County, 26 km from central Christchurch, near the middle of the South Island and has places for 98 women (since July 1998). This prison holds all female remand and sentenced prisoners from the South Island and those not considered suitable for Arohata. It has the only maximum security accommodation for women prisoners. There is no public transport directly to the prison from Christchurch city and it is a time-consuming procedure to get there, even for those with their own transport, as the prison is situated some kilometres (about a 5 minute drive) from the main highway at Templeton, in the same vicinity as the Paparua Prison for men. Buses run from Cathedral Square in the centre of Christchurch to Templeton and may, on request, drop visitors off at the prison and collect them on the return journey. Otherwise, the prison is at least a 20-30 minute walk from the main bus route.

Christchurch Women's Prison was the first purpose-built prison for women in New Zealand and was opened on 1 June 1974. Prisoners and staff from Dunedin Prison for Women and the Women's Division at Paparua Prison were transferred in that month. As with Arohata, male prisoners have been housed at various times (from July to December 1988 and from July 1990 to April 1993) at Christchurch Women's Prison.

The first thing that strikes a visitor to Christchurch Women's Prison is the seemingly idyllic setting. The prison is situated on the Canterbury Plains and there is a clear view across to the majestic Southern Alps. A wire fence surrounds the perimeter and access is through a locked gate which is opened from the main building when visitors state their identity through an intercom. There is also an intercom outside the main door of the administration building. As with Arohata and Mount Eden, access to the cell block area is through the administration building and the wings are all accessed from a spacious main corridor area, with the control room situated to the left of the access door from the administration block.

The wings themselves are similar to those at Arohata, and open onto courtyard areas planted with flower gardens. The building itself has the same "hospital-like" feeling of Arohata, with the locked doors and the grills at the end of the cell blocks. The maximum security wing has a barbecue area where the women can sit outside during the summer. Also situated along the main corridor are: the gymnasium, where visits take place; small rooms used for special visits; and interview rooms.

The isolation of women in prison

According to a Department of Justice (1988) submission to the Ministerial Committee of Inquiry into the Prisons System (1989), most of the women in prison in New Zealand come from areas in which there is no prison. Furthermore, only Christchurch Women's Prison takes women convicted of serious offences in the early years of their sentence and Mount Eden can only take women serving relatively short sentences, irrespective of where they have lived prior to their sentence. This, of course, means that a large proportion of women in prison are far from their families and communities. This situation inevitably increases the difficulty of visits and creates an added stress for those women attempting to maintain relationships with their children, their families and others they are close to. Research overseas has also commented on this aspect of women's imprisonment (Catan, 1992; Carlen, 1990; Grace, 1990; Howard League for Penal Reform, 1993; Farrell, 1996, 1998; Johnston & Gabel, 1995; LeFlore & Holston, 1989; Prison Reform Trust, 1996; White, 1989) and adds that as fathers are less likely to be imprisoned as far from their home communities as mothers (due to larger numbers and therefore more regional facilities) they often receive more visits from their children (Koban,1983).[26]

Mothers in prison and their children

The fact that there has been more focus placed on imprisoned mothers and their needs than on those of imprisoned fathers is possibly due to the fact that women still traditionally fulfil the nurturing and care giving role in our society (Baunach, 1979, 1984, 1985; Beckerman, 1991;

---

[26] Hairston (1995) debates this, stating that contrary to a widespread belief most fathers in prison have limited contact with their children, which very much depends on their relationship with the child's mother (or other caregiver). A Ministry of Justice report (Gray Matter Research, 1996) provides an insight into the situation of imprisoned fathers in New Zealand who were their children's primary caregivers before their imprisonment.

Bloom, 1993, 1995; Caddle & Crisp, 1997; Henriques, 1982, 1996; Richards, 1992). As discussed previously, however, apart from the data published in the biennial prison census, nobody knows exactly how many women in prison have dependent children. Census data do give some indication of the numbers involved and what is of concern is that approximately three-quarters of those women who had dependent children said that they were sole parents compared with slightly more than a quarter of the men. Nobody really knows what happens to children when their mother is imprisoned. There is no agency with responsibility for their care and hence no policy for ensuring their wellbeing. However, the Children, Young Persons and Their Families Agency (CYPFA)[27] may become involved in individual cases if asked by the mother, a family member or friend on her behalf, or the police where a woman is arrested and detained in police custody. This involvement is not always to the benefit of the mother as it may result in her child/ren being placed in the care of the state if other satisfactory care arrangements are unable to be made - for example, if the woman's family/whanau[28] or friends are unable to care for the child/ren.

Caring for prisoners' children

The experiences of children who have a parent in prison will differ according to which parent is imprisoned. The children of imprisoned fathers are more likely to be cared for by their mother or father's partner, whereas the children of women inmates tend to be looked after by extended family/whanau (Harris, 1996; Koban, 1983; Richards et al, 1996: cited in Caddle & Crisp, 1997) her friends (Prison Reform Trust, 1996; Woodrow, 1992a, 1992b) or placed in foster care (Adalist-Estrin, 1986; Bloom & Steinhart, 1993; Harris, 1996; Johnston, 1995a; McGowan & Blumenthal, 1976, 1978).[29] According to the 1997 prison census, 71% of the children of male prisoners were looked after by their current or ex-partner. In contrast, slightly less than a third of the children of female prisoners were cared for their by their current or ex-partners; a further 26% were being looked after by the women's parents (Lash, 1998). There was no indication of how many children of either male or female prisoners were in state care.

There is evidence from overseas research to suggest that there is a greater instance of family disintegration after a mother's imprisonment. The children of women prisoners are often separated from their siblings, especially if their mother is a single parent and has sole responsibility for their financial care (Catan, 1988; Dobash, Dobash & Gutteridge, 1986; Howard League for Penal Reform, 1993; Larman & Aungles, 1991; Stanton, 1980; Zalba, 1964). Therefore, when a woman goes to prison, her children are at risk of separation from each other whilst those whose father goes to prison quite often still have one parent at home.

---

[27] The Department of Social Welfare through CYPFA has prime responsibility for the implementation of the Children, Young Persons, and Their Families Act 1989 which enables them to assist such children where required. One of the functions of the Agency is to make provision for children and young persons who are in need of care or protection and the Act specifies a range of different circumstances in which this may be appropriate. In terms of the children of women in prison the section of the Act which has relevance is 14(1)(f): that the parents or guardians or other persons having the care of the child or young person are unwilling or unable to care for the child or young person.

[28] Whānau is the Māori word used to refer to family and/or extended family.

[29] Research carried out in the United States estimates that between 7% and 15% of the children of imprisoned mothers are in foster care with non-relatives (Bloom & Steinhart, 1993; Henriques, 1982; McGowan & Blumenthal, 1976, 1978; Stanton, 1980; US Department of Justice, 1991, cited in Bloom, 1995).

The effects of separation on children

There is little known about the children of either male or female prisoners. They are indeed the forgotten victims of the criminal justice system (Larman & Aungles, 1991). One study of the children of a small sample of imprisoned fathers in England (Shaw, 1987) decried the lack of information on the children themselves and the social and psychological effects of their father's imprisonment.[30] As might be expected, there is considerably less information on the children of the even fewer mothers. Yet it is widely believed that the impact of a mother's imprisonment is likely to have a more detrimental affect on children.

Although there has been very little research on the effects of separation on children as a result of parental imprisonment, there is much information on the emotional and psychological effects of separation.[31] The bonding of a child with his/her primary care-giver is seen to take part principally in the first two to three years of life and to be essential for the psychological and emotional development of a 'well adjusted' individual (Hatty, 1984).[32] Available literature on the effects of maternal separation on young children indicates that bonding and attachment are products of a complex set of factors: for example, the age of the child at separation, the sex of the child [33] and the duration and circumstances of the separation experience[34] are all variables which have an effect on the emotional and behavioural

---

[30] Studies which have been carried out into the effects of men's imprisonment on their families have tended to focus on their relationships with their partners and other members of their families rather than their children (e.g. Brodsky, 1975; Deane, 1988; Fishman, 1990; Morris, 1965).

[31] The majority of studies of distress following separation have been conducted with children admitted to hospital or to a residential nursery (Rutter, 1972, 1981).

[32] Bowlby (cited in Bremner, 1994), who coined the term "maternal deprivation", concluded that bonds were formed between the mother and child between the age of 6 months and 30 months. The claim was that a range of personality and behaviour problems were likely to result in later life if a satisfactory attachment was not formed during infancy, or if an attachment once formed was disrupted through separation. Bowlby's view was that if a temporary separation occurred in the first 6 months of the child's life, before a bond had started to form, that the effects would be less severe. Bowlby's focus on the crucial nature of the bonding process between mother and child has subsequently been criticised by others who have come to less pessimistic conclusions about the effects of maternal deprivation (Clarke & Clarke, 1976; Rutter, 1972, 1981; Schaffer, 1971; cited in Bremner, 1994). Indeed a study carried out by Schaffer & Emerson (1964, cited in Bremner, 1994) found that by the age of 18 months the majority of the infants in their sample had formed attachments to more than one person. What seems to be important is the quality of stimulation and the continuity of care in a child's life rather than the exclusive bond with his/her mother (Rutter, 1981). Bremner (1994) suggests therefore, that the term 'social deprivation' may be more appropriate than "maternal deprivation".

[33] Rutter (1981) notes that studies that have found sex differences show that males have generally been found to be more vulnerable to the adverse effects of separation experiences.

[34] Studies on the separation of children and parents have also focussed on the effects on children of parental divorce or death. Such research has indicated that children who lose a parent through death are less likely to suffer long-term negative effects than those who lose a parent through divorce (Richards, 1992). It has been suggested that this may be due to the nature of the home environment before the occurrence and that homes broken by divorce or separation are more likely to have been characterised by discord and disharmony preceding the break (Rutter, 1972, 1981). Richards (1992) also notes that the negative effects of divorce on children can be the result of many factors including a drop in income for the household, a move of house, a change of school, the loss of childhood friends and the child possibly being given a negative picture of his/her absent parent. He adds that studies of divorce have shown, parents who are preoccupied with their own problems, or depressed, are less likely to be able to supply the extra support and attention that their children need at this time. Richards (1992) suggests that the effects of parental imprisonment on children may be similar to those of parental divorce.

14

consequences that mark the child's deprivation experience (Hatty, 1984). Rickford (1991) quotes a child psychotherapist as describing the separation of very young children from their mothers as: *"An appalling way to build up problems for the future"* (p 12).

Separation of women offenders from their children can begin at the point of arrest. The Roper Report (1989) notes that for young children caught up in such events the effects can be devastating and enduring, hampering their future behavioural and emotional development. That report describes the possible effects on children separated from their mothers in this fashion (1989: p 164):

> *Changes from independent to clinging behavior; regression in toilet habits; fear of strangers including a phobia of police; inability to sleep alone; fretting and depression, form part of what is described as a normal reaction to unexpected and sudden separation of young children from their mothers. At times the reaction is so severe as to include suicidal tendencies.*

There are no published data which tell us how many children of women in New Zealand prisons were present when their mothers were arrested. However, research from the United States gives some indication of the numbers of children involved. Johnston (1991, cited in Johnston, 1995e) estimates that about one in five children are present at their mothers' arrest; half of these children are between the ages of 3 and 7, and are in their mothers' sole care. In addition, in her research on mothers in prison, Baunach (1979, 1985) found that a significant number of children were present at their mother's arrest. It was also observed that mothers taken into custody frequently had no opportunity to make immediate or long-term child-care arrangements. Children were thus often reliant upon the goodwill of whoever was present at the time. They were usually cared for on a temporary basis by family or friends until long-term arrangements could be attended to. Kampfner (1995) adds that these children witness their mothers' powerlessness and violation, whilst their own emotional needs are essentially ignored; such experiences leave children feeling vulnerable. Furthermore, they are likely to be subjected to the same search and arrest procedures as their mothers.[35] A study carried out by Kampfner (1995) to assess the incidence of post-traumatic stress reactions in the children of imprisoned mothers found that each child could remember vividly his/her mother's arrest, even two to three years after the event. Approximately 75% of the children reported feeling depressed, having trouble sleeping and concentrating, and experiencing flashbacks about their mothers' crimes or arrest.

However, it is not only the very young that are adversely affected. Stanton (1980) found that school-age children of imprisoned mothers had low self-esteem, were poor academic achievers and posed discipline problems at school. In relation to the possible perpetuation of offending by those from a criminal background, a recent New Zealand report to the Minister of Justice, Police and Social Welfare on persistent child offenders (i.e. 10-13 year olds) indicated that over a third (38%) of the children identified (N=109) were known to have lived in families with a history of criminal involvement (Maxwell & Robertson, 1995). Similarly, an American study carried out by Robins et al (1976, cited in Baunach, 1979) to determine the

---

[35] Similarly, Woodrow (1992b) noted that some children remained with their mothers throughout the whole procedure of them being charged. This meant that they were often subjected to such experiences as being held in cells with their mothers and/or being present for their mothers' photographing and finger-printing. Woodrow commented that this usually occurred where the mother had not been allowed to arrange for someone to care for her children.

effects of parental arrest on the behaviour of adolescents found that children's delinquency could be predicted from parental arrest records.

Catan (1988) presents evidence, from her research in England, that the negative effects of a parent's imprisonment are also evident in accounts of imprisoned mothers' views of their children's situations. Children were perceived to have shown signs of disturbance since the imprisonment of their mothers.[36] They appeared to be unhappy at home, to be doing poorly at school, to be withdrawn, to be unwilling to play and to be prone to emotional outbursts and nightmares. Most mothers felt that the children's emotional, physical and academic problems were being brought about or exacerbated by the formers' incarceration.

The maintenance of family-ties

The Department of Corrections believes that the successful reintegration of offenders into the community is the best way to protect society (Department of Justice, 1988). Thus the concept of 'case management' in New Zealand prisons is geared towards providing each offender (whilst in prison and on parole) with the programmes and services he or she needs to aid this reintegration (ibid, p 20) with the ultimate aim of reducing re-offending. It is well documented both in New Zealand and overseas that the maintenance of prisoners' family ties and their relationships within the community facilitates this aim (Boudouris, 1996; Deane, 1988; Hairston, 1991a, 1991b; Light, 1993). In the case of women with children, it has been shown overseas that their ongoing relationships with their children are of crucial importance to their successful assimilation back into society (Baunach, 1979; Beckerman, 1989; Datesman & Cales, 1983; Kiser, 1991; McGowan & Blumenthal, 1976).

During imprisonment, the maintenance of a prisoner's family ties is seen to serve three important functions: the maintenance of the family unit, the enhancement of the well-being of individual family members, and the facilitation of the prisoner's post-release success (Bayse et al, 1991; Cobean & Power, 1978; Hairston, 1988, 1990, 1991a, 1991b; Holt & Miller, 1972; Howser & McDonald, 1982). In addition, Hairston (1991b: citing Richards, 1978) suggests that the preservation and development of contacts/relationships within the community plays an integral part in the management of the mental health of long-term prisoners.

Although most studies have been carried out with male prisoners, their findings seem to apply equally to imprisoned women and indeed may have more relevance as they are more likely to be single parents. Adalist-Estrin (1986) cites a need for prison programming aimed at holding families together in an effort to decrease recidivism and to combat the ever-increasing intergenerational patterns of criminality. There is evidence that, over the years, second-generation inmates and second-generation drug addicts have begun to enter prison; that is, either the children of former inmates are now being imprisoned or parents and their children are 'serving time' together (Caramouche & Jones, 1989: p 27). Therefore, it seems essential that penal policy should recognise the importance of women prisoners being able to maintain regular contact with their families.

---

[36] In another English study, Caddle & Crisp (1997) also found that 44% of the mothers in their study on imprisoned women and mothers, reported that their children had exhibited behavioural problems following their mother's imprisonment. Another 30% said their children had become withdrawn. These problems did not occur in isolation; for example, behavioural problems were often associated with problems related to eating, sleeping, bedwetting and withdrawal.

With this in mind the New Zealand Department of Corrections has a national policy on Family/Whānau Relationship Maintenance and Enhancement[37] which applies to all prisoners. It states:

> *Inmate relationships with their family/whanau are maintained and enhanced, in a culturally appropriate manner, to assist their wellbeing and effective reintegration into the community.*

The performance standards related to this policy[38] include the provision of culturally appropriate family/whānau visiting areas which reflect the needs of visitors including access to toilets, adequate seating, a play area for child/parent interaction and a suitable area to feed and change babies/toddlers. The following sections describe how these standards are currently being met in the three women's prisons.

Visiting

Sentenced prisoners[39] are entitled to weekly visits during set visiting hours, usually during the weekend (unless they are being punished and are being denied such "privileges"). At Mount Eden, women may have visitors by invitation only (i.e. they are required to send out visitors passes) and they are entitled to a one and a half hour visit per week, time permitting. Visiting hours are between the hours of 1.00 pm and 3.45 pm Monday to Friday and between the hours of 8.00 am and 10.45 am or 1.00 pm and 3.45 pm on a Saturday. Neither Arohata nor Christchurch Women's Prison require visitors to have passes[40] and both facilities allow sentenced prisoners two hourly visits on a Saturday. These can take place either in the morning or the afternoon, or in some circumstances women may be entitled to both. Visiting hours at Arohata are between the hours of 9.30 am and 11.30 am and 1.30 pm and 3.30 pm and those at Christchurch Women's Prison are broadly similar. In special circumstances and for visitors travelling from outside the area, visiting outside of normal hours or special extended visits may be allowed subject to prior approval being sought from the prison. All three of the prisons allow such exceptions to their usual visiting regimes.[41]

Visits at Arohata and Christchurch Women's take place in the gymnasium where there is minimal if any privacy and where the conditions can best be described as "spartan". Chairs are wooden and are linked together, with prisoners and visitors sitting opposite each other. Whether or not contact is allowed between a woman and her visitors is very much dependent on the staff supervising the visits. There is an outside playground at Christchurch Women's -

---

[37] Policy and Procedures Manual, A.02 (Public Prisons Service, 1998).

[38] These are listed in full in Appendix 1.

[39] Those on remand are subject to different regulations and have separate visiting times, usually during weekdays. For example, Mount Eden allows one half hour visit during the week between the hours of 1.00 pm and 3.45 pm. At Christchurch Women's Prison visiting for remand prisoners is between the hours of 1.45 pm and 2.45 pm Monday to Friday and those who intend to visit must phone and advise the prison prior to the desired date. At Arohata the hours for visiting those on remand varying according to the day of the week i.e. 1.00 pm to 3.00 pm on Mondays and Tuesdays and 2.00 pm to 3.00 pm on Wednesdays, Thursdays and Fridays.

[40] Although at the time I was conducting interviews passes were required at Christchurch Women's Prison and the present policy was being reviewed as at January 1999.

[41] All visiting hours and conditions cited are those that were in force on 19 January 1999.

the only women's prison with such a purpose-built area.[42]   At Mount Eden, there is a dedicated visiting room which is quite small. There is usually a limited range of donated toys provided by voluntary agencies in all of the prisons' visiting areas. However, these are usually damaged fairly quickly and often go missing. Other than these, there are no special facilities provided for mother and children.

Special visits often take place at Arohata in the chapel, which is situated on the ground floor of the administration block. This is a pleasant environment with plenty of space for women and visitors to move around, unless there is more than one woman at a time that has visitors. Sometimes, the kitchen will provide refreshments for lengthy special visits. At Christchurch Women's Prison, special visits may take place in the small rooms adjacent to the main cell block area previously mentioned, or in a larger room which has windows which overlook the garden and the chapel. This room also may be used for more than one visiting group at a time.

Family days

Family days are held at two of the three women's prisons - Arohata and Christchurch Women's. The women send out invitations to family and friends and may invite a limited number of adults; there are no restrictions placed on the number of children who may attend. Families are invited to bring food to share with the women and to spend the day. Activities may be arranged by the women for the children who attend. For example, at one family day I attended at Arohata, games and competitions with prizes were arranged for the children and the women who belonged to the Māori kapa haka[43] group performed for their families and friends. Staff, prisoners and their visitors mingled freely and there was a general picnic atmosphere even though the activities were confined to the exercise yard adjacent to the wing.

Family days at Arohata are scheduled to be held every two months. However, since each wing in the prison has a separate family day, the women may go for several months without spending quality time with their children. Family days are held at Christchurch Women's Prison on an average of every three months. Prison management, usually the Unit Managers, decide when family days will be held. There are no facilities to hold family days for women at Mount Eden.[44]

Kids' Camp

Shortly before Christmas 1996, a camp was run at Arohata for some of the women (those serving sentences of more than 5 years) and their children. Te Araroa was used, as the wing is somewhat self-sufficient, and the camp lasted from Friday to Sunday afternoon. Four staff members (the Programmes Manager, the Chaplain and two others) and their children participated with the women prisoners and their children and all slept in a "marae-style"[45]

---

[42]   Women reported to me, during follow-up interviews in mid 1996, that their access to this had recently been curtailed in an attempt to stop the flow of drugs into the prison. Thus they were denied the opportunity to interact with their children in this environment.

[43]   Māori performing arts.

[44]   However, my understanding is that family days are held for the men there.

[45]   A marae is a Māori community facility that usually consists of a carved meeting house, a dining hall and cooking area as well as the marae ātea (sacred space in front of the meeting house).

situation. The prisoners ran the camp themselves and the staff were just there to supervise. Most of the women who took part did not come from the Wellington area, although one of them had her child living nearby - in the Hutt Valley.

As part of the camp, a prison van was used to transport the children and the three women who were minimum security on an outing. Two of the children visited their fathers at the Rimutaka Men's Prison and time was spent at the children's play area at Avalon Park, situated in the Hutt Valley.[46] This camp is reported to have run smoothly and no problems (e.g. around security, discipline or drugs) were encountered.[47]

Phone calls and letters

Phone calls and letters also help women in prison to maintain relationships with their families and children. Restrictions are not usually placed on the number of letters that a woman may send and stationery is provided by the prison. Only the additional cost of sending large parcels or letters by fastpost is required to be met by the women themselves.

Telecom payphones are available for use by prisoners.[48] However, this depends on whether or not they can afford Telecom prepaid phone cards. Sentenced prisoners are able to nominate a maximum of 10 telephone numbers,[49] subject to approval by staff.[50] There is no limit to how many calls a day a prisoner can make other than whether nor not they can afford to do so. Calls have to be no longer than 15 minutes. A warning beep is heard by both parties 30 seconds before this time is up and a final beep sounds before the system disconnects the call. Prisoners cannot receive incoming calls. At both Arohata and Christchurch Women's Prison, the women have access to a card phone during their leisure hours. At Mount Eden, the use of the card phone must be pre-booked due to the demand. All three women's prisons allow prisoners to make additional or extended calls in special circumstances and the cost of these calls may sometimes be met by the prison.

Temporary releases from custody

Prisoner may be granted a temporary release from prison under section 21 of the Penal Institutions Act 1954 for the purpose of enabling them to maintain home contacts (Public Prisons Service, 1998). This is known as home leave and is limited to a maximum of three days (72 hours) plus travelling time. Once granted, home leave may be taken at two monthly intervals. Leave is granted only on application by the prisoner. It must be recommended by the prisoner's case management team and supported by his or her partner, family, or sponsor. The prisoner must also have an established home to go to or have made other suitable

---

[46] The Salvation Army has offered the use of their camping facility at Arawhata in the Akatarawa Valley. However, most of the women who meet the criteria for the camp are restricted from leaving the prison due to their security classifications.

[47] Personal communication with the Programmes Manager at Arohata 24/11/97.

[48] Prisoners are advised that telephone access is a privilege and not a right, and such access may be withdrawn or reduced, or the length of calls reduced at any time by the discretion of the prison General Manager.

[49] If sentenced prisoners wish to keep in touch with their lawyer for any reason they must do so via this system. Free telephone access to legal counsel is only available to those on remand.

[50] All intended recipients of calls are contacted to ascertain whether or not they wish to receive calls from the prisoner.

arrangements for accommodation. Prisoners may also be granted day releases to assist with the maintenance of family/whānau relationships: for example to attend a family group conference. The criteria which govern a prisoner's eligibility to be granted home leave or other temporary releases from custody include: his or her security classification; the nature of the conviction; the length of the prison sentence; and the stage of the sentence that the prisoner is at.[51]

National policy for female prisoners

A national policy and related performance standards for female prisoners were drafted and trialled in 1993 and were implemented generally from 1 December, 1994. These were due to be reviewed by 30 November 1997. However, this policy is still in place and is part of the current Policy and Procedures Manual.[52] It states:

Women prisoners are contained in separate secure facilities and are managed in (a) manner which respects women as adults, takes into account their particular needs as women and acknowledges their family/whanau circumstances and personal histories.

It is this latter statement relating to the family/whanau circumstances of women which is crucial to mothers in prison. There are twelve standards[53] indicating what is seen as good practice in New Zealand's women's prisons. Importantly **none** relate to women's unique role as mothers. The only provisions which are made to ensure the maintenance of family relationships and to address the needs a parent may have are general (i.e. the national policy on Family/Whanau Relationship Maintenance and Enhancement) and apply both to male and female prisoners. However, the prison service does have a national policy which recognises the needs of pregnant prisoners and those mothers with babies up to the age of 6 months and this will be discussed further on in this chapter.

New Zealand policies on mothers in prison

There are no facilities provided in New Zealand women's prisons for the accommodation of imprisoned mothers and their infants or young children. In contrast, prisons in many overseas countries provide such facilities.[54] Sections 21 and 28 of the Penal Institutions Act 1954

---

[51]   For example, minimum security prisoners (except those with convictions for violence against the person) are eligible to apply for home leave after serving 1 year since effective sentence date,* or one-third of the time between this date and final release date, whichever is the sooner. The criteria for minimum security prisoners with convictions for violence against the person are the same, once they are within 12 months of their final release date. Medium security prisoners may apply once they are within three months of their final release date and after serving at least two months since effective sentence commencement date. Those serving sentences of life imprisonment or preventive detention are eligible to apply for home leave once the Parole Board supports the temporary release as a pre-release measure. (The effective sentence commencement date refers to the date received in prison either on remand or as a sentenced prisoner.)

[52]   Policy and Procedures Manual, D15 (Public Prisons Service, 1998).

[53]   These are listed in full in Appendix 2..

[54]   For example, in England there are four mother and baby units in women's prisons providing a total of 66 places between them. They are situated at Holloway prison in North London, Askham Grange in York, Styal prison in Cheshire and New Hall prison in West Yorkshire (Caddle & Crisp, 1997). The majority of states in Australia have facilities which allow mothers and their infants to be together (Hartz-Karp, 1983). Some examples of these are: Brisbane Women's Prison in Queensland and Fairlea and Tarrengower prisons in Victoria (Farrell, 1998). Mother and baby units are also to be found in countries such as West

allow women likely to give birth while in prison to be given temporary release on parole to church or welfare agencies and section 94 of the Criminal Justice Act 1985 authorises the early release of prisoners likely to give birth while in prison. However, not all women are eligible for such release since security reasons are taken into account. Also, these provisions do not take into account women with very young children.

New Zealand law theoretically allows for the provision of mother and baby units in women's prisons. Regulation 55 of the Penal Institutions Regulations 1961 states that:

> *Any female prisoner who gives birth to a child, or who on admission has a child less than six months old, may keep the child with her until proper provision is made for its care.*

However, this does not happen as there are no facilities in prisons for babies and the Department of Corrections does not see prison as a suitable environment for children.[55] In the case of a woman who gives birth whilst serving a sentence it is more common to grant her a special release under section 94 of the Criminal Justice Act 1985, as mentioned previously in the section on sentencing policy and practice. The rationale for current policy was stated in 'Prisons in Change' (Department of Justice, 1988: p 392):

> *The department is strongly in favour of the present policy of release wherever possible for inmates who wish to keep their babies. The other possibilities, separating mothers and babies, or providing facilities for mothers to keep their babies while remaining in custody, are both seen as undesirable. Separating mothers and babies is seen as undesirable because of the large body of evidence suggesting that this may cause considerable psychological damage and distress to both. Separate facilities for mothers and babies would not be feasible in cost terms given the low numbers, and the department also believes that a prison is not a suitable environment in which to rear a baby.*

National policy for pregnant women in prison and women prisoners with babies

The needs of women who have the care of babies, or who are pregnant at the time they receive a prison sentence, are catered for under the Department of Corrections national policy on Pregnant Inmates and Women Inmates with Babies,[56] which states:[57]

> *Women inmates who are pregnant or have babies up to six months of age are managed in a sensitive manner that takes into account their particular risks and needs while optimising the wellbeing of the baby.*

Germany and the United States (The Alliance of Non-Governmental Organizations on Crime Prevention and Criminal Justice, 1987; Roulet, 1993).

[55] The Roper Report (1989) recommended that children up to the age of 2 should be kept with their mothers in prison in nursery units where she was the sole caregiver and wished to continue to care for her child. This has not been implemented.

[56] Policy and Procedures Manual, D16 (Public Prisons Service, 1998).

[57] Regulation 55 of the Penal Institutions Regulations 1961, previously cited, is incorporated as performance standard x of this policy.

Performance standards[58] relating to the care of pregnant prisoners cover such issues as: the health of the pregnant woman, both before and after the birth; and information and counselling regarding the pregnancy itself or other options available to the women (e.g. termination, adoption, early/temporary release options). Provision also exists for a pregnant prisoner's partner to be involved in decisions/activities relating to the pregnancy and to be present at the birth if the woman requests. The cultural and religious beliefs of women who give birth whilst in prison, or who miscarry (within 20 weeks of gestation), are taken into account when the disposal of the afterbirth or foetus is undertaken.

Performance standards relating to women prisoners with babies up to 6 months of age recognise the importance of the bonding process between the mother and the child, hence the provision for daily visits. Suitable, safe, secure and private facilities and equipment are to be provided for women who are breastfeeding babies up to the age of 6 months. The importance of bonding between the mother, her partner, and their child, along with other whanau or the child's caregiver (if not the father) is also recognised and is to be facilitated.

The Ministerial Committee of Inquiry into the Prisons System

In 1989, the report of the Ministerial Committee Inquiry into the Prisons System (the Roper Report), was published. This Committee made several recommendations in relation to the needs of imprisoned mothers and their children.

- Section 23.12 recommended that the police should inform an appropriate voluntary community agency when arresting the sole care-giver of a young child and there was no parent substitute at hand.

- Section 23.29 recommended that children between the ages of two and five years be allowed daily visits.

- Section 23.41 recommended for the provision of mother-child units in the grounds of women's prisons.

- Section 23.46 recommended the provision of visiting centres in prisons where children and their mothers could spend quality time together.

- Section 23.48 recommended the implementation of all-day visiting for children during the weekend in a properly equipped and supportive environment for children in all women's prisons.

The Department of Justice Working Party on Women in Prison

The Department of Justice Working Party on Women in Prison[59] was convened early in May 1990 to report on the recommendations made in the Roper Report and it subsequently reported (Department of Justice, 1990) later in 1990 to the Prison System Review Steering Committee. This was made up of representatives from the Ministry of Women's Affairs, the Justice Department, prison custodial staff, the Prisoner's Aid and Rehabilitation Society and

---

[58]   The performance standards for this national policy are quoted in full in Appendix 3.

[59]   The Working Party also investigated several recommendations made in the Department of Justice submissions to the Ministerial Inquiry, however, these were generally related to women's imprisonment rather than addressing the needs of mothers in prison. For example, the provision of a new women's prison in the Auckland area and where men and women were housed in the same prison separate accommodation, facilities and resource allocations should be provided.

the Māori community. Sections of the Roper Report relating to women and their children that were considered and approved in principle were 23.12 and 23.48. Sections 23.29, 23.41 and 23.46 do not seem to have been considered by the Working Party.

In relation to providing greater mother-child contact through all day visiting, the Working Party (Department of Justice, 1990) suggested that there were two possibilities. The first was all-day visiting on weekends (as recommended in the Roper Report) and the second was all-day visiting during the entire week. They also noted that New Plymouth men's prison currently allowed all-day visiting from Monday to Saturday inclusive within prison visiting hours (i.e. morning and afternoon). This arrangement was seen by the prison superintendent to have resulted in reductions in tensions within the prison and in less pressure on visiting facilities. There was also said to be minimal disruption to programmes and employment within the prison and few resourcing difficulties were encountered. It was further recognised that the provision of educational programmes for mothers in prison would help the mothers to deal with issues relating to the effects of the separation on their children and other parenting concerns. It was believed that mothers and children needed to be able to interact in as normal a way as possible during visits, and to this end it was envisaged that children could either spend time with their mother or take part in organised activities. With this in mind, it was suggested that additional staff be provided to cater to the needs of younger children, for whom restricted visiting conditions become tedious after a while, by providing supervision and developing creative play activities for them. The Working Party consequently accepted section 23.48 in principle and made the following proposals (Department of Justice, 1990: p 32):

- All-day visiting over the whole week should be instituted for inmate mothers and children in all women's prisons as a matter of priority.

- A properly equipped environment should be provided for mother-child visiting, including provision of equipment and resources (staffing, space etc), and indoor/outdoor space.

- Special priority should be given to creating an environment for visiting which is conducive to the cultural needs of Māori female inmates or those inmates whose children and whanau identify as Māori.

- Indoor and outdoor spaces should be provided, and advice sought from people with appropriate expertise for design and equipment provision considerations.

- Specialist staff should be appointed to establish appropriate child-care/supervision provisions and activities for regional women's prisons. This would include the possibility of developing child-care training opportunities, and also educational training in child development and parenting skills.

- Women's prisons should establish on-site facilities for the preparation and sale of refreshments for visitors at the prison.

These recommendations were not addressed by the Steering Committee because they were seen as a 'parenting issue' and as such should be discussed along with visiting issues relating to all prisoners, not just to women.[60] After being raised at the first two meetings of the Steering Committee, this recommendation (23.48 - Roper Report) was not discussed in any of the subsequent Committee meetings (as recorded in its minutes).

---

[60] These were being addressed by another Justice Department Working Party which was dealing with the 'Rights, Privileges and Complaints' section of the Roper Report.

In accepting the Roper Committee recommendation 23.12, the Working Party recognised that arrangements made for child-care at the point of arrest are frequently *'sudden, unsupported and often ill-conceived'* and may have negative effects on the children involved. Their proposal (in an amended form)[61] stated (Department of Justice, 1990):

> *The police should ascertain whether an arrested woman has dependent children and make adequate and appropriate arrangements for their care. The arrested woman should be asked to indicate who would be best to provide care in her absence and to indicate her preference as to a community organisation of the Department of Social Welfare being contacted in the event of a relative being unavailable.*

This proposal was accepted in its amended form by the Steering Committee. However, the police had already responded to the Roper Report recommendation 23.12 and in 1989 had implemented a General Instruction to address issues relating to the arrest and custody of sole caregivers of young children and breast-feeding mothers.[62]

Preparing women for reunification with their children

The specific needs of mothers on their release from prison have been well documented by overseas researchers (Eaton, 1993; McGowan & Blumenthal, 1978; National Policy Committee on Resettlement, 1993, Wilkinson, 1988). Trying to re-establish themselves in the community can affect the ability of such women to reunite with their children. In order to regain the custody of her children a woman will need suitable accommodation and a means to support her family. Such difficulties are exacerbated in that women prisoners in New Zealand, like those overseas, are predominantly from the lower end of the socio-economic scale.

Pre-release programmes in New Zealand prisons are directed generally at all prisoners and are usually run by community based organisations contracted to the Department of Corrections. These programmes are pragmatic in nature and the emphasis is on the provision of information, rather than on the delivery of practical and effective assistance. Programme content is usually based on the needs articulated by those prisoners due for release. For example, topics covered may include: welfare benefit entitlements, job preparation, stress management, budgeting, dealing with grief and basic legal rights.[63] Therefore, it would appear, that any pre-release (or indeed post-release) assistance to aid the reunification of mothers and their children would need to be specifically requested by the women themselves, rather than being part of the pre-release orientation package.

Summary

The profile of women in prison in New Zealand is comparable to that of women in overseas prisons. These women are relatively young, predominantly criminally unsophisticated, and serving relatively short sentences of imprisonment. They are more likely to have been the

---

[61] The term 'whānau member' was seen as being open to various interpretations and so was replaced with 'relative'. The Department of Social Welfare was added as it was viewed to be an appropriate option.

[62] This General Instruction is quoted in full in Appendix 4.

[63] These examples were provided by Challenge 2000, a group which has run pre-release programmes for women at Arohata prison.

victims of abuse and to experience higher levels of addictions that their male counterparts. Because they are few in number, women in prison are likely to be imprisoned far from their homes and families which makes it difficult for them to maintain relationships with family and friends.

Such difficulties are exacerbated for those women in prison who have children. Separation of a mother and her children can have negative effects on both parties and pose problems for the successful reunion of the family on the mother's release from prison. Department of Corrections' national policies have related performance standards which take into account the importance of maintaining and enhancing the family/whanau relationships of prisoners. However, apart from policies relating to women with babies under the age of 6 months, there is no specific policy which addresses the unique needs of mothers in prison by taking into account the fact that they are more likely to have been their child/ren's primary caregiver before their imprisonment.

The following chapters in this book will examine the experiences of imprisoned mothers and the caregivers of their children. How both groups perceive that their needs, and the needs of the imprisoned women's children, are being met by current policy and practice, and their ideas for improvements, play an integral part in this analysis. Finally, suggestions for changes in policy and practice to address the needs of mothers in prison, their children, and the caregivers to those children will be discussed, with the aim of ameliorating the effects of separation on both the imprisoned women and their children.

CHAPTER 2   RESEARCH DESIGN AND METHODOLOGY

Introduction

This chapter describes the aims of the research, the premises which underpinned the project and the perspectives which informed the research process. Also described are the methods used: to obtain the sample, to collect the data, to collate and analyse the data, and to present the results. The difficulties that I had in obtaining a sample will be detailed, along with the pitfalls and frustrations I encountered along the way. Finally, the constraints and limitations of a study of this nature will be discussed.

Aims of the study

As described in Chapter 1, the principal aim of this study, based on the initial premise that imprisoned mothers and their children are a vulnerable population, was to find out what happened to children when their mothers were sent to prison. I decided to accomplish this by asking the mothers themselves where their children were, what problems they were having as imprisoned mothers and how the children were affected by this separation from their mothers. I was also interested in obtaining information on who was looking after the children and information on how the women perceived that these caregivers were coping. To provide an added dimension, I asked selected women if they would give me contact details of the caregivers of their children so that I could contact them and talk to them about their experiences in this role. By the end of the initial interviews it became obvious to me that the women's relationships with their children and the care situations of their children did not remain stable throughout their period of separation. With this in mind it was decided to extend the study and conduct follow-up interviews with the women some months later to ascertain how things had changed both for them and their children.

Theoretical basis of research design and methodology

This research has been informed principally by aspects of feminist methodologies.[64] Gelsthorpe (1990) notes the main themes of feminist research methods: the choice of topic, the research method, issues of power and control and the recording of the subjective experiences of the research. This research project is feminist through both its principal aims (i.e. choice of topic) and the research process chosen. The aims of the project (as listed above) were concerned with making mothers in prison visible by describing their reality, albeit through the medium of my narrative. This research is essentially qualitative in nature, which gives an added depth to the women's experiences and allows them to "tell it how it is".

A feminist paradigm also exposes the myth of unbiased, objective interviews and thus acknowledges the subjectivity of the researcher and the researched (Gelsthorpe, 1990; Sommers, 1995). This was the situation with the interviews I conducted. I continually found that the women and I were able to establish common ground through our experiences as mothers or as women and this helped to establish a rapport (however slight) between us. It was impossible not to become involved in what were, at times, very emotional experiences. Such reciprocal experiences also negate the power imbalance inherent in the traditional

---

[64]   For a detailed discussion on feminist perspectives in criminology see Gelsthorpe & Morris (1990). Similarly, Stanley & Wise (1993) challenge existing styles of feminist research thus creating a context for current debates concerning feminist research principles and practice.

relationship between the researcher and his/her subjects. Such positivist objectivity is described by Stanley and Wise (1983) as being obscene in that people are treated merely as objects to be researched, which, they state, is *"morally unjustifiable"* (p 170). Thus, the interview methodology used was interactive in nature, engaging both the researcher and the interviewee in the process (Rapoport & Rapoport, 1976).

As part of this study, I kept a field diary in which I not only described the research as it progressed, but also reflected on my experiences and feelings along the way. The concept of "reflexivity" is used by Roberts (1981) to describe the process through which feminist researchers locate themselves within their work. This personal involvement of the researcher in the research process has sometimes led to accusations about a lack of objectivity: as Loraine Gelsthorpe and Allison Morris succinctly state (1990: P 1-2):

> *To say that you are a feminist usually evokes preconceived notions of identity, role or behaviour. These notions are often negative rather than positive, and you are popularly assumed to be an aggressive, self-seeking, banner-waving woman who prefers work to family life and who, if a mother, abandons her children to a hen-pecked partner, or, worse still, to the state. To say that you are adopting a feminist perspective in an academic discipline or a feminist methodology in research usually leads to puzzlement, claims that there is no such thing, or accusations of bias.*

However, as discussed previously, it is this notion of objectivity which feminist researchers have queried and scrutinised. Du Bois (1983) concludes that a concern with accuracy is not contingent on the practice of objectivity.

The coding and analysis of the data from the interviews conducted centred on the identification of themes which emerged to provide a picture of the women's experiences. These were then quantified, where possible, and illustrated through the use of the women's words. Therefore, this research has also been informed broadly by the principles of grounded theory.[65] That is, the themes (or theories) which emerged were grounded in the data collected and presented in a manner which: *"uses (respondents') words, ideas and methods of expression wherever possible,"* (Glaser & Strauss, 1967: p 125) but which goes beyond these through the interpretation, or analysis, of what has been said (Gilbert, 1993).

Research methodology

The initial stages of this research involved interviews with a sample of female prisoners in the three New Zealand women's prisons (Arohata, Mount Eden Prison Women's Division and Christchurch Women's Prison) during the months of June, July, September and October 1994. During a series of group meetings, usually of women in each wing, held at each of the three women's prisons, the women were fully briefed on the aims of the project and invited to put forward their names for individual interviews. I issued an invitation to all women present, not just those with children. Others were also given the opportunity to take "time out" to discuss any concerns they might have. It was made clear to the women that they could withdraw their consent at any time. Subsequently, 63 women put forward their names, including four women who just wanted to talk. Five of these women (including two who had just wanted to

---

[65]   For a comprehensive overview of grounded theory see Glaser & Strauss (1967).

talk) later withdrew for personal reasons. Subsequently, I interviewed 56 women[66] and chatted generally with another two.

The final sample consisted of 51 women (three of whom were pregnant) who had children under the age of 18 at the time they were interviewed, one woman who was pregnant with her first child, and four women who only had adult children and grandchildren. Follow-up interviews took place at a later date with 36 of these women and the caregivers of the children of 11 of them.[67]

Researching in the prison environment

Spending time within the prisons I was constantly aware of a feeling of isolation - I was neither a staff member nor a prisoner. Nor was I part of any of the other groups which come and go in prisons - e.g. contract therapists, counsellors, educators and so on. I was constantly being referred to as a 'social worker', both by staff and the women, which meant that the women would ask me questions about their children or families, which I could not answer. However, although I was probably part of the 'official system' in that I could leave at the end of the day, the fact that I did not have free access to all parts of the prisons and had to ask staff to unlock doors for me, even to go to the toilet, meant that I received a brief glimpse of what it is like to lose the freedom and autonomy that most of us take for granted.

Moreover, being part of neither camp, so to speak, created problems for me as a researcher. The reaction of staff to my study was not always supportive. I had the feeling that a lot of them thought I was wasting my time and theirs. Why was I only asking the women for their side of the story? Why not interview the staff as well? How did I know the women were telling the truth? It was also clear that my presence enabled some staff, who were disgruntled about internal politics and the perceived lack of communication between management and other staff, to use me as a scapegoat. For example, I was told one day that prison psychologists were complaining that they had come out to see women who were being interviewed by me, when no-one had known that I would be there. This added to my feeling of awkwardness.

I was continually receiving messages from some of the staff such as: *"We know what happens to kids when their mothers go to prison - the families look after them."* I was also told that women in prison do not really care about their children. In contrast, they said that at men's prisons the women arrive to visit with a child under each arm and the men at least take an interest in their children. I found this statement intriguing considering the small number of women in prison who have current partners who both look after the children while they are away, and bring the children to visit them! One of the women provided a brilliant illustration of this situation.

> *I've done the male prison visiting thing for years. There's women trudging out there from fucking miles away week after week after week, putting money in the account, bringing the drugs or whatever, going without. Women go to jail and where's all the guys queued up?*

---

[66]   The majority of these women (53) were sentenced prisoners; three were on remand and were awaiting trial.

[67]   The criteria that I used to select these women are described fully in Footnote 232, Chapter 7.

Subsequently, during interviews another of the women had her own comment to make on staff members who had made similar observations about the nature of the relationship, or more accurately lack of relationship, between women prisoners and their children.

> *That's a load of rubbish because if you go into a cell that a woman with children is in the notice-board has got their (children's) photos up all over the place. They've been to crafts and everything they make is for their children: y'know, photo-frames and teddy-bears ... knitting jerseys, all for children. No, they care about their children, they do. I don't think that people should say they don't. because no-one who runs this prison really knows anyone in here. They don't know us; they just see how our attitude is in here. Most of the time it is an "anti" attitude 'because you're in here because of the system ... coping the best way you know.*

Consequently, I found having lunch or a tea break in the staff room an awkward experience, especially when I was being questioned about why I was there, or when the staff were talking in negative terms about the women.

Even though I did not spend a great deal of time in each prison, the more I was around the more acceptance I gained from both staff and prisoners. For example, women who had not taken part in the study would often express an interest in the project and ask me how things were progressing, when I met them in the corridors. Moreover, women whom I had interviewed would call out to say *"Hello"* when we saw each other. I also noted that while, during interviews, most women were forthcoming and quite open, on leaving the interview room I could almost see the change of attitude in some of them as their barriers went back up. This was obviously how they survived in prison. I never felt entirely at ease and was always conscious that I should not 'blot my copybook' in any way. An example from my field diary illustrates how I was always on tenterhooks. At Arohata, I sometimes conducted interviews in unused offices upstairs in the administration building. When I was using this venue, I had been told that I could make the women a drink if they would like one. On one occasion, I left a woman in the room and went down the hall to make a cup of coffee. When I came back she was not there! I wrote: *"I couldn't find her and freaked out!"* It transpired that she had wanted to go to the toilet and had been told by the staff that she had to go back to the wing to do so. When she returned, I was never so relieved to see anyone in my life.

Obtaining a sample

The initial interviews

Arohata Women's Prison

The initial phase of this project was undertaken at Arohata Women's Prison as I had carried out research there on a previous occasion.[68] The Site Manager of the prison was approached with a proposal for the research during April, 1994 and by May I had received a reply stating her support for the project. Subsequently group meetings were arranged in each of the three wings, for the first week in June.

---

[68]   At this stage, I had not obtained any funding. Therefore, travelling within the Wellington region where I lived was all I could manage.

The women were fairly enthusiastic in principle at these initial meetings and seemed happy to talk about the problems they were having with their children and families. Several of the women remembered me from previous visits that I had made to the prison. I was concerned that the women should not feel pressured into taking part in the research and so I told them to take some time to think about whether or not they wanted to participate. The Programmes Manager said that she would put notices up in each of the wings so that women could indicate if they were willing to take part and what time would suit them. At this stage I felt encouraged by the women's positive responses to what I had to say. In retrospect, asking the women to indicate publicly whether or not they were prepared to take part in the research raises issues relating to preserving confidentiality and respecting their privacy. However, as I had issued an invitation to all women to come and talk to me, for whatever reason, no-one other than the individual woman herself would be aware of the content of the interview.

Due to various misunderstandings, the notices did not go up immediately and it was not until two weeks later that I was told that none of the women had indicated their willingness to be interviewed. It was then suggested by the Programmes Manager that I should come back to the prison and approach the women again. This I duly did and, although the reception I got from the women was definitely cooler than at the first visit, five women from the first wing I visited said they were willing to participate. I then went to another wing and sat around for half an hour before I was told that some of the women did not want to attend the meeting. However, another three women volunteered to be interviewed, making an initial total of eight. I set up interview times with these women for the next week.

During the first week in July, I made another attempt to encourage more of the women to participate in the research. The Programmes Manager had suggested that I should visit the women whilst they were working as this involved talking to smaller groups of women. This was to be followed by a group meeting in the last of the three wings. I subsequently visited the women at work in the sewing room, the kitchen and the laundry, and several more women volunteered to be interviewed. After the last meeting on the wing, I had a total of 25 names; 23 women who were willing to take part in the research and two who just wanted to come and talk to me. I subsequently interviewed 22[69] women from Arohata, 19 of whom were sentenced prisoners and three of whom were on remand.

Mount Eden Women's Division

I telephoned the Custody Manager at Mount Eden Women's Division and arranged to visit during the last week of September, 1994.[70] After an initial meeting with the Custody Manager, I was taken by one of the custodial staff and shown around the women's living areas. During this process, I talked to women on the wings following the same format as I had at Arohata, that is: I introduced the project, answered any questions the women had, and invited them either to take part in the research or just to come and talk to me. Again, interest

---

[69]   I talked to one of these women twice: once to interview her and another time so that she could talk about issues which were upsetting her. She had not been in prison for very long at that stage and was still quite emotional. Another of the women who had put her name forward to take part in the research withdrew for personal reasons. One of the other women told me that this woman had not been in prison for very long and was finding the separation from her small children very distressing.

[70]   By this stage, the project was being jointly funded by the Department of Justice and the Department of Social Welfare Social Policy Agency; the Crime Prevention Unit later made a contribution. Subsequently letters were sent to the management of Mount Eden and Christchurch Women's Prison by the National Manager of Prisons, introducing me and supporting my research.

in the project was greater on some wings than others depending on how many of the women had children and were concerned about them. Twelve women put forward their names to be interviewed, 11 sentenced prisoners and one who was on remand. In addition, one of the women who had been on remand for several months called out to me as I was walking past and asked if she could come and talk to me. As I only had a limited period of time at Mount Eden prison, I obtained the sample and conducted the interviews within a period of three and a half days. All of the 12 women were interviewed then and I spent an hour talking to the woman who had been on remand for some time.

Christchurch Women's Prison

I arranged to visit Christchurch Women's Prison towards the end of October, 1994. My liaison there was the Staff Training Officer, who was very helpful and who showed me around the prison and introduced me to other staff members. The Education Officer at the prison was supportive of my research in principle but she was concerned to know what safeguards I had put in place for the women in terms of informed consent. She said that there had been quite a few researchers who had talked to the women in the past and who had taken advantage of them by using information that they had told them in confidence.

Again, the procedure was similar to that followed at the other prisons. On the first day, I visited two of the wings and found that the women were somewhat suspicious and challenged me to tell them why they should take part in the research. They wanted to know what was in it for them. They could not see any benefit in participating as they believed that nothing ever came out of projects such as this. I had decided that I was not in a position to promise them that the outcome of this study would result in any changes to policy and practices for mothers in prison. Consequently, I said to them that if no-one collected the information on what happened to their children while they were in prison and what problems occurred for them, their children and the caregivers, they would remain a forgotten minority in the prison system. I also asked them: *"When was the last time anyone asked you what you wanted?"* Later, during an interview, one of the women from this wing told me that she had been thinking about what I had said and that she could not remember ever being asked what she wanted or how she felt.[71] Twelve women from these two wings subsequently put their names forward to be interviewed. The next day I visited the third wing where 11 more women volunteered, making a total of 23 women. Later, two of the women decided for personal reasons that they would not participate. However, another two women who had heard of the research and who had not been on the wings at the time of the group meetings, approached me to take part.[72] I interviewed a total of 22 sentenced women at Christchurch Women's Prison and spoke with one who just wanted to talk. Again my time at the prison was limited and this entire process was completed within four days.

---

[71]   Hairston (1991b) reported a similar experience. She said that several of the imprisoned women who were taking part in her study had cried during their interviews and had stated that this was the first time that anyone had shown any interest in them or their children.

[72]   One of these women stopped me in the corridor and indicated that she would like to take part and the other woman indicated her interest through a staff member.

Obviously the women were suspicious of me and my motives, although I stressed my independence from the criminal justice system.[73] One of the women at Arohata had asked me what I would do if I visited a caregiver in their home and smelled marijuana or saw a roach in an ashtray. I replied that it was none of my business. However, later, when I was reflecting on this incident, I thought it was ironic that she assumed that I would recognise the odour of marijuana and know what it looked like.

Women at both Arohata and Christchurch Women's Prison talked about how they were often the subjects of research projects or data gathering and were not informed fully of either what the aim of the project was or what the outcomes were. This added to their feeling of powerlessness as a 'captive population'. In recognition of this, I made sure that all of the women that I re-interviewed received a summary of the results of the first interviews. I then made a point of asking them what they thought about my conclusions and the recommendations that I had made for changes in policy and practice. In principle, the women generally agreed with these but were doubtful whether any changes would actually take place.

The follow-up interviews

From October 1995 through to December 1996 I again visited the three prisons and re-interviewed those women who were still there (11) and obtained contact details, where available, for those who had been released. This process will be discussed further in the section on how I established contact with the women in the community.

The caregivers

Fourteen of the women gave me contact details on the caregivers of their children. I provided a letter for the women to sign which introduced me to the caregiver and which informed caregivers that I was contacting them with the women's consent. Two of the women who had provided such details were on remand and did not subsequently receive a custodial sentence, so I decided not to contact these caregivers. The majority of caregivers had a phone and initial contact was made through this medium. I had addresses for the other two caregivers and contacted them by visiting the address. One of them had moved and I finally located her through being given her address by a former neighbour. All of the caregivers who were contacted, except two, agreed to be interviewed.

Data collection - interviews

Data were collected by means of in-depth semi-structured interviews. Initially, I had decided to obtain demographic information on the women from their files. However, it soon became obvious that it was more efficient to ask the women themselves for this. Files were sometimes not easily found and the demographic information in them had been obtained from the women initially anyway. Questionnaires were designed to be utilised mainly to keep the interviews on track rather than to follow a strict format and were adapted as new issues emerged. Although questions were structured to obtain specific information, they were not always applicable in each case and therefore the circumstances of each interviewee dictated the format and the wording of the interview.

---

[73]   Henriques (1982) and Woodrow (1992b) also reported similar findings.

The process of 'funnelling' was used in the design of the questionnaires, to ease those being interviewed into the process. The assumption made in using this strategy is that those involved in the interview process (the interviewer and the respondent) will find it uncomfortable to begin by talking about issues which may be personally threatening or upsetting to think about (Minichiello et al, 1990). Therefore, general questions formed the first part of the interview and as rapport developed interviewees were asked about their own personal histories. I did not ask the women specifically about issues relating to their children until well into the interview, and I finished the interview by asking them to make suggestions to improve the lot of imprisoned women and their children. This method was also used in the follow-up interviews with the women and in interviewing the caregivers.

Before each interview, the prospective interviewee was given a consent form to sign which explained that what they told me would remain confidential and that they were free to withdraw from the project at any time. I also provided them with details on how to contact me if they wished to do so for any reason, including withdrawing from the project. After the interviews with caregivers and follow-up interviews were completed with the women, I sent all the participants a card thanking them for their involvement in the project and reminding them that they could contact me at any time. I felt that it was important to acknowledge my appreciation of their willingness to participate in the study, which, after all, would not have existed without their contributions.

Where practicable, interviews were taped and supplemented by handwritten notes on the questionnaires. Researchers have noted that the tape recording of interviews can have both positive and negative aspects. It is obviously a means of obtaining a full and accurate record of the interview and can enhance greater rapport by allowing a more natural conversational style (May, 1993; Minichiello et al, 1990). However, some participants are resistant to it. I must admit that I had not thought through the implications of taping interviews with women who had been in contact with the criminal justice system. At Christchurch Women's Prison, the Custody Manager, asked me if I had had any trouble in obtaining the women's permission to tape the interviews. I replied that I had not encountered any. He said that that was interesting because for many of the women the use of tapes to record interviews could remind them of unpleasant experiences they had had during police taped interviews.

All of the interviews with the mothers in prison were taped. A few of the women were suspicious of the tape recorder; one in particular told me that she had been apprehended and charged during a police under-cover drugs operation. However, I explained to the women that the reason for using the tape recorder was so that we could, in effect, just chat without them having to worry about what I was writing down and why. I told them that no-one else would have access to the tape and that it was just for my reference. None of the women in prison objected to the use of the tape recorder; if they had I would not have used it. Although I was concerned with collecting accurate information, I also felt that the women should have as much say in the conditions under which the interview took place as was possible.[74] I felt that this would assist in putting them at their ease.

---

[74] Young (1993) stated that the taping of interviews with women in her research at Mount Eden was seen to be necessary in the interests of accurately recording all that was said. Consequently, the women were not given a choice, if they did not like the idea of being taped they were free not to participate in the study. However, she notes that no-one objected.

Many of the women were often desperate for someone to talk to,[75] especially if they had not been in prison for very long, as was the situation with many of the women I interviewed. Moreover, this appeared to be true also for many of the caregivers. I was contacted by one of the caregivers and one of the mothers some months after I had spoken with them. Both women wanted to discuss the problems they were having and asked for my advice.

The women in prison

Interviews ranged in length from 20 minutes to slightly over an hour and were carried out wherever there was available space. Therefore, recording conditions were not always perfect. Unfortunately, I did not always discover this until I transcribed the tapes, even though I listened to a section of each one immediately after the interview to ensure that the recording had worked. At Arohata, interviews took place in interview rooms, in staff offices, in the chapel and in the chaplain's office. It was arranged that I should ask for the women at the control office and they would be brought down to me wherever I was. At the end of the interview, I escorted them back to the control office, and they then went back to what they had been doing before the interview. At Mount Eden, interviews were conducted upstairs in the original old building. I was given the use of the room which had been the prison remand dormitory. Women had slept in there in bunks and the switches for the lights in the room were located outside in the corridor. The floor was bare boards which meant that voices echoed and interviews were punctuated by the screeching of birds in the roof. This area was separated from the main administration area of the prison by a locked grill. I was told to shout through this when I was ready to come out. I found myself physically unable to do this, so I just stood there until I could catch someone's eye. If I had one of the women with me they would shout out to get the attention of the staff one of whom would come and let us out. When I told the women how I felt, they said they had all felt like that when they first came to prison, but had soon got over this. Again, the women were sent down to the control room as I requested them and I met them there. At Christchurch Women's Prison, interviews took place in a small interview room situated off the main corridor. This room was opposite the control room and so, as I was ready for each woman, I would just go across and ask the staff who would contact the woman and bring her down to me.

Financial constraints meant that I only had limited time at both Mount Eden and Christchurch Women's Prison. This meant that I was sometimes interviewing up to nine women in a day. Although a lot of these interviews were not very long, this was a physically and emotionally draining experience, especially following on from the stressful experience of introducing the project to the women and trying to encourage them to take part. Indeed, in Christchurch I interviewed 22 women in the space of three days. This is the only group of women whom I have trouble visualising; all the other women whom I talked to are clear in my mind. I recorded how I was feeling at the time in my field diary: *"I feel shell-shocked and have difficulty remembering individual women - the day tends to go by in a blur when you interview so many."*

As a result of this stress, and trying to be economical by using both sides of each tape, I taped over a major part of one interview. However, although I lost a lot of the detail, which is what really tells the women's stories, I retained enough information from what I had written and what was still audible on the tape to analyse the data. Also, by the end of that week, as a

---

[75]   Loraine Gelsthorpe (1990) made similar comments when describing her participation in a research study involving five men's prisons in England.

result of sitting in a small room for hours each day talking with women who usually smoked (when I do not), I had almost lost my voice. This was not helpful when I went to interview caregivers the next day.

The caregivers

Interviews with caregivers followed the same general format as those with the women in prison. Interviews were taped where this was practicable and supplemented with handwritten notes. Four interviews were not taped. One was conducted over the phone as a suitable time to visit the caregiver could not be arranged, and another two were not taped as both of these interviews took place in conditions which were not suitable for taping to take place; that is, one was conducted out the back of a busy shop and the other was conducted outside. All except one of the other interviews took place in the caregivers' homes; the exception was conducted at a caregiver's place of employment. Most of the interviews took place amidst the various comings and goings of caregivers' families.

Although some caregivers were hesitant about me talking to them when I first contacted them, during the course of the interviews they became more at ease and were quite happy to discuss issues with me. One example of this was the mother of one of the women in prison, who had been caring for her son for some time. When I phoned her she was not very keen on talking to me; however, she said she would see me if this was what her daughter wanted. She set out one condition: I was to be introduced to her grandson as her friend. I agreed to that and after a two hour drive I arrived at her home. However, the first thing she did when I arrived was tell the boy that I had been to see his mother in prison. By that stage, she seemed quite happy to talk to me. I was made very welcome by all those I visited and more often than not was offered refreshments.

Women in the community

Interviews with women in the community followed the same format as those within the prison. Twenty-three women were interviewed in person and three were interviewed over the phone. Interviews usually took place in the women's homes where it was not unusual for other family members or children to be present. However, before these women could be interviewed, I had to find them and this proved to be by far the most complicated and exhausting part of the whole project.

My plan was to try to contact all of the 43 sentenced women[76] who had been released from prison by the time I was conducting follow-up interviews. To this end, I asked the prisons for access to the women's files so that I could record any information which might help me track them down: for example, their last address or phone number, family/friend contact details or the address of the Community Corrections Office that they had had to report to. Neither files nor contact details could be found for three of the women. Furthermore, most of the information on the other women's files turned out to be out of date, the women having moved either from the address listed or from that area altogether.

---

[76] Forty-five of the women from my sample had been released from prison, however, as two of them had been on remand at the time I interviewed them and did not receive a subsequent custodial sentence I decided not to attempt to track them down. In addition both of these women had problems with addictions, were recidivists and led transient lifestyles: neither current files nor contact addresses could be found for either at the prison.

My first attempt to contact the women was usually to write to them. I wrote letters to 21 women, either directly or through their families.[77] I received only three replies. Only one of these women was living at the address which had been recorded on her prison file. The most common method for finding women's current addresses or phone numbers was either from family,[78] other women who I had managed to contact[79] or through writing to Community Corrections[80] who, I must add, were very helpful in assisting me. As a final attempt to locate nine of the women, I checked the electoral rolls in the areas where they had last been living. Although this often appeared to produce a recent address for the woman in question, this was not a fool-proof method. For example, I thought I had the relevant details to contact one of the women in the sample whom I had not previously been able to get in touch with, although I had written to her family. On arriving at the address which had been listed on the electoral roll, I found that, although a woman of that name did in fact live there, she was not the woman that I knew. At this stage, and to prevent any further embarrassment to all concerned, I decided that the electoral rolls were not a reliable source of information. Also, due to the time involved in tracking the women and funding constraints, I decided at the end of 1996 that I would not make any further attempts to contact those women whom I had still not talked to - however many 'clues' emerged as to their possible whereabouts. By this stage, I could readily identify with Julie Leibrich's (1993) comments about how she tried to develop a *"detective's mentality"* when trying to track down and interview ex-offenders in the community.

Making contact with the women often involved many and varied processes and took a lot of time and energy. There were too many such instances to record in detail. However, the following are a few examples of the types of difficulties encountered. I visited the address I had obtained for one of the women from her file. This was in a large house which had been divided up into flats. There was no-one at home. I also visited the address I had for her mother whom I found out had moved. I then phoned the Community Corrections office who verified the woman's address and suggested that I might try phoning the methadone programme at a local hospital, as it was thought that the woman was still attending this. I decided not to follow that option. The next day I went back to the first address, where again there was no-one at home. As I was leaving, a woman from one of the adjacent flats asked me who I was looking for. When I told her she invited me in and proceeded to tell me a story about the woman I was looking for and her partner, which included scenarios involving the police armed offenders' squad, gang members, drugs and violence. She concluded by telling me that she had seen the woman I was looking for coming out of a house which was situated in a street just up the road. I subsequently made two visits to this new address and, on the second occasion, I encountered people who were moving furniture out of the house. When I asked them if they knew the whereabouts of the woman I was looking for, I was told that she lived a few houses down on the same street. I proceeded to go to that address where I met up

---

[77] See Appendices 14 and 15 for copies of the letter sent to women and the form which was included so that they could indicate whether or not they were willing to see me and provide details of when and where they would prefer this to take place, if they were agreeable.

[78] Nine of the women were contacted through a family member, including in one case, a current partner.

[79] Six of the women were contacted through information given to me by women whom I had been successful in contacting. It was clear that the relationships that some of the women had formed in prison were maintained on the outside.

[80] Where a woman had been released on parole I often contacted the Community Corrections office that she had had to report to. This method was successful in putting me in touch with five of the women I re-interviewed. Community Corrections' staff were also very helpful in verifying addresses of the women who were on their prison files.

with the woman, who was agreeable to talking with me, and conducted the interview. Understandably, she was interested in knowing how I found her!

On another occasion, I wrote to the address of one of the women and informed her that I would be in her area on a certain date. I asked her to respond telling me whether or not she would be prepared to see me. I did not get a reply. When I arrived in the area, which was on the west coast of the North Island, I visited the address, and was told that the woman no longer lived there. I had arranged to interview another of the women in the sample who lived in an adjacent area and, whilst I was there, she told me that she and the other woman still kept in touch. Consequently, she provided me with an address in a city located in the far north of the North Island. I wrote to the woman at this new address, but did not receive a reply. On visiting this area five months later, I called at the address I had been given and was told by the woman's partner that she had just moved out. He said she was staying at a house for which he could only give me a sketchy physical description, with a friend that he only knew the christian name of. I found the road he had directed me to and drove up and down until I saw what looked like the house. I then went in and asked if the friend lived there. Luckily it was the right address; however, the woman I was looking for was not there at that moment but happened to ring the house and so I was able to talk to her on the phone and arrange an interview for the next day.

A final example is where I was unable to contact the woman I was looking for. I had arranged an interview with a woman who lived in a town on the east coast of the North Island. I had the address of another of the women who had been living further up the east coast in a country area at the time she was sent to prison. I drove for more than an hour and finally reached the small seaside settlement where the address was located. While I was psyching myself up to knock on the door of every house (I only had general rural delivery details),[81] I saw a shop and so I decided to ask the shop-keeper for directions. He told me that the young woman no longer lived there but her father lived down the street. I drove further down the road to this house, where the cousin of the woman I was looking for told me that she had moved to Auckland, several hundred kilometres to the north. I had just come from there! Although I subsequently found an Auckland address on the electoral roll for this woman, or one with the same name, I decided not to follow it up. Being away from home, travelling throughout the country, knocking on doors and trying to contact and interview as many women as possible was often emotionally exhausting and depressing. I must admit there were days when I thought: *"I can't face another person."*[82]

Therefore, of the 43 sentenced women from my original sample who had been released from prison, I was able to successfully contact 28 and complete interviews with 26. Only one of the women contacted did not want to take part in this phase of the study. Another woman had been willing to be interviewed over the phone; however, due to unforeseen circumstances I lost contact with her. Three of the interviews were carried out over the phone. I had been playing 'telephone tag' with one of these women unsuccessfully for several weeks and had left my home phone number with her flatmate not expecting her to call me, even though I had

---

[81] The delivery of mail in country districts in New Zealand is regulated by the division of such localities into numbered RD (rural delivery) areas. Therefore a person's address might consist of a road name followed by the name of the closest settlement/town, followed by RD (1,2,3,.....). However, in this situation the address details were even more cryptic, all I had was: "State Highway X" (which, by the way, traversed a sparsely inhabited farming area) followed by the name of the nearest seaside settlement.

[82] Leibrich (1993) aptly refers to this as *"the research blues"* p 257).

left instructions that she could call me collect, as she was in Auckland and I was in Wellington. However, to my surprise, she did. All of the others were face-to-face interviews.

The women were usually more forthcoming during the follow-up interviews and were interested in how the project was proceeding. It was evident that they were no longer as suspicious of me as they had been when in the prisons. They were happy to invite me into their homes and they were willing to give me the phone numbers or addresses they had of other women that I had not been able to contact. All but two of the face-to-face interviews were conducted at the women's homes (or where they were currently staying), usually with other family members or children present.[83] One was carried out in the home of the partner of one woman as it was easier for her to meet me there and another was carried out in a community centre because this woman did not want her husband to know of my visit.

Safety issues

As with any research which involves fieldwork, I had to consider issues of personal safety. Although the prison environment in itself is threatening, I did not at any time feel threatened by any of the women prisoners, although, as I mentioned before, they often challenged me. The situation was the same when I interviewed women and caregivers in the community. At no time did I feel that I was in any danger. However, I must admit that there were times when I was driving by myself on deserted country roads that I did think about what would happen if my car broke down. Also, when I was going into a situation which I perceived might be risky, for example, interviewing one woman whose partner was a gang member, I made sure that I let someone know where I was going to be (although, in that particular case the address turned out not to be the correct one and I ended up somewhere else). So much for safety measures! Generally, however, I did try to make sure that someone knew of my whereabouts most of the time.[84]

I was also fortunate in that, for two trips away from home, either my son or my partner was able to come with me, and wait in the car while I interviewed the women or caregivers. Having someone else to drive and navigate while I 'detected' was a godsend on these occasions. Interestingly enough, if the people whom I was visiting saw that I had someone in the car, they often told me to invite them into the house for refreshments.

Analysis and presentation of the data

The first step in the analysis of the data collected was the transcription of the tapes. This was a long, tiring, and tedious process. Tapes could take anything up to five or six hours to transcribe depending on factors such as: the quality of the recording, how much the woman had to say and how well the woman could express herself. This was often a problem with women for whom English was not their first language, or even for women who were not used to analysing their thoughts and feelings.

After the tapes had been transcribed, a coding schedule was drawn up based on the answers that the women had given and the themes that had emerged from the data. Transcribed interviews were then coded and frequencies produced to present the data in a quantifiable

---

[83]   When interviewing ex-offenders in the community, Leibrich (1993: p 275) noted that "life doesn't stop for interviews and I just joined in what was happening".

[84]   Leibrich (1993) also discusses the precautions she took to try to ensure her safety during fieldwork.

form. This information was supplemented by quotes illustrating how the women themselves felt about the issues we discussed.

The analysis of the information from the interviews has been presented in this book in a predominantly qualitative form, with quantitative descriptions, or frequencies, where this is appropriate. Throughout, I have tried to present the women's realities through the medium of their own voices.

Research limitations

It was not possible to randomly select the sample in this study due to several factors. Firstly, the exact number of women in prison at any one time who have children is not known, and the number of women in prison in New Zealand is small to begin with. Secondly, there are problems with getting imprisoned mothers to participate in a study of this nature due to the vulnerability of their family situations in the community and the fear that their children may be taken into State custody. Also, many women do not want to talk to a stranger about sensitive private issues. These factors also meant that it was not possible to conduct an initial pilot study. However, despite this fact, the questionnaire design was effective in enabling me to obtain the information I needed to describe the women and their children. In addition, although the sample is relatively small, it was generally representative of the national profile of women in prison in New Zealand in that it represents: different ethnicities, geographical spread, spread of offences, and spread of previous criminal experience.

Because I was concerned with presenting the women's reality and their perceptions of their problems and those of their children and the caregivers, questions of the reliability and validity of the data collected did not have a great deal of bearing on this project. I found that the women's versions of events were sometimes coloured by their perceptions of certain situations or what they felt it was wise to say at that particular time. But generally what they told me was borne out by their consistency on issues throughout the two interviews. In fact, the main discrepancies I found in the women's stories between the two interviews related to whether or not they had a live-in partner at the time they were sentenced to prison, especially if they had been welfare dependent at that time. Of course, the caregivers' and the mother's assessment of the children's problems were not always identical, but considering both groups were viewing these from different perspectives this is not surprising. Furthermore, themes which emerged from the data also replicate those which have been reported from research in countries overseas such as Australia, Canada, England and the United States.

CHAPTER 3   A PROFILE OF THE WOMEN

Introduction

This project was undertaken to ascertain what happens to children when their mothers go to prison. The initial stages of this research involved interviews with a sample (56) of female prisoners in New Zealand women's penal institutions (Arohata, Mount Eden Prison Women's Division and Christchurch Women's Prison) during the months of June, July, September and October 1994. This chapter provides a profile of the women who took part in the research.[85]

This sample (of 56) consisted of 51 women who had children under the age of 18 at the time they were interviewed (three of whom were also at the time pregnant), one woman who was pregnant with her first child, and four women who had adult children and grandchildren. Nearly three-quarters (73%) of the women in the sample had only been in prison for a relatively short period of time (less than 6 months) at the time they were interviewed.

Age and ethnicity

Women were asked their age and ethnic origin during the collection of demographic data. Initially, it was thought that this information would be obtained from the women's files: however, this was not as straight-forward as it first seemed as in some cases files were missing. Consequently, the majority of this information was obtained from the women themselves.

Twenty percent (11) of the women were under the age of 25 and 43% (24) were under 30 years of age. Eighty-four percent (47) of the women were less than 40 years old. The ages of women in the sample ranged from 19 to 55 years with the average being 32 years.

All of the women identified with one only ethnic origin. Forty-one percent specified New Zealand European (or Pakeha), 46% as New Zealand Māori and 9% as Pacific Island. A further 4% of the women specified one other ethnic origin group.[86]

Table 3.1 shows the age group distribution for each ethnic origin group. This shows that those who identified as New Zealand Māori were on average slightly younger than the other ethnic groups the women specified. Nearly half (46%) of those who identified as New Zealand Māori were under 30 years of age whilst just under two-fifths (39%) of those who identified as New Zealand European were in the same age bracket.

---

[85]   Sixty-three women put forward their names, including four women who just wanted to talk and five who later decided to withdraw for personal reasons. Two of these women had also just wanted to talk.

[86]   A comparison with Pacific Island and Other ethnic groupings would be misleading because of the small numbers involved.

Table 3.1   Ethnicity by age for women: numbers and percentages

	NZ European		NZ Māori		Pacific Island		Other	
Age	n	%	n	%	n	%	n	%
15-19	-	-	1	3.9	1	20.0	-	-
20-24	4	17.4	5	19.2	0	-	-	-
25-29	5	21.7	6	23.1	2	40.0	-	-
30-34	6	26.1	7	26.9	2	40.0	1	50.0
35-39	3	13.0	4	15.4	-	-	-	-
40-49	4	17.4	3	11.5	-	-	1	50.0
50+	1	4.4	-	-	-	-	-	-
Total	23	100.0	26	100.0	5	100.0	2	100.0

Education level and economic situation

In general, the women interviewed had limited educational skills and little or no work experience. The majority of them (86%) had had some secondary school education whilst two (3%) had attended University for a short time. Seven percent of the women (4) had not been educated in New Zealand but seemed to have reached secondary school level, whilst another of the women had only attended primary school. Data were unavailable for one of the women.

Forty-eight (86%) of the women cited welfare as their main source of income (this included sickness, unemployment and domestic purposes benefits). Another five (9%) women stated that they had been in full employment when sent to prison and two (3%) of the women had been supported by a partner who was employed. Only one of the women reported that she had no legitimate means of support.

Living arrangements

Over half (59%) of the women in the sample indicated that they had lived in rental accommodation prior to their coming to prison. Another fifth had owned their own homes or were paying a mortgage themselves or with their partner. The rest of the women either lived with family/whanau (5%) or had various places of residence (15%) including boarding houses or sharing accommodation with friends. Only one of the women stated that she had no fixed abode at the time she came to prison.

Sixty-one percent (34) of the women said that they had had a partner or were involved in a significant relationship at the time they were sentenced. The partners of 13 (38%) of these women were also in prison. A significant number of these women (20) indicated that they were living with their partners at this time. Slightly less than 40% (22) of the sample stated that they did not have a partner at the time they received a custodial sentence.

Drug and alcohol use

During the course of the interviews, it became obvious that a significant number (64% or 36) of the women in the sample had problems related to substance abuse. However, it was also apparent that around half of these women had already been in rehabilitation or counselling unsuccessfully.

From the women who stated that they had a problem with or used alcohol or drugs, 39% (14) said that they had a problem with drugs and alcohol, 11% (4) reported problems with alcohol only and another 31% (11) stated that their problem lay with drug use only. Nineteen percent of this number (7) described themselves as 'social users', mainly of marijuana. This description of social use may, however, be misleading. One of the women who had described her drug use as 'social' said that she did not think she had a problem until she was asked how many 'joints' (marijuana cigarettes) she smoked a day. She then decided that her usage may have become a problem she needed to address

Experiences of victimisation

Although women were not specifically asked about histories of abuse, a number of them volunteered this information during the course of the interviews. Thirty percent (17) of the women talked about the sexual, physical, or psychological abuse they had experienced either at the hands of their families and/or partners. It was not uncommon for these women to mention experiencing more than one form of abuse. The most frequently reported combination involved psychological abuse and either sexual or physical abuse, with two-fifths of the women saying that they had been subjected to these.

Previous imprisonment

Twenty of the women indicated that this was not their first time in prison, this included previous periods spent on remand.[87] Eighty percent (16) of these women had had children under the age of 18 years the last time they had been imprisoned. Two of these women, who were chronic drug addicts and who had spent several terms in prison, already had children in long term care at this stage.[88] However, for others, their imprisonment led to the loss of custody of at least one of their children.[89] By the time of this current term of imprisonment, although they all had at least one child still under the age of 18, only five of them had all, or some, of their children living with them. Seven had lost custody of their children to family/whanau or ex-partners[90] and two women had children under the age of 18 who were living independently.[91]

Current term of imprisonment

The sample was comprised of both sentenced (52) and remand (4) prisoners. For 36 (63%) of these women it was their first time in prison and for 14 of these women it was also their first offence.

---

[87] At least 45% (9) of these women also had a history of being in the care of the State as children or teenagers.

[88] The son of one of these women lived with her mother and the two children of the other woman had been in CYPFA care for five years, one year prior to her last period of imprisonment.

[89] Three of the women lost custody of children at this time to other family/whānau members.

[90] This number does not include the two women who had lost custody of their children prior to their last term of imprisonment. These children were still in care.

[91] One 15 year old boy and another 17 year old girl who had lost the custody of her own children to her mother who was now in prison.

Offences leading to the women's current term of imprisonment were broadly categorised into four groups. For approximately one-third (34%) of the women, the offence that lead to their imprisonment was one involving violence (including offences such as aggravated robbery, sexual assault, manslaughter and murder). Thirty percent had been sentenced to imprisonment for property offences and 29% for drug related offences. The remainder of the women (7%) had been sent to prison for traffic offences. Table 3.2 presents the length of sentence imposed on the 52 sentenced women.[92]

Table 3.2   Women's sentences: numbers and percentages

Sentence	n	%
< 3 months	3	5.8
3 months and < 6 months	6	11.5
6 months and < 1 year	12	23.1
1 year and < 2 years	10	19.2
2 years and < 3 years	5	9.6
3 years and < 4 years	5	9.6
4 years and < 5 years	1	1.9
5 years and < 7 years	2	3.9
7 years and < 10 years	1	1.9
10 years and over	2	3.9
Life	5	9.6
Total	52	100.0

As indicated in Table 3.2, nine of the women were serving sentences of less than six months, with the largest percentage of the women sentenced to periods of between six months to one year (23%) and between one and two years (19%). Slightly less than 10% (5) of the women were serving life sentences.

Family/whānau imprisonment

Almost half (46%)[93] of the women said that a member of their family had also been in prison.[94] Those family members most commonly mentioned were siblings[95] or a parent, although three of the women said that some of their older children had been in prison at one time or another. Most of the family of one young woman had been in prison; that is her mother, uncles and sisters. She and her siblings had been brought up by her mother and did not know who their father was.

---

[92]   The majority of these women will, of course, be released on parole or remission before the actual date that their sentence expires.

[93]   A total of 26 women reported this.

[94]   This included the ex partners of four women.

[95]   This was so for 12 of the women.

Summary

The women included in this study share the characteristics of the New Zealand female prison population in general, even though this sample was not randomly selected. As in the discussion in the previous chapter, many of the women were in prison for the first time, had committed property or drug offences and were serving relatively short prison sentences. Other similarities that the women had in common with the national profile of imprisoned women were that they generally had few (if any) educational qualifications, they were predominantly welfare dependent before coming to prison and they were often single parents. There were slightly higher numbers of Māori women in this sample which parallels the statistics that indicate that Māori women are over represented in the numbers of women who are sent to prison. Also, a significant proportion of the women reported problems related to the abuse or misuse of drugs and/or alcohol and told of histories of victimisation, as do many other women in New Zealand prisons.

The next three chapters present the data from both the initial and follow-up interviews with the women and explore how the separation through imprisonment has affected these women and their children and their relationships with each other. The characteristics of the children's caregivers are discussed as part of this section. The caregivers' views on the problems they experience as substitute parents and their perceptions of how the children are coping with the separation from their mother follow in chapter 7. Suggestions made by the mothers and the caregivers as to how the situation could be improved for all concerned have been amalgamated and are presented in Chapter 8. The final chapter discusses what has emerged from this study and the implications that these findings have for policy and practice changes within women's prisons, the welfare sector and the wider community.

CHAPTER 4   MOTHERS, CHILDREN AND THEIR CAREGIVERS

Introduction

This chapter presents the data collected from the initial interviews with the 56 imprisoned women. The focus is on the women in their role as primary caregivers and the information that they provided: about themselves, about their concerns as mothers, about their children and about their children's caregivers. All the women in the sample were mothers already, except one who was pregnant with her first child. Another three were also pregnant.

Children

The 56 women had a total of 148 children[96] between them. More than a third (37%) of these women said that they had only one child, whilst just under a quarter (22%) said they had two children. Another nine (16%) reported having three children and five (9%) said they had four children. Almost a fifth (16%) stated that they had five or more children.

The women were asked the current age of their children and this was used to calculate the age of their youngest child when they were sentenced to imprisonment. Over half (52%) of the women had pre-school children (under the age of 5 years) when they were sentenced, including 15 women whose youngest child was aged 2 years or less at this time. The youngest child of more than a fifth (21%) of the sample was aged between 5 and 10 years whilst, for a similar number (21%) of women, their youngest child was between 11 and 18 years of age.

The majority (91%) of the women had children who were under the age of 18 at the time they came to prison[97] and almost two-thirds (63%) of them indicated that they had sole financial responsibility for these children and that these children were living with them. Another five women were contributing financially towards the keep of children in care or of independent children, under the age of 18 years, on limited incomes. Other women (7) indicated that they and their partners were financially responsible for dependent children who were living with them both.

Women who had children living with them at the time they went to prison

There were 39 women[98] who had at least some of their children living with them alone, or with them and a partner, before their imprisonment.[99] These women were caring for a total of

---

[96]   These numbers are based on information collected from the women. As there is no method of verifying the reliability of these data, actual numbers of children concerned could be different (possibly greater). Mothers are often reluctant to divulge the exact numbers of children that they have due to concerns of interference by welfare agencies, which could lead to their children being placed in care (Woodrow, 1992a, 1992b; Carlen, 1983; Stanton, 1980; Rosenkrantz & Joshua, 1982).

[97]   For one of the women, who was serving a long sentence, this was about 6 years before the time that the interviews took place.

[98]   More than half (56%) of these women said that their children had been present at the time of arrest. For four of the women this was also the time of the offence. This was usually where a woman's home was the subject of a drugs-related search warrant or where, in one case, the offence was a driving charge and the woman had all of her children in the car with her. The experience of arrest was often traumatic for both women and children.

79 children. Table 4.1 describes the children's living arrangements before and after their mother's imprisonment.

Table 4.1   Children's living arrangements before and after their mothers' imprisonment: numbers and percentages[100]

	Before imprisonment living with									
	Mother only		Mother and father		Mother and partner		Other		Total	
After custody	n	%	n	%	n	%	n	%	n	%
Natural father[101]	8	13	9	90	3	60	1	33	21	27
Family/whānau	18	30							18	23
Grandparent/s	14	23	1	10					15	19
Mother's friends	9	15							9	11
Foster care	5	8							5	6
Mother's partner	3	5			2	40			5	6
Older siblings	3	5							3	4
Other[102]	1	2					2	67	3	4
Total	61	100	10	100	5	100	3	100	79	100

Slightly less than a quarter (23%) of the children were described by their mothers as either not knowing or not knowing very well the caregivers that they went to live with. These children were: those in foster care and those living with family/whānau or with friends of their mother, with whom they had had little contact.

Almost half (46%) of the children experienced little disruption to their living conditions when their mother went to prison. These children either stayed in their own homes with their caregivers, or went to caregivers with whom they had spent a lot of time. Most of the children who stayed with their father or their mother's current partner, or who were living with family/whānau, were in this category.

In the cases where the women had more than one child (23), there was a 50% likelihood that the children would be separated from each other when their mother went to prison. This type of situation was sometimes complicated. For example, one of the women in the sample had six dependent children living with her at the time she was sentenced: four of her own and two

---

99   Seven of these women also had a total of 10 children who were not living with them at the time they were imprisoned; these children are included in Table 4.3.

100   This table includes an 18 and a 19 year old who were still living at home and financially dependent on their mother at the time she went to prison.

101   Those children being cared for by their father included two who were being fostered by one of the women and when she went to prison they went back home to their father.

102   This category includes two grandchildren who were in the custody of one of the women. These children went back to their mother on their grandmother's imprisonment. Also included in this category is a child of whom the mother said she was sharing custody with her ex partner, the child's father; and a teenager who was at boarding school, but who lived with his mother when it was not term time.

foster children who were family members. When she went to prison, the two foster children went back to their father. Her eldest son went to her sister, the next eldest boy went to his grandmother (her mother) and her two youngest children stayed in the family home with a couple who had been boarding with the family.

By far the majority of the children knew that their mother was in prison. The women said that those children who did not know were too young to understand. One woman with five young children, two of whom had lived with their paternal grandmother since before their mother's imprisonment, spoke of how upsetting this was when the family came to visit.

> *Well they come here, but they really don't know what's going on. I think they think it's a bad place because when they leave and (they're saying) "Come on Mummy, come on." ... And I can't go and then they scream and then I cry. I freak out and I turn the other way so they don't see it. But I think they really think that this is a bad place because they're not allowed ... to run around n'all that in the visiting room and stuff like that.*

The only other exceptions were the two small children of one woman who had been told that she was on holiday and two young brothers who were living separately with members of their father's family. Their mother did not know what they had been told.

Almost one-fifth (15) of the children had had a change of caregiver since their mother went to prison. These changes usually took place at the beginning of their mother's sentence. They often took place when a caregiver who had taken siblings discovered that they could not cope with all the children; when the children did not settle with the caregiver; or when the placement was just a temporary measure until a more permanent solution was found. The teenage children of one woman had decided to sort out their own care whilst she was in prison.

> *My family agreed to move into my house to look after them and a week after I was in jail I rung home and my sisters answered ... and my kids weren't there any more, they run away to their father ... (but) when I rung him he said it was all right ... he'd look after them.*

> *People meant well and offered ... but they'd last a week or two weeks and then they couldn't cope ... I think his (son) behaviour was quite erratic ... and this happened quite a few times until he went to a complete stranger.*[103]

Another woman described a horrific scenario where a change of caregiver resulted in her daughter being placed in a family environment where she had been sexually abused previously while her mother had been in prison on another occasion.

> *I was staying at my sister's place, so my daughter just stayed with her because I got locked up. She came home from school and I wasn't there. My sister had a hole-in-the heart baby and ... couldn't cope. So she sent her (daughter) back to my mother, not knowing what had happened (previously) ... and the abuse took up again.*

---

[103] This child eventually ended up living with his mother's sister in Australia.

At the time of the interviews, this young woman was 17 and living independently.

Caregivers of children who had been living with their mother at the time of her imprisonment

There were 52 caregivers responsible for the care of those children who had lived with their mother[104] before her imprisonment. Who they were is set out in Table 4.2.

Table 4.2   Caregivers of children living with their mother at the time of imprisonment: numbers and percentages

	Caregivers (n=52)	
Relationship to child	n	%
Family/whānau	16	31
Natural father	15	29
Grandparent/s	7	13
Mother's friends	7	13
Mother's partner	4	8
Foster care	3	6

The largest number of caregivers came from the child's own family with almost half (44%) being grandparent/s or family/whanau members. These were almost always[105] female members of the mother's family; in more than two-thirds (68%) the carer was the woman's mother, sister, aunt or niece. The exceptions were where the carers were the older children of one woman, the brothers of two women and the uncle of a fourth. Friends of the mothers often cared for children; they made up another 13% of the caregivers.

The next largest group of caregivers were either the child's natural father (15 caregivers) or their mother's current partner (4 caregivers). Where the woman had a partner she was living with, he often cared for the children. There was only one situation where this did not happen and this was when both the woman and her partner were sentenced to prison. In this case, one son went to stay with his natural father and the other[106] went to his paternal grandmother. However, in 60% of these situations (that is where the caregiver was either the child's father or the mother's current partner), the child had been living with his/her mother alone before her imprisonment. The remaining three caregivers were foster parents, that is they were either not known personally to the mother or were arranged through the Department of Social Welfare (CYPFA).

---

[104]   In two cases, the woman was either the children's grandmother or stepmother.

[105]   In four cases paternal relatives looked after the child/ren. These were a paternal uncle, a paternal aunt, one pair of paternal grandparents and a paternal grandmother. This category also includes the mother of the two children who had been in the care of their grandmother - referred to in Footnote 8.

[106]   This was the child of the woman's current partner.

Almost two-thirds (32) of the caregivers were either single or single parents;[107] only 17 caregivers had a current partner that they were living with. It was not known if three of the caregivers had a partner. By far the majority (60% or 31) of caregivers were welfare dependant. A further 31% (16) were either working, self employed or supported by a partner who was working.[108] There was no information on the other five caregivers. The women said they had little, if any, knowledge of the caregivers' home situations or how they were managing with the extra children in their homes. For example, women were unsure, or did not know, how many of the caregivers had their own children, or, if they had children, how old these children were. However, the information available indicated that at least one-third had dependent children of their own. This number included the current partners of three of the women who had children from previous relationships. These children did not live with their fathers.

Children who did not live with their mother at the time of her imprisonment

Forty-nine women had children living with caregivers at the time I interviewed them.[109] Eighteen of these women had not had either any, or all, of their children living with them at the time they came to prison; half had been in prison before. There were a total of 31 children who had not been living with their mothers before they went to prison. Table 4.3 details where these children were living.

Table 4.3   Children not living with their mothers at the time of imprisonment: numbers and percentages

	Children (n=31)	
Child lived	**n**	**%**
Grandparent/s[110]	8	26
Natural/step father	8	26
Mother's friends	6	19
Family/whānau	5	16
Foster care	4	13

Although women who did not have their children living with them before they went to prison were not the primary focus of this research, they made up a significant proportion of those women who had children under the age of 18 at the time of the interviews. Furthermore, if a woman had a drug or alcohol problem there seemed to be a greater likelihood that her children were, or had been, in long-term care, often with family/whānau. This was so for over

---

[107]   This number includes situations where the mother and father had been living together before she went to prison and the father was caring for their children.

[108]   Where a single parent is imprisoned the caregiver may be entitled to either a partial continuation of the mother's benefit or alternatively to the Unsupported Child's Benefit depending on circumstances such as: the length of imprisonment of the mother and the ability of the other parent to support the child. Those who are caring for children under the guardianship of the Director General of Social Welfare are entitled to board payments from CYPFA.

[109]   The 17 year old of one woman was now flatting.

[110]   Grandparents were usually maternal grandmothers without partners; only two children were living with both maternal grandparents.

four-fifths (83%) of the group of women who did not have some, or all, of their children living with them. Moreover, a whole different range of issues and concerns arise relating to these women and their children, one of which is trying to minimise the damage caused to the relationship between mother and child/ren especially if the aim is for the reunification of the family unit at some time in the future. If this is not possible, or even desired, the women still express a desire for either contact with or information about their child/ren. And it is also crucial for us to have some idea of where these young people are placed and who is looking after them.

Mothers who had all of their children in care before prison

Eleven women did not have any of their children living with them before their imprisonment. Between them, they had a total of 21 children ranging in age from 3 to 14 years.[111] Only the two children of one woman were not living with relatives; even those in the care of the State had been placed with family/whanau. One young woman described a typical care scenario for the children of young mothers whose lifestyles were often characterised by alcohol, drugs and crime:

> *I had him till he was 13 months old and I got heavily into the drug scene and the crime scene ... the gang scene ... because the father of my son is a Nomad ... So my mother took (son) off me, she said ," Look you can't handle him," so she took him. She wants to legally adopt him. Like he is much better off with her, I'd rather him be brought up than dragged up ... if he was with me he would've been dragged up ... A lot of young people I know have given their child to their mother, you know - to the grandmother.*

It was not unusual for these children to have been living away from their mother due to her lifestyle and/or concerns[112] for the well-being of the children.

> *When I had him I kind of gave him (son) to my mother, he was really small ... he was a drug baby. I'd been taking heaps of Valium right throughout my pregnancy and I was working (prostitution) when I had him. I couldn't bring him out of hospital for three weeks because he wasn't feeding ... they were tube feeding him. When I did bring him out of the hospital I just didn't have it there for him ... so I said to my mum - you can have him and she's really over the moon about it ... the thing is when she goes (dies) he come back to me.*

All of these mothers talked about living with some of their child/ren again at some point in the future.[113] The only exceptions were one woman who had adopted one of her sons to whānau at the age of six months and another who had also sent two of her four children to

---

[111] All but one of these women had long term addictions and seven (64%) had been in prison before.

[112] Concerns about the children could have been raised by the mother herself, her family or the State.

[113] One woman had had her children uplifted by CYPFA and had been told that she would never get them back; however, she still talked in terms of "working towards" regaining custody. It was also not unusual for women to say they expected to have their children back to live with them when their family, especially grandmothers, could no longer cope. Expectations such as this may have been unrealistic for the majority of these women as they may have grown apart from their children by the time of their release or, conversely, the children may have become old enough to be independent.

live with family/whanau when they were babies. The majority of these children, who were old enough to understand, knew their mothers were in prison.[114]

Seven of the women had more than one child and in only one of these situations were all of the children living with the same caregiver.[115] Separated siblings did not have regular contact with each other. All of the children, except the brother and sister in professional foster care, knew their caregivers before going to live with them.[116] Another baby had three changes of caregiver (all non family) before he went to live with family when he was nine months old. There had been multiple changes in caregiver for the brother and sister in foster care; their mother estimated there had been five during the five years they had not been living with her.

Mothers who had some of their children in care before prison

There were seven women who did not have all of their children living with them when they were sent to prison. These women had a total of 10 children ranging in age from 4 to 17 years who lived with other caregivers.[117] In the majority of these cases, children lived in a family/whanau environment. Five children, including one set of siblings, lived with their natural father[118] and another two sisters lived with their paternal grandmother. One teenage girl who had spent a period of time in State care in a secure institution had been placed into the guardianship of her whanau. Only two of this group of children were living in professional foster care situations and they were also the only two siblings who were separated. In fact, their mother had lost touch with the elder and was not sure where he was.[119] The women were not asked to provide details of the caregivers of these 10 children[120] as it was obvious that these were either long standing arrangements or that the mothers had little or no knowledge of the care situations.

Long-term caregivers' profile

There were 13 caregivers responsible for the long-term care of the children of the 11 women who had all of their children in care;[121] three were couples, four were maternal grandmothers, one was a child's maternal grandparents, two were female members of the woman's family (her sister and her cousin) and another was a female friend. The final two were male: the child's father and another's stepfather (her mother's ex-partner).

---

[114] This does not include the three adopted children, and the daughter of one woman who said even her parents, the caregivers, did not know she was back in prison again. She felt that if they knew they would use it against her in some way. She said, *"They're real bastards man!"*

[115] These were four young brothers aged from 4 to 8 years of age. Two brothers in another family were placed together; however, their baby brother was living elsewhere. Also another two boys lived with their grandmother whilst two of their siblings had been adopted out to family/whanau as babies.

[116] This does not include those children who had been adopted as babies.

[117] For two of the women this had been some years prior to the interviews I conducted with them so these young people were now independent and, indeed, had their own children. Both girls had been teenagers, about 16 years old, when their mothers were imprisoned for the current offence.

[118] This number included one boy who had always been in his father's custody and the stepson of one of the women. Both women included these boys when asked how many children they had.

[119] She had not been kept informed of his whereabouts and was not sure whether he was in a Department of Social Welfare family home or a boy's hostel; he was 16 years old.

[120] There were eight caregivers in all caring for these children.

[121] This does not include caregivers to those three children who had been adopted as babies.

Over half (46% or 7) of these caregivers were welfare dependent, three were self-employed and three were working. Five were either single or single parents. Approximately a third (4) lived in rental accommodation.

Five of the caregivers had, between them, eight dependent children ranging in age from 7 to 15.[122] The women had concerns about how caregivers who were beneficiaries were managing financially, yet the majority were satisfied with how their children were being cared for.[123] However, two mothers did express concerns about the negative messages they felt their children were receiving from caregivers.

I hear my mother ... "Oh you're no good. You're never going to be any good for anything." And those are messages that they hear ... and they grow up with it. No wonder I ended up the way I was - it's pretty powerful stuff.

When I saw my daughter for the first time in two years it was just so natural, you know how it is between parents and children ... They (caregivers) don't want her (daughter) to know that I'm in prison, they don't want to bring her in here ... and they'll do their damnedest to make sure it happens and they have.

Children in foster care

Placements often broke down for children in professional foster care (CYPFA) situations. One woman who did not have a family had placed her two pre-school children in foster care voluntarily when she realised she was coming to prison. In the 3 months that these children had been in care they had had three placements. The only information their mother had on their current caregivers was a name and an address. She had also been informed by a social worker that she may not get these children back when she left prison, even though she was the one who had initially placed them with foster parents. Another of the women, who had two children in long-term foster care (with separate caregivers) and two in foster care (together) for the term of her sentence, had lost touch with one of the older children and was not sure exactly where he was. This was causing her concern, even though the teenager had not been living with her for three years at the time she came to prison.

Plans to reunite with children after release

Of the 49 women who had children who were living with caregivers at the time the interviews took place, the majority (69%) said that they intended to resume the care of their children when they were released from prison. Another 27% said they were working towards regaining custody of their children, some of whom were in long-term care situations. For these women, their expectations about the ease with which this would happen may have been unrealistic as a number of these women had addiction problems. The difficulty that addictions might pose for some is illustrated by one woman's story. This woman[124] talked

---

[122] The woman with children in foster care did not know much about the family situations of the caregivers. She thought one couple had their own children and had done quite a bit of fostering and that the other couple had just adopted a small boy.

[123] Only one woman expressed concerns about the safety of her children. The mother whose children were in foster care had little, if any, information about the care situations of her son and daughter.

[124] Both of her sons were in long-term care with family/whānau; however, she stated that she would like to live with the eldest one at some stage.

about 'turning tricks' (i.e. engaging in prostitution) since the age of 13 to support both her own and her mother's drug habits. She explained that when she is stressed she feels like a concrete lid shuts down on her and the only way that she can lift it is to take drugs.

Contact – visits, phone calls and letters

The 39 women who had had children living with them at the time they were sentenced to imprisonment were asked whether or not they had had visits from their children. Thirteen of these women said they had not seen their children at all since they had been in prison. On the other hand, two-thirds (26) of the women indicated that they had received at least one visit from their children. Thirteen of these had seen at least one of their children within the last week and another 10 had had a visit within the last month. These data would appear to indicate that women were having regular contact with their children. However, more than half (7) of the women who said that they had had a visit within the last week had been in prison for 1 month or less and none of these women had been in prison for longer than 4 months. These figures may therefore be misleading. Three of the women in the sample had not seen any of their children for over six months. Only three of the 11 women who had children in long term care had received a visit from their children. Women who had spent some time at Mount Eden before going to Christchurch or Arohata frequently said that they had not had any visits since they had been transferred.

A number of women (6) had only had one visit and were concerned that this was all they were going to get. Reasons for this were many and varied but included: the distance the carers lived from the prison; the relationship the women had with the caregivers; financial difficulties where families were on benefits; carers without vehicles or not allowed to drive; and the need for more than one car seat where there were several small children in a family. For one of the women who was serving a life sentence and who had only had a single visit from one of her children in the 12 months since she had been in prison, this lack of visits was a real concern. However, the other five women had only been in prison for relatively short periods of time (ranging from one week to two months) at the time they were interviewed and so it was not yet clear that their concerns, though real, were realistic.

Women who had to rely on PARS (Prisoner's Aid and Rehabilitation Society) or CYPFA to bring their children to visit because of the care situation found it difficult, if not impossible, to arrange for regular visits even if the children were with carers in the area, especially if the children were in separate care situations. If a woman had a supportive family they were more likely to make the effort to bring her children to visit even though they could only do so rarely, depending mainly on the availability of funds and transport. Consequently, whether or not a woman saw her children very much depended on her relationship with the children's caregivers and whether or not she had a supportive family.

> *I've been told by my sister that she won't allow (son) to visit me on his own. (Would she bring him to visit you?) I honestly don't know.*

Those women who had to send out visitors' passes found that this limited the number of their visits. That is, if someone who did not have a pass was able to visit and those who were sent a pass were unable to come, then the woman ended up without visitors. However, conversely, it enabled the women to choose who came to see them. This situation existed only at Christchurch Women's Prison. The justification for this difference in policy is unclear.

Sending out visitors' passes also limited contact by letter for the women at Christchurch. As at the time of the interviews, they were only allowed free postage for three letters a week; this meant that if they sent out three visitors' passes they used up their entitlement. This also meant that outside contact was limited for those women who had no financial support from family/whānau.

Thirty-one of the women indicated that they were able to phone their children. But again whether or not women could speak to the children depended very much on the goodwill of the caregivers. Moreover, a woman's children were often living with separate caregivers which exacerbated the problem. Maintaining contact by phone was an expensive exercise and so many women could not phone regularly or even at all. Women at Christchurch Women's Prison were unable to make collect calls and so were only able to phone their families when they could afford a phone card. There was also a toll bar on the payphone in this prison which meant that women who were not from the district usually had to use the phone in the social worker's office if they needed to make a call.

> *Plus it's a double jeopardy, because a hell of a lot of us are North Islanders or come from out of town. The people who live in Christchurch and can make local calls can also get visits. So the ones that actually need the phone contact more, have less opportunity to use it.*

Those women who were able to make collect phone calls were always worried about the amount of the phone bill their families had to pay. Therefore, this was seen by the women as a no win situation: they could not afford to phone home as their weekly prison earnings amounted to just a few dollars and their families could not subsidise them. Yet if they were able to make collect calls their families ended up in debt.

> *I'm ringing home everyday and the last phone bill that he (partner) got, the first one of me being in here, was $1257.00.*[125]

If, during their separation, the women's only method of contact with their children was by telephone, it was not unusual for that to be curtailed due to the size of the toll bill incurred when the women phoned collect.

> *Yeah, it (phone bill) went up to $800 in three months ... and then the phone got cut off - so that was the end of my contact, apart from three letters.*

Two-thirds of the women kept in contact with their families through letters, sometimes continuing to send mail when there was no response. A number of these women (14) were not sure if their children were receiving their letters, whereas others (22) found that even quite young children could respond by drawing pictures for their mothers.

> *I write to my children fortnightly to monthly and I get nothing back, I don't even know if they're getting those letters.*[126]

---

[125] This was a woman who had concerns about her teenage daughter and was trying to sort out problems over the phone.

[126] This woman did not have a good relationship with the caregivers of her children.

Home leave

At this stage none of the women had been home on temporary release. The reasons for this included not being able to afford to and not yet being eligible. However, all of the women were aware that those who were eligible could apply for home leave and most said that they intended to do so when they were able. Only one woman expressed doubts about the benefits of temporary releases.

A lot of people say they find it traumatic for their children to suddenly have you there and then suddenly you are gone again. I think it's easier when the children come to you and can see where you are and see that you're okay. You know, be able to see where you sleep and see where you eat and then it's sort of like a bit of rest for their minds ....

Furthermore, not all of the women were aware that the cost of home leave had to be met either by themselves or their families and it was felt by some that this might create barriers for them. One woman's comment sums up the prevailing situation in relation to temporary releases.

If you can't afford to go home - well you just don't go!

Difficulties with contact

Fifty of the women stated that there were difficulties associated with contact with their families. A significant number (37) cited the distance families had to travel to visit; others (33) said the cost involved was a factor and a further 18 women indicated problems with the care situations (primarily strained or nonexistent relationships with carers) posed difficulties for them in maintaining contact with, or receiving visits from, their children. Other difficulties that were reported were work or family commitments that prevented caregivers and children from visiting and a lack of transport or accommodation for those who had travelled from a distance. It was also often difficult for families to visit when there were several small children to bring, or when carers were elderly or infirm and were unable to drive for long periods of time.

There are a lot of women in here who haven't had a visit since the day they came in ... because the people who are looking after their children are their parents and they're old and you know, they cannot just cope with the drive all the way up here.

Visiting facilities

Generally, those women who had served previous terms of imprisonment appreciated the changes to visiting facilities that had been made over time. Some of the other women who had had visits were just happy to have had contact with their families and had not really thought about the conditions under which visits took place.

However, when the 30 women who had received at least one visit were specifically asked if they felt that the visiting areas provided catered to their needs, 80% (24) thought that the facilities provided could be better. The rest felt that facilities were adequate or were unsure if they were adequate or not. When the women were questioned about the facilities available they cited problems such as: damaged toys that were dangerous for children to play with; uncomfortable seating; the lack of refreshments; the lack of privacy - staff often stood or sat close enough to overhear conversations; visiting areas which were all non-smoking areas which made it difficult for smokers especially if the visit was stressful; and small visiting areas which were often too crowded which limited communication.

> *In the gym it's so impersonal. Like you know, you just have to whisper n'you know - if you wanna know anything. And the officers are usually sitting, you know, staring ...*

> *I don't think it's a relaxing situation at all really, because they're (staff) watching you like hawks you know, to see that you're not smoking or eating, or you know.*

> *Well, if you're a smoker it's really more of a punishment than if you're a non-smoker. Because I mean you know, when the nicotine levels get low and you're in that stress situation anyway.*

Visits were often emotional times for both mothers and children.

> *They didn't cry, they promised me that they wouldn't cry because they didn't want me to cry. But as soon as they got out of sight they broke down and I couldn't hold it that long.*

> *I can't help myself crying all the time when they come in.*

The women also mentioned that toilet facilities for visitors were often not freely accessible. This meant that precious visiting time was sometimes used up getting staff to unlock doors to take visitors to the toilets. This was especially the case for small children who often wanted to go to the toilet frequently.

> *All mine are toilet kiddies - so when they want to go to the toilet they go outside and I sit there and wait until they come back in.*

Women who had had a visit from their partner and their children also found that they could not easily divide the visiting time between the two. Women said that if they spent the time catching up with their children's news and playing with them, there was no time to discuss adult concerns with their partner or vice versa. One woman said that if she spent too much time talking to her partner, her daughter got jealous and demanded attention.

> *I think your kid's visits should be separate ... I find it really hard when I've got my partner here and I've got my daughter here and it's like I need to talk to him and I need to spend time with her and she gets jealous of me talking to him and like it just ends up being a bit of a hassle ...*

The tenseness of this situation was compounded by the fact that the child lived permanently with an ex-partner of her mother and so did not spend much time with her mother. In addition, the mother's current partner, who was visiting, was a recovering alcoholic and therefore not coping well with her being in prison. Visiting times were particularly fraught for all concerned, but particularly for the mother in that she was trying to spend time with her daughter, who she did not see on a regular basis, whilst at the same time trying to support her current partner.

Another woman who had three small children felt bad that she spent all the time during visits with the children and did not get enough time to talk to her partner who was caring for them whilst she was in prison.

> *I don't have enough time to spend with each child and then when the visit's over I haven't even spoken to him (partner), all I've said is "hello" and "goodbye" y'know, I'm hogging the visit with the kids.*

Visits - a right or a privilege?

I asked all of the women whether they felt that being allowed contact with their children by means of visits was their right as a mother, or whether this access should be a privilege: dependent on their good behaviour. All but one of them stated categorically that visits should be a right of both mother and children and were beneficial for all.

> *They should be a right. The children need to see us as much as we need to see that they're being well looked after.*

> *No I think they should be a right because I don't think families should be penalised for what we've done. They're being penalised, we've been taken away from them. We're the ones that should be punished: not the families.*

> *I think they're a right. I mean your children need to see you. Well I know myself okay, I haven't got little kids but if I had little kids you need to see them. They need to see you each week, I don't care how long you're here for. Even big kids they worry, they wonder how you're getting on ...*

> *They should be a right - no matter what you do, because you still need visits and family can help you, you know if you're going through stress. People in here can't help you.*

Although some women also felt that visits were seen as a privilege by prison staff.[127]

> *Well according to them, they're a privilege.*

One woman who felt that visits were in fact a privilege was, at that stage, on remand and hoping that she would not get a custodial sentence.[128]

> *It's a privilege I think to have your kids (visit) ... but if you want to muck it up it's your fault eh? I think if you're gonna play up and cause shit that's your problem eh?*

---

[127] Farrell (1998) also noted that interviews with staff in the Australian Women's Prisons where her research was undertaken, confirmed that in their view family visits were a privilege rather than a right. The comments of one prison officer in Victoria reflected this view: *"(Mothers) have to maintain that good conduct to have their kids in, it gives them something to work for"* (Farrell, 1998: p 109).

[128] Both her and her husband were subsequently sentenced to terms of imprisonment.

Women's concerns about their children

Interviews with the women were invariably centred around their anxieties about their children. Table 4.4 lists issues of concern for the women who had children who were living with caregivers. This includes children both in short-term (i.e. whilst their mother was in prison) and long-term care situations.

Table 4.4   Women's concerns about children and families: numbers and percentages[129]

Concerns	Women (n=49)	
	n	%
Health of children	22	45
Regaining custody of children	20	41
How families are coping financially	17	35
Children being angry with them or society	15	31
Little or no knowledge of children	14	29
How caregivers (especially women's partners) are responding to children's emotional needs	14	29
That they can't be there when their children need them	13	27
First time away from child for any length of time	12	26
Still trying to be a mother in prison - trying to deal with problems/maintain control of family	12	26
Children bonding with someone else/forgetting them	9	18
Children getting negative messages about them	9	18
Re-establishing relationships with children	8	16
Children being separated	7	14
Safety of children	7	14
Little or no knowledge of care situation or caregivers	6	12
How child/ren are coping at school (mainly academic)	6	12
Losing custody of child/ren to ex-partner whilst they are in prison	4	8

Note: Percentages do not add up to 100 as many of the women had multiple concerns.

As indicated in Table 4.4, the main focus for the women's concerns was the needs of their children and families. Children were often seen to be the innocent victims of the mother's crime.

> *I know we're the one's being punished, but really it's the children that suffer the most and while they're punishing us I don't know if they understand that our children are being punished as well. They're not the ones that did the crime you know? They're innocent.*

---

[129]   This table includes the concerns of all those women who had children living with caregivers at the time of the interviews.

I can take responsibility for my part and I know I'm doing my time for my part in the crime. What about my son? He's an innocent. He had nothing to do with the crime and yet he's getting punished.

A number of women related that it was difficult to feel that you were still a mother while in prison, especially if contact with their children was limited.

Y'know I don't even remember I'm a mother half the time because I don't even hear from him.[130]

On the other hand, those who had served numerous terms in prison said that they found it difficult being a mother when they were actually with their children.

See, I spent most of my life in institutions. Like, he's (son) 10 now and I spent about years of his life with him and that was just about 2 years ago. When I got out (of prison) I was out for about 2 years up until now and then - yeah, I did find it difficult being a parent.

Concerns about the effects of separation

For 26% of the women, this was the first time they had been away from their children for any length of time, and both mother and child/ren were having problems adjusting.

My son was all I had you know, and I was all he had. ... He depended on me and I depended on him and then all of a sudden not to have that because of one stupid moment in my life ... You know I accept my punishment but why should he have to?

We've never been apart you know, we're sort of like the same person ... we're one ... I never thought I'd be apart from her (daughter) ... and the pressure of being away from her - I can't sleep ... it's very bad emotional[ly] ... and not just for me, it is for her too.

One 15 year old boy, who missing his mother, found his own solution to the problem, which resulted in his coming into contact with he police. This caused his mother a great deal of anxiety as he had never been in any trouble before her imprisonment

My eldest got picked up by the police for pinching things from the dairy just across from college where he goes. He did it on purpose, because he just went in and picked up the whole box of chewing-gum while the shopkeeper was there and he ... just walked straight out with it. And when the man came over and told him, "What are you doing?" He says, "I'm taking it what're you going to do?" And so the shopkeeper rang the cops and they came n'pick him up and took him to the station to question him. And they asked him where his parents were and he was really upset that he's done it, but he actually turned around and he says, "My mum's in jail. Take me to jail, I want to stay there with Mum." My ex brought him over to Mt Eden so I can have a talk with him ... and I said, "Look you're not making it any easier for me and you're not doing any good for yourself ... it's not

---

[130]   This woman's son was being cared for by her sister in Australia.

like I'm going to be in jail forever; if you hang in there ... I said, "Look I don't want you to do that sort of thing again" (crying).

Consequently, almost 30% (14) of the women were concerned about how caregivers, especially the children's fathers or step-fathers, were responding to the children's emotional needs in their mothers' absence. About the same number of women (27%) talked about how it was stressful for them when they could not be there for their children in times of need. Children's problems at school (mainly academic) were seen by some women (6 or 12%) as indicative of how the children were affected by their mothers' imprisonment.

It was not unusual for the women to talk about their children being angry with them or with society in general; this was so for 31% of the women.

He's a bit more settled now; but he was wetting the bed, attacking people, destroying things, you know - angry, very angry.

Well my oldest hates me for it - it's her excuse for everything she does now. Everything she does: well, who am I to judge her? I'm a crim ... now that I'm in prison.

A number of women (18%) were concerned about what their children were being told about them, either by the caregivers or by others in the community. Therefore, it is not surprising that some women (16%) had concerns about re-establishing their relationships with their children on their release.

They've just taken me out of society but they've sentenced my kids ... my kids are expected to grow up with other people and when mothers come out of jail they're expected to pick up where they left off.

A similar percentage (18%) felt that their children were bonding with their caregivers and forgetting their mother. This was especially true in the case of those with babies or young children. Trying to fulfil the mothering role from prison was causing concern for a quarter of the women, especially if the principal form of contact they had with their children was either by letter or over the phone. For one of the women this meant that she was not able to guide her daughters through the process of becoming young women. She talked about trying to cope with her teenage daughter telling her over the phone that she had just had her first sexual experience. This woman was really concerned about her daughter's wellbeing and felt that in her absence there was no-one to guide her through this experience and offer advice on contraception.

We had this arrangement that when he (boyfriend) started getting hot and heavy she would come and talk to me ... she didn't have to go into the details of everything, but she would come and say to me, "Okay Mum, I think I'm getting to the point where I might be making some decisions. Could you please put some joeys (condoms) in the bathroom drawer and don't ask me questions about them, just keep them topped up." ... It was all fine and dandy and we had discussions about Aids and all that. But now it's just happened - I got her on the telephone and I've been informed that she's a woman now, she's no longer a virgin and, "Stick that in your pipe when they lock you at night." She can't talk to my partner about it ... she's doing it at home - there's no one to talk to about protection or precautions; she didn't do it with protection or precautions. They just got hot and heavy and did it and I can't discuss it with anybody out there because they'll go back to my partner and he'll come down on her like a ton of crap! A big part of it is getting back at me because who the hell am I to have all these morals? I'm a bloody prisoner!

Concerns related to children's health

Concerns about the health of their children mainly centred around on-going complaints such as asthma and eczema, or were related to feeding problems experienced by babies who were being breast-fed at the time that their mother was sentenced.

And the little one, well I was breast-feeding her at the time that I came to jail and that just dead stopped, so she lost a lot of weight not taking to the formula straight away.[131]

Some women expressed concerns that they had been told by caregivers that their young children had started wetting the bed again. They said that they felt that this was due to the separation: their children were fretting for them.

Concerns about little knowledge of caregivers

A concern for 29% of the women was that they had little or no knowledge of how their children were. One young mother whose two infants were being cared for their paternal grandparents said that although she knew her children were being well looked after, she would just like some communication with the carers.

They don't write to me and that's what I'd like ... about once a week, (to know) how my kids are doing. I know they're doing good, but you know?

Another 12% of the women knew very few details about their children's carers or the care situations. This especially caused concern for those women with children in CYPFA foster care. The children of one woman had had three changes of caregivers in the space of three months.

I've heard that they're a Māori couple. I've heard that ... the guy's a Māori and the lady's Pakeha. I've heard that she's the Māori and he's the Pakeha - (I know) nothing. I have to make the effort to contact them ... and if my phone card runs out here in the jail I've got no way on contacting them.

I've rung him (social worker), left messages, asked them (CYPFA) to include me to meet the new foster parents of my daughter. Everyone else (family) is invited, except for me because I'm in prison. I feel that I haven't got any rights.
I don't know who's fuckin' got them, you know. I don't know. I haven't seen these people - I haven't seen their house. I don't know if they're black, blue, or purple.

---

[131]   This woman had four children under five years of age.

Women whose children were in care arranged by CYPFA stated that they seldom received reports on the children even though they had been informed that these would be provided on a regular basis.

I had to hassle him (social worker) because the kids had psyc (psychological) reports done earlier this year and I had to hassle to get those reports and it took me three months to get the reports.[132]
She (social worker) promised: she said, "I'll keep in touch about where the children (are) or how they're progressing," and she hasn't ...

Ignorance of how the law works often meant that women were not aware that they had signed away custody/guardianship rights which meant that they would lose parental rights over their children. This was particularly a concern for those women whose children were being cared for by their natural fathers, but whom the women were no longer living with. The words of one woman summed up the general feeling.

A lot of us are very ignorant of what happens with the law.

Mothers' participation in and satisfaction with care situations

Fifty-seven percent of the women stated that they were involved in making decisions concerning their dependent children whereas 43% were not consulted by caregivers. Over half (61%) indicated that they felt that issues concerning their children were being concealed from them - primarily so that they would not worry.

Yes, she (caregiver) would be (keeping things from her), but if they were really, really, bad she would tell me. They're (family) not telling me much on the outside, they're just saying they're all good, y'know.

The women said that as they had a lot of time to think, they often worried unnecessarily about trivial matters concerning their children. However, they worried even more if they felt that information was being kept from them. Thirty-two (65%) of the women said that they were satisfied with their child/ren's care situation, whilst 17 (35%) were not satisfied or felt that they had done the best they could in a bad situation.

Whether I am or not (satisfied) is immaterial. I don't ... like a lot of things that are happening, but ... they've got a roof over their heads and they're in a stable home.[133]

Well not a hundred percent but, you know, it's the best that we can do at the moment. I wanted them all to be together but it just can't happen.

Those women who were not satisfied with their children's care arrangements stated reasons such as concerns for their children's safety and poor relationships with caregivers. Women who felt that they had done the best that they were able to for their children mentioned: children being separated from their siblings; children being left with elderly grandparents; not

---

[132] This woman described herself as a *"drug addict and a criminal offender"*. Her two children had been in CYPFA care for the last five years.

[133] This woman had six dependent children when she went to prison.

knowing the caregivers very well; having to ask ex-partners (the children's fathers) who were in new relationships to care for their children; and children being in foster care. Where families were caring for children, some women (35%) expressed concerns about how they were managing financially.

Concerns of women with independent children

The women in the sample had a total of 38 adult children (i.e. 18 years of age or over)[134] who were not living with them at the time of the current offence. Even though these children were legally adult and financially independent, their mothers still had concerns about them and mentioned: taking drugs; not coping with their own children; being angry with their mother; having to take on the responsibility of caring for younger siblings; and keeping things about the family/whanau from them so that their mothers did not worry. The women felt that they had let their families down by not being able to be there for them to offer practical or emotional support and it was not unusual for these women to have completely lost touch with one or all of their children. Visits tended to occur in an artificially cheerful environment as adult children were often worried about how their mother was coping in prison and so shielded her from a lot of the problems the family was facing. This resulted in women reporting that there was a loss of closeness and honesty between the two parties.

The imprisonment of these women had not only had an affect on their children but on their grandchildren also. These children often hated the fact that their grandmother was in prison and were not happy visiting her in this environment. Women were also worried about teenage grandchildren who were acting out and in danger of coming to the notice of the police.

Women's support systems

All of the women in the sample were asked if there was anyone with whom they could discuss concerns that they had about their children. Over half (52%) responded negatively.

> I've never tried ... not about my personal things - I just keep them to myself. But deep in here (inside) I really hurt ... I'm just missing my family eh?

> No, not really - I write it in my diary, for me that's a release.

> I don't know - I've never gone to anybody, I'm not good at that .... I'm not a needy person I just get on with things.

> Not that I know of. They all just tell you to fill in a form. Fill in a form: that's it! If you want to see (social worker) fill in a form.

Many of the women relied on their families for both financial and emotional support which posed difficulties for those without families or whose relationships with them had broken down. Of the 27 (48%) women who said that there was someone they could talk to, most mentioned either the prison social worker or a member of the custodial staff (usually a unit or case manager). However, most women did not feel that they could discuss personal problems

---

[134] This figure includes one 15 year old who has been classed as adult as he was living in rented accommodation and was financially independent (i.e. receiving a Social Welfare benefit).

with prison staff and usually only approached them for practical help (e.g. sorting out payment of children's school fees).

You can only say so much to those people in authority because you don't want to let yourself go. Those people are here, keeping you here, you don't want to really have much to do with them.

I don't get into the habit of discussing my personal problems with strangers - because that's what they are ... I've been to (social worker) once to sort out the school fees ... but other than that I don't talk.

Like you know ... they say that there's help and that but it's bullshit you know, what can they do?

But when it comes to the staff I actually don't trust a lot of the staff ... I have had dealings with the social worker and I find her to be untruthful and untrustworthy .

Ironically, one young mother who had a long history of offending and institutionalisation considered that prison was the only place where she could find the support she needed.

It's the only reason why I came back here: so I can get help

Conversely, another young woman with a similar personal and offending history felt that her concerns were dismissed out of hand by staff when she sought help.[135]

They don't take me serious enough (laughs). Only what I've done they take seriously, but they don't take me seriously.

However, even those women who said that they had no support talked about how many of the women relied on each other for support.

Some of the other women in here we sort of have a support network you know, certain people get together and we fill each other's needs

No, not really, no. No-one that can do anything ... just the women in the wing I talk to them ... we're all in the same boat. I suppose it depends a lot on personalities and understanding of the situation

Summary

In this chapter, I presented a profile of imprisoned mothers, their children and the children's caregivers which reflects that provided by researchers both in New Zealand (Aikman, 1981; Young, 1993) and in several countries overseas: namely the United States (Baunach, 1979, 1985; Bloom & Steinhart, 1993; Hadley, 1981; Henriques, 1982; Hungerford, 1993; McGowan & Blumenthal, 1976, 1978; Stanton, 1980, Zalba, 1964), Canada (Wine, 1992),

---

[135]   Both of these young mothers had problems with addictions and both had daughters in the long-term care of whānau.

England (Catan 1988, 1989; Caddle & Crisp, 1997; Dobash, Dobash & Gutteridge, 1986; Gibbs, 1971; Woodrow 1992b), and Australia (Farrell, 1996).[136]

The majority of the women had children under the age of 18 at the time they came to prison; a significant number were single parents and more than half said that their children had been present at the time they were arrested. The fact that a significant proportion of imprisoned mothers are single parents has been well documented by other researchers (Caddle & Crisp, 1997; Catan, 1988; Gibbs, 1971; Hairston, 1991b; Hungerford, 1993; Kiser, 1991; McGowan & Blumenthal, 1978; Shaw et al, 1990; Stanton, 1980; Wine, 1992; Woodrow, 1992b, Zalba, 1964). The presence of children during their mothers' arrest and the consequent trauma suffered by them has also been discussed in other studies (Baunach, 1979, 1985; Butler, 1994; Henriques, 1982; Kampfner, 1995; Kiser, 1991; McGowan & Blumenthal, 1976, 1978; Smith et al, 1994; Stanton, 1980; Wine, 1992; Woodrow, 1992b). Over half of the women had children under 5 when they were sentenced, including 15 women whose youngest child was aged two years or less at this time. Over two-thirds of the mothers had all or at least some of their children living with them before they were sent to prison. These findings also parallel those of other studies which note that significant numbers of imprisoned mothers have dependent children who are living with them before their imprisonment (Arias-Klein, 1984; Baunach, 1979, 1985; Bloom & Steinhart, 1993; Caddle & Crisp, 1997; Catan, 1992; Farrell, 1996, 1998; Gray et al, 1995; Hairston, 1991b; Koban, 1983; McGowan & Blumenthal, 1978; O'Neill, 1989; Snell & Morton, 1994, cited in Chesney-Lind, 1997; Woodrow, 1992b).

Almost half of the children who had been living with their mother at the time she was sent to prison experienced little disruption to their living conditions. These children were usually being cared for by their father, their mother's current partner or family/whānau. These findings parallel those of Datesman & Cales (1983) and McGowan & Blumenthal (1976, 1978). The latter researchers noted that the imprisoned women in their study appeared to rely heavily on extended family and informal social networks for child-care resources. Conversely, almost a quarter of the children of the women in this sample who had lived with their mother before her imprisonment were placed with caregivers that they either did not know or did not know well. It was not unusual for siblings to be separated when their mother was sent to prison. This separation has been commented on by other researchers both in England (Dobash, Dobash & Gutteridge, 1986; Wilkinson, 1988; Woodrow, 1992b) and the United States (Hungerford, 1993; Johnston, 1995a; Koban, 1983; Michigan Women's Commission, 1993; Stanton, 1980; Zalba, 1964).

Almost one-fifth of the children had had a change of caregiver. This usually took place early in the mother's sentence. Other studies have also found a lack of stability and continuity in children's care arrangements early in the mother's sentence (Catan, 1989, 1992; Morris et al, 1995, Woodrow, 1992b). And Woodrow (1992a, 1992b) in particular draws attention to the fact that the nature of the children's placements, either at the time of their mother's imprisonment or as subsequent placements break down, can impinge on whether or not they are able to maintain ongoing contact with not only their mother, but also their siblings, friends and other members of their extended family.

The largest number of caregivers came from the child's own family; almost half were grandparent/s or other family/whanau members. Caregivers were usually female members of

---

[136]   Farrell (1996) conducted a comparative study in Australia and England on the impact of imprisonment on mothers and their children up to the age of 8 years.

the mother's family, particularly maternal grandmothers. Another third of the caregivers were either the children's natural father or their mother's partner. Where a woman did not have family that she could leave her children with she often relied on her friends to care for them or they went into foster care. These findings are similar to those of other studies which have noted that the majority of children stay with extended family when their mothers go to prison and that maternal grandmothers most often care for these children (Baunach, 1984; Bloom & Steinhart, 1993; Farrell, 1996; Hairston, 1991b; Hungerford, 1993; McGowan & Blumenthal, 1978; Snell & Morton, 1994, cited in Chesney-Lind, 1997; Stanton, 1980) or other female relatives (Caddle & Crisp, 1997; Catan, 1989; Dobash, Dobash & Gutteridge, 1986; Gibbs, 1971; Hadley, 1981; Henriques, 1982; Woodrow, 1992b). The gendered nature of the children's caregivers and the women's support systems has often been commented on by researchers (e.g. Farrell, 1996; Fuller, 1993).

The findings from this chapter indicate that caregivers shared many of the characteristics of the imprisoned mothers; they were also predominantly single or single parents and the majority were welfare dependant. At least a third had dependent children of their own. Other researchers have made similar comments regarding the characteristics of the caregivers of the children of women prisoners (Catan, 1989, 1992; Bloom & Steinhart, 1993; Henriques, 1982; Kampfner, 1995; Prison Reform Trust, 1996; Woodrow, 1992b; Zalba, 1964). In a study carried out to assess the quality of care received by the children of imprisoned mothers, Gaudin and Sutphen (1993) compared the substitute care given by low income family and friends with that provided by foster parents of a higher socio-economic status. They noted that, when compared with infants, older children (3 - 6 year olds) appeared to be disadvantaged by being placed with family and/or the women's friends. They concluded that family caregivers found it difficult to meet the children's increasing needs for social and intellectual stimulation through the provision of toys, games and reading materials and also by providing the children with encouragement and affection and a safe physical environment. However, Gaudin and Sutphen (1993) caution against the generalizability of these findings due to the size and nature of the sample and the significant differences in income between the two groups of caregivers.[137] Despite this caveat, these findings are significant in that they show that the majority of children of women prisoners are being cared for by under-resourced families.

In this study, there were a number of women who did not have any or all of their children living with them before their imprisonment. Other studies have noted that a number of the children of imprisoned women have not been living with their mothers prior to imprisonment (Gibbs, 1971; Hairston, 1991b; McGowan & Blumenthal, 1978; Woodrow 1992b). These were mothers whose lifestyles were often characterised by alcohol, drugs and crime and it was not unusual for their child/ren to be in care because of the mother's lifestyle and/or concerns for the children's well-being. Studies carried out elsewhere have reported similar findings (Baunach, 1979; 1985; Woodrow, 1992b).

For half of the women who did not have either all, or any, of their children living with them when they were sent to prison, this was not their first sentence of imprisonment. Studies carried out in the United States (Hairston, 1991b; McGowan & Blumenthal, 1978; Stanton, 1980; Zalba, 1984) and England (Dobash, Dobash, & Gutteridge, 1986; Gibbs, 1971;

---

[137]   Gaudin and Sutphen (1993) interviewed a small, self-selected sample of 31 extended family caregivers and nine foster parents. The socioeconomic status of the foster caregivers was higher than that of the extended family caregivers.

Wilkinson, 1988) have concluded that the more times a woman has been in prison the less likely she is to have her older children living with her. The children of women who have been in prison previously will, therefore, have been separated from their mothers and possibly their siblings on previous occasions. Hungerford (1993), for example, found that 49% of the children of the imprisoned women in his study had been separated from their mother previously due to her imprisonment. He stated that, therefore, these children had experienced multiple mother-child disruptions during their formative years. Moreover, findings such as this have led researchers (Gibbs, 1971; Hairston, 1991b; McGowan & Blumenthal,1978) to link women's imprisonment to the long term severance of family ties as the likelihood of mother-child reunification decreases with each term of imprisonment the mother receives.

Placements often broke down for children in foster care. This suggests, as has been found in other studies (e.g. Kampfner, 1995), that foster care does not necessarily offer stability to the children of imprisoned women. Mothers seldom had up-to-date knowledge of their child/ren's welfare or progress or of the caregivers themselves. These women often faced the risk of loss of custody/guardianship due to their ignorance of the law. Other studies (Barry, 1985; Baunach, 1979, 1985; Beckerman, 1989, 1991, 1994; Hairston, 1991b; Henriques, 1982; Johnston, 1995a; McGowan & Blumenthal, 1976, 1978) have also suggested that contact between social workers and mothers is strained and infrequent and that mothers are uninformed about their legal status and responsibilities. Recent research carried out by Beckerman (1994) confirmed these perceptions. She noted that imprisoned mothers with children in foster care often did not receive letters or reports from their children's caseworkers, and a significant number (one-third) did not even receive notification of custody hearings. A somewhat dated study carried out by Zalba (1964) reported that the Californian child welfare workers she surveyed regarded the opinions and desires of imprisoned mothers as irrelevant to any plans that were being made for their children in care. The comments made to me by women with children in care indicated that they felt that this was still the situation today in New Zealand.

Almost all of the children knew that their mothers were in prison except those who were too young to understand. These findings are consistent with those from other studies (Baunach, 1979, 1985; Butler, 1994; Caddle & Crisp, 1997; Datesman & Cales, 1983; Henriques, 1982; Woodrow, 1992b) which have also noted that whether or not children know of their mother's imprisonment is largely a function of their age and level of understanding of the situation and the nature of the mother's offence and/or her relationship with the caregivers.

Research on imprisoned mothers indicates that most women plan to reunite with their children on their release from prison (Baunach, 1979, 1985; Caddle & Crisp, 1997; Datesman & Cales, 1983; Hairston, 1991b; Henriques, 1982; Koban, 1983; McGowan & Blumenthal, 1976, 1978; Woodrow, 1992b; Zalba, 1964). The expectations of the women that I interviewed were identical: the majority of the women planned to resume the care of their children on release; others said that they were working towards having their children live with them again. However, the expectations of this latter group may have been unrealistic as these women had usually not been living with their children prior to their imprisonment and many had addictions to deal with. Both Hairston (1990) and McGowan & Blumenthal (1978) reached similar conclusions. This idealized view women in prison can have of their relationship with their children and of their ability as mothers has also been commented on by other researchers (Baunach, 1979, 1985; Henriques, 1982; Hungerford, 1993). For example, Hungerford (1993) reports that throughout discussions and interviews with the imprisoned mothers in his sample, a theme which was common was "how they were good mothers and how they will continue to be good mothers upon release and reunification with their children" (p 88). However, the mothers' perceptions of their relationship with their children were not often validated by their teenage children: mothers rated themselves higher on scales measuring mother-child attachment norms than their teenage children did.

The women in this research primarily maintained contact with their children through visits, letters and phone calls. Few women, however, received regular visits from their children. These findings duplicate those from other studies (Baunach, 1979, 1985; Bloom & Steinhart, 1993; Catan, 1989; Hadley, 1981; Hungerford, 1993; Kiser, 1991; O'Connor, 1996; Snell & Morton, 1994, cited in Chesney-Lind, 1997; Stanton, 1980; Young, 1993). Whether a woman received regular visits depended to a large extent on the nature of her relationship with the caregivers and whether or not she had a supportive family. Women with children in foster care rarely had visits from their children. It has been suggested by Koban (1983) that having to depend on an extended network of family, friends and social agencies for contact with their children works to the women's disadvantage. It is important to note, however, that other studies have found that some women do not want to see their children whilst they are in prison as they feel it would be too upsetting for all concerned or, conversely, they do not want their children exposed to the prison environment. These findings have emerged from research carried out both in New Zealand (O'Neill, 1989; Young, 1993) and in other countries (Bloom, 1995a; Datesman & Cales, 1983; Hairston, 1991b; Henriques, 1982; Kiser, 1991; Sack et al, 1976; Stanton, 1980;).[138] None of the women in this sample voiced such sentiments.

Attempting to maintain contact with their children by letters and phone placed restrictions on those women with very young children. The cost of phone calls made it difficult for women to be able to talk their children on a regular basis. This expense was exacerbated by the women's imprisonment far from their home areas which meant that phone calls inevitably incurred long-distance call charges and by the fact that their children could be living with separate caregivers. The prohibitive expense of phone calls for women prisoners has been remarked upon by other researchers (Farrell, 1996, 1998; Gray et al, 1995; Wine, 1992; Woodrow, 1992b) along with the limited access women have to telephones and the lack of privacy when using them (Caddle & Crisp, 1997; Henriques, 1982; Morris et al, 1995; Stanton, 1980). For example, Caddle & Crisp (1997) found that the expense of phone calls was the problem most frequently mentioned by the women prisoners in their sample,[139] although other problems such as long queues, noise and lack of privacy when using the phone were also cited.

Women who maintained contact with their children through letters often kept writing even if there was no response. Others found that even young children could respond by drawing pictures for their mothers. Other studies have also noted that most imprisoned women maintain contact between themselves and their children in the form of letters and phone calls (Baunach, 1979; 1985; Bloom & Steinhart, 1993; Caddle & Crisp, 1997; Datesman & Cales, 1983; Farrell, 1996; Morris et al, 1995, Young, 1993; Woodrow, 1992b) - although, admittedly, some children will be too young to read or write, or even to respond by drawing

---

[138] However, Hairston (1991b) found that the mothers' stated desires for visits were related to whether or not they in fact received visits from their children. None of the women who said they did not want their children to visit had received a visit. She conjectured that it was possible that some women who did not receive visits compensated by saying that they did not want them.

[139] Forty-nine percent of the women in Caddle and Crisp's sample said that they could not afford to buy phone cards.

pictures (Baunach, 1979, 1985; Wilkinson, 1988). Conversely, Stanton (1980) found that few of the women prisoners in her study kept in contact with their children by means of letters. More than one-third of the mothers never wrote to their children and approximately 62% never received letters. She concluded that if there was no communication between a mother and her child/ren by means of letters or phone calls, it was unlikely that there would be any visits.

Geographical distance, lack of transport, cost, and the woman's relationship with her children's caregivers or families were those reasons most often cited by the women for the scarcity or non-existence of visits by their children. The main barriers to visiting or other contact with their children talked about by the women in this study have been noted by other New Zealand studies (Young, 1993)[140] and have been found by other researchers to be similar to the problems faced by women in prisons in other countries such as Australia (Butler, 1994; Farrell, 1996), England (Caddle & Crisp, 1997; Morris et al, 1995), the United States (Baunach, 1979, 1985; Bloom & Steinhart, 1993; D'Arcy, 1994; Datesman & Cales, 1983; Hadley, 1981; Kiser, 1991; Sametz, 1980) and Canada (Faith, 1993) For example, Bloom & Steinhart (1993) cited the distance between the child's place of residence and the prison as the primary reason for infrequent or non-visitation by children of imprisoned mothers in their study. More than 60% of the children lived over 100 miles from the mother's place of imprisonment. They also noted that caregivers were often angry with the mother for prolonged periods of substance abuse, criminal activity, or repeated imprisonment, and were reluctant to take the children to visit their mother. These difficulties are compounded for those women with children in foster care (Beckerman, 1991; Henriques, 1996; Johnston, 1995a; Wine, 1992), especially where the foster parents may see the mother as an "unfit" parent or where they have established a relationship with the children that they fear may be lost if the mother and her child/ren maintain contact (Bloom & Steinhart, 1993).

The women in this research described the prison visiting facilities as under-resourced and lacking; visiting areas were too crowded and afforded little privacy to the women and their families. Staff maintained a visible presence and were often close enough to be perceived to over-hear conversations. These sentiments echo those of the women in Dobash, Dobash & Gutterdige's (1986) study carried out in Cornton Vale women's prison in Scotland. The pervasiveness of this under-resourcing of visitors' areas in women's prisons has been noted by other researchers both in New Zealand (Aikman, 1981; Phillips, 1992; Young, 1993) and overseas (Butler, 1994; Farrell, 1996, 1998; Hampton, 1993; Rosenkrantz & Joshua, 1982; Shaw et al, 1990; Morris et al, 1995) Farrell, describes the facilities provided in such areas as 'neglected, inhospitable', and 'abysmal' (1996, p 299).

The findings in this chapter are centred around the women's perceptions of the problems that their children and the caregivers are facing and how the children are coping with the separation from their mothers. This is so too of the majority of studies which have been carried out elsewhere (e.g. Baunach, 1979, 1985; Caddle & Crisp, 1997; Farrell, 1996; Fritsch & Burkhead, 1981; McGowan & Blumenthal, 1976, 1978). Only a few studies have included the perspective of the children themselves (Stanton, 1980; Henriques, 1982; Hungerford,

---

[140]   Young (1993) carried out a study at Mount Eden prison to discover how imprisoned mothers reacted to, and coped with, being separated from their children. She interviewed 17 women, 13 of whom were mothers.

1993; Woodrow, 1992b)[141] and/or of their caregivers (Bloom & Steinhart, 1993; Henriques, 1982; Hungerford, 1983; Woodrow, 1992b).

The primary focus of the women's concerns was the needs of their children and families. A number of women voiced concerns about re-establishing relationships with and/or regaining custody of their children and were worried about their children becoming distant with them. Other concerns the mothers talked about related to problems concerning their children's health and/or their children's behaviour and emotional state; and problems related to their children's schooling and to the mother's lack of knowledge of caregivers. Other studies have also noted the concern of women prisoners for their children's health and welfare, for the continuation of the mother-child relationship and for the reunification of the family after release (Baunach, 1979, 1985; Butler, 1994; Caddle & Crisp, 1997; Hairston, 1991b; Henriques, 1982; Hungerford, 1993; Kolman, 1983; McGowan & Blumenthal, 1978; Woodrow, 1992b). Approximately a quarter of the women echoed sentiments expressed by New Zealand women prisoners interviewed during two previous studies carried out at Mount Eden prison (Clark, 1979; Young, 1993) when they said that they found it difficult still trying to maintain their role as a mother whilst in prison. Mothers were also concerned about their children getting negative messages about them from either their caregivers or others in the community. These findings parallel those of Woodrow (1992b) and Henriques (1982) who commented that mothers were afraid that their children might develop negative attitudes towards them because of the influence of caregivers. For a quarter of the women in this research, it was the first time they had been away from their children for any length of time. This is also a common theme in other studies of women prisoners (Baunach, 1979, 1982, 1985; Caddle & Crisp, 1997; Koban, 1983; Woodrow, 1992b). Concerns about how their families were coping financially were also discussed by over a third of the women as they have been by imprisoned women in other studies (Datesman & Cales, 1983; Young, 1993).

Researchers have also documented a range of behavioural and psychological problems in children precipitated or aggravated by the imprisonment of their mothers which are similar to the findings described in this chapter. Children are noted to be having problems at school (Baunach, 1979, 1985; Bloom & Steinhart, 1993; Fritsch & Burkhead, 1981; Henriques, 1982; Stanton, 1980) and as displaying anger and aggression (Butler, 1994; Johnston, 1995d; Woodrow, 1992b) which often led children, particularly teenagers, into contact with the police (Baunach, 1979, 1985; Hungerford, 1993; Stanton, 1980). Of course, it is important to note that the problems that children may be having do not exist in isolation for, as Baunach (1979, 1985) remarks, poor school work or health problems may be related to underlying emotional or psychological problem and children's problems may have existed before their mother's imprisonment (Woodrow, 1992b; Stanton, 1980). Indeed, Stanton (1980)[142] found

---

[141]   Woodrow (1992b) obtained a sample of 15 children of women prisoners and ex-prisoners by means of a national advertising appeal launched in various newspapers, magazines and journals. These children had been aged between 7 and 16 years of age at the time of their mother's sentence and the majority were either in their late teens or their 20s and 30s at the time of responding to the advertisements. Woodrow describes their experiences as similar in nature and the information that they gave her as supporting much of that obtained from the caregivers and imprisoned mothers in her study.

[142]   This is the only study which has measured outcomes directly upon the children and provided quantifiable comparative data. Stanton (1980) compared the school behaviour, self-esteem and academic achievement of 49 female prisoners' children aged 4 to 18 with that of 35 similarly aged peers whose mothers served non-custodial sentences. Her findings indicated that children experienced a variety of emotional and school-related problems after their mother's imprisonment.

that the mother's socio-economic status and prior criminal record had more bearing on a child's academic performance than whether or not she was currently in prison. Furthermore, teachers surveyed were unable to distinguish between the behaviour of children before and during their separation from their mother.

Women felt that issues were being kept from them by caregivers, especially family, so that they would not worry, as did mothers in Young's (1993) sample and those interviewed by Woodrow (1992b): unfortunately, this caused them to worry even more, especially since they had a lot of time to do little else! However, the majority of the women said that they were satisfied with their children's placements and caregivers; those who were not invariably had a poor relationship with the caregiver. These findings are similar to those of Baunach (1979, 1985), McGowan and Blumenthal (1978), Caddle and Crisp (1997) and Woodrow (1992b) who reported that mothers generally expressed more satisfaction with their children's living arrangements when they were being cared for by an immediate relative.

A mother does not cease to have concerns about her children when they become adults. The women talked about how they were worried about their adult children and often said that they felt that they had let their families down by not being available to provide support for them. Grandchildren were also seen to be affected by their grandmother's imprisonment. Similar conclusions were reached in a study carried out to explore the family relationships of female prisoners at the Dwight Correctional Center for women in Illinois (Kiser, 1991). Researchers found that even adult 'children' may find the arrest and imprisonment of their mother an unsettling experience. One of the women who took part in the study reported that her adult son, a father of three, wept uncontrollably when told of her arrest and when he visited her in prison she said: "We cried most of the 30-minute visit every Saturday. It was the only thing we were able to do. Words were lost to us" (Kiser, 1991: p 58).

The main source of support, both financial and emotional, for women was their family/whanau, a factor which has been noted by other studies (Bresler & Lewis, 1983;[143] Farrell, 1996; Shaw et al, 1990; Young, 1993). This posed problems for those without families or whose families had disowned them. In addition, almost half of the women said that if they had a practical problem they could go to prison staff for assistance; however, most felt that they could not discuss personal problems with those in authority. These findings are consistent with those of Genders and Players (1988) who reported that long-term women prisoners sought practical assistance from prison staff, but kept personal anxieties to themselves. It has also been documented that issues relating to a lack of trust and concerns over confidentiality may also prevent women prisoners from seeking help from or confiding in prison staff (Morris et al, 1995).

In conclusion, the key findings from the initial interviews indicate that imprisoned women are often single mothers with dependent children. Some of these women will not have their children living with them especially if they have been to prison before and/or suffer from addictions. Siblings are often separated when their mother goes to prison and if there are no family members to care for the children they may go into foster care. Caregivers themselves are often from the disadvantaged end of the socioeconomic spectrum and are usually members

---

[143] It should be noted, however, that these authors reported that this was predominantly true for the imprisoned black women in their sample, even though most came from "broken" homes. White women, on the other hand, appeared to be emotionally, as well as geographically, distanced from their families and often spoke bitterly of them.

of the women's families. Few imprisoned women have any sort of regular contact with their children whilst they are in prison and voice concerns about their children's well-being.

Women are still in the main the primary caregivers of their children and the key findings from the initial interviews indicate that when a woman goes to prison her family is often split up, especially if she is a single parent and solely responsible for the financial support of those children that she has living with her. This was so for 32 of the women in this sample. One of the women who was serving a long sentence put it this way:

> *I don't necessarily believe that it's right, that it should be this way, but the reality is it's women that maintain family relationships. When a hub's pulled out the whole wheel falls apart - when a guy goes to prison it (the wheel) keeps on turning, it's just one spoke missing ...*

The maintenance of the mother-child relationship during a woman's incarceration is crucial - not only to her sense of self-esteem and her potential for rehabilitation, but also in minimising the impact of the separation on both her and her child/ren. The data from the initial interviews reinforce that information which is already available: the need for additional resources to assist women in prison to maintain contact with their children and family.

Some of the data presented in this chapter appear to give the impression of a static picture, especially that relating to the whereabouts of the women's children and the contact that they have with their mother. However, I became aware during the data collection of the fragility of many of the care arrangements. When families were contacted it soon became apparent that situations were in fact dynamic and had often changed within a fairly short period of time. Sometimes, this took place at the request of the mother herself. Examples such as these gave rise to the question of whether or not placements that the women were satisfied with at the time they were interviewed were maintained throughout the sentence and until the women were released from prison. The instability of children's placements whilst their mother is in prison has implications for the well-being of the children for, as studies have shown, children who are subject to several changes of living environment and/or caregiver may exhibit behavioural and/or developmental problems (Richards, 1992).

Subsequently, I decided to track these women over time (both in the prison and in the community) with a view to providing a more extensive picture of what happens to children when their mothers are imprisoned and the effects of imprisonment on the relationships between women and their children. These data are presented in Chapters 5 and 6.

CHAPTER 5   STILL BEHIND BARS

Introduction:

The next two chapters present the results of the follow-up interviews with the women. This chapter discusses the experiences of those women still in prison and the following chapter discusses the experiences of the women who had been released. The total sample re-interviewed was 11 women still in prison, and 26 women in the community: a total of 37 (66% of the original sample). I decided not to seek to re-interview two of the original 56 women as they had been on remand at the time of the initial interviews and did not subsequently receive custodial sentences. Two women contacted were not re-interviewed: one declined and contact was lost with the other who had earlier been prepared to be interviewed over the phone. Therefore, of the 54 women I attempted to re-interview, contact was made with 39 (72%) and successful interviews were conducted with 37 (95%). Interviews took place between late October, 1995 and early December, 1996.[144]

Women in Prison

Eleven women were re-interviewed in prison:[145] interviews took place between late October, 1995 and early June, 1996. The majority of these women (64%) were re-interviewed more than eighteen months after the initial interviews. All except one were serving their original sentences at the time of the follow-up interviews. The one woman who was not had been serving her first term in prison at the initial interview; by the time of the follow-up, she was serving her third.[146]

Current location of the women

Seventy-three percent of the women were still serving their term of imprisonment at the same prison where they had been at the time of the initial interview. One woman categorised as still being in the same prison (Christchurch Women's) had spent four months at a prison closer to her family (Mount Eden). All of the women who had transferred had requested this themselves. Although wanting to be nearer their children was a factor in this request, it was not the sole factor. Other reasons included: wanting a change of environment and wanting to be closer to a partner who was also in prison.[147]

---

[144]   Forty-three percent (16) of the women re-interviewed were New Zealand Māori, 38% (14) were New Zealand Pakeha/European, 14% (5) were of Pacific Island origin and 5% (2) were English. The description of the ethnicity of the women is based on their own identification from the initial interviews.

[145]   Five (46%) were Māori, 4 (36%) were New Zealand European (Pakeha) and 2 (18%) were English.

[146]   This current sentence was for theft and receiving and she was given a three month prison sentence in addition to having to serve a 12 months suspended sentence received previously. Previously she had completed half of a nine month sentence and had only been out of prison for five weeks or so before she went back in. Since she had been in prison this last time she had had her sentence increased by a month for possession of drugs.

[147]   For two of the women, these requests may have had their basis in more serious reasons. One had been assaulted by two female prisoners and the other had barricaded herself in her cell and tried to hang herself. This latter incident was described to me by the aunt of the woman, who was the caregiver to the woman's son.

Length of time women had been in prison

Table 5.1 shows that nearly half of the women (46%) had been in prison for more than three years at the time the follow-up interviews took place.

Table 5.1   Length of time in prison: numbers and percentages

	Women (n=11)	
Months in prison	**n**	**%**
6 months and < 12 months	1	9.0
12 months and < 18 months	1	9.0
18 months and < 24 months	2	18.0
24 months and < 30 months	1	9.0
30 months and < 36 months	1	9.0
> 36 months	5	46.0

The woman who had spent the least amount of time in prison was the one, mentioned previously, who was serving her third term of imprisonment since the first interview. The five women who had spent more than three years in prison at the time they were re-interviewed were all serving sentences for violent offences. Three of these women were serving life imprisonment. These five women had all been in prison for at least four years and one had been there for eight years of her sentence plus a period of several months on remand. The two women who had been in prison for between 18 and 24 months were both in the early stages of a life sentence.

The children

The 11 women had a total of 43 children, including adult children. Over four-fifths (9) of the women had three or more children. Four of the women had only adult children and grandchildren. Sixty-four percent of the women (7) had at least one child under the age of 18 at the time of the interviews. These seven women had a total of 17 children under the age of 18.[148] As can be seen from Table 5.2, only three of the 17 children under the age of 18 years were pre-schoolers, and approximately three quarters were aged between 11 and 17 years.

---

[148]   Twelve of these children were still with caregivers, one 16 year old was flatting and two teenagers (aged 16 and 17) in the same family had left school but could not find work; one stayed most of the time with her Aunt, and her 17 year old brother and a younger 15 year old sister (who had been expelled from school) were being cared for by their father. There was an older brother who had spent some time in prison and it was not clear whether or not he was at home with his father also. The 17 year old son of another woman was presently serving a term of Corrective Training at Rangipo prison.

Table 5.2   Ages of children: numbers and percentages

Ages	Children (n=43)	
	n	%
3 - 4 Years	3	7
5 - 10 Years	6	14
11 - 17 Years	8	19
Over 18	26	60

The care situation of the children under 18

Three of these 17 children had had a change of carer or living situation since the initial interview with their mother. One teenager could not cope with the rules set in place by his caregivers and had rebelled against them. He ended up getting into trouble with the police.[149] The other two children who had had a change of caregiver were both from the same family. One had been living with her maternal grandmother and two siblings and went from there[150] to another care situation with friends of her mother. This placement broke down due to her mother's dissatisfaction with the carers and she was placed with another friend.[151] Her older sister went from a placement with one of her siblings - again with 'friends' of her mother[152] - to live with her father in Australia. She had recently left home to go flatting; she was 16. The 14 children who had not had a change of caregiver included the three teenagers mentioned above. Approximately 90% of the children were said to have maintained a stable home and school environment since the first time their mothers were interviewed.

The mother's perceptions of the care situation

The women had little or no real knowledge of caregivers' living or financial situations, particularly in the situations where there was no contact or ongoing relationship between the carers and the mother or between the mother and her child/ren.[153] When asked if they felt the caregivers were experiencing any financial difficulties, the majority[154] of the women indicated that as far as they were aware there were no problems. However, two of them were quick to point out that they felt that, even if the carers were having problems, they would not worry the women with them. This applied to situations where caregivers were either family/whanau or friends of the women.

Generally, the women with children in care considered that their children were being well looked after, even if they did not have a good relationship with the caregivers themselves. However, one woman had concerns about the health and safety of two of her children, who were with the same caregiver, and felt that her other son was only receiving adequate care

---

[149]   This is the young man undergoing Corrective Training at Rangipo, mentioned previously.

[150]   Her grandmother was not coping well with the three of them.

[151]   This woman was a single parent and part-time student with a nine year old son.

[152]   This was a girl whom there had been problems with the first time I interviewed her mother. She had been angry with her mother and this had posed problems for their relationship.

[153]   This was the case for three of the women.

[154]   Five out of the six women (83%) with children living with caregivers responded in this manner.

from her sister. This mother had lost custody of her three children due to the offence that she had been imprisoned for.

Contact between mother and child/ren

This section relates to the levels and frequency of contact that the women had with all their children, including adult children and grandchildren. Table 5.3 sets out when the women had last seen any of their children and relates to all the women who were re-interviewed, not just those with children in care.

Table 5.3 Length of time since mothers have seen their child/ren: numbers and percentages

	Women (n=11)	
Contact	n	%
Within last week	3	27
Within last month	3	27
Within last 6 months	2	18
Over 6 months	3	27

Three women had seen at least one of their children in the last week. One of these was a woman with adult children and grandchildren whose family travelled a long way each weekend so that they could visit her. Another had transferred to a prison further from her son and had just had a special visit from him and his caregiver. She had effectively gone from a situation where he was able to visit her every week to one where this could be the only visit she got until she was released. The third woman was serving a long sentence and fought hard to maintain contact with her children. She had four children with three different caregivers and was fortunate in having a strong support network that she could call on to transport the children to visit her at least once, and sometimes twice, a week.

Those women who had seen their children within the last month felt they had fairly regular visits from at least one of their children. One of the women had three teenagers still at home and did not expect them to visit her very often. She was soon to be released and lived in the area where the prison was situated. On the other hand, the majority of the women who were serving long terms of imprisonment had limited or no contact with their children. The three women who had not seen their children for over six months all had children living with caregivers who would not bring them to visit for reasons other than the cost and distance they had to travel: for example, the relationship between the caregiver and the mother was poor or having contact with their mother was not seen (by social workers or the court) as being in the best interests of the children. There were seven children in this last category: five were in the care of CYPFA and two were in the care of family.

Prison family days

For many women, prison family days were the only opportunity they had to spend quality time with their children and others close to them.[155] For nearly three-quarters (73%) of the women, however, there had not been a family day at their prison since the previous year: that is more than six months ago. For two of the women there had been a family day within the last month. One woman was at a prison that did not hold family days due to restricted facilities.

Over half of the women had had family members present at the last family day at their prison. Once again, however, things are not always as they seem. The majority of these women (67%) had adult children, grandchildren or teenagers[156] as their visitors. Only two women had younger children visit.[157] It was not uncommon for friends to come to spend the day with a woman if her family could not, or would not, come. However, such visits were dependant on whether or not the woman had friends in the area where the prison was situated or within a reasonable travelling distance. The three women whose families had not been present at the last family day stated that distance, expense, family commitments and poor, or non existent, relationships with caregivers, were the principal reasons.

Changes in type or frequency of contact

Two of the women reported that the type of contact that they had with their children had changed since they were first interviewed; both of these women had maintained contact with their children through fairly regular visits at that stage. This meant that for most of the women the situation had remained the same; that is, if contact was usually maintained through visits it had remained so over the intervening period. Of course, this also meant that if contact had been one sided or unsatisfactory (for example, women writing and not getting replies or phoning and not always being able to speak to their children) this status had also been maintained.

The same two women reported that they were having less contact with their children compared to when they were first interviewed. One had moved to a prison further from her family and the other was serving her third prison sentence since the first interview. Her ex-partner was reportedly not keen to keep bringing their teenagers to visit her. In addition, he had a new partner and so was not visiting the woman herself any more.

The three women who had been transferred to other prisons were asked whether or not this transfer had affected their contact (either negatively or positively) with their children. One, who had been agreeable to being transferred to Arohata which was further from her son who lived with whanau in Christchurch, reported that for her the level of contact was worse than when she was at Christchurch Women's Prison. Two other women who had transferred to prisons closer to where their children were living, in order to facilitate contact with them,

---

[155] Mount Eden prison did not hold family days for the women there as the limited nature of the facilities would not allow it. With regard to Christchurch Women's and Arohata the women were asked when the last family day had been at that particular prison.

[156] The youngest of the teenagers was 15 years of age.

[157] This woman had five children aged: 12, 11, 9, 8 and 4.

reported that they still had little or no contact with their children.[158] It had not made a difference.

One of the other women had been on temporary transfer to a prison closer to her two children to try to initiate some sort of contact with them. However, in the three and a half months she was able to stay at the prison before increases in the muster necessitated her return to the South Island, the caregivers of one of her sons would only bring him for a single one hour visit, and she only managed to speak to the other once on the phone. She felt that if she had been able to stay in the area where her children were it would have been easier to apply to the court for access:

I'd have better chances of fighting it up there being on home turf than what I can from here. I mean I'm miles apart from them; I'm on the other side of the ocean.

This woman's oldest son had just turned 6 and she had sent him a birthday card for the first time. She did not know if it had been given to him. During the brief contact she had had with her boys, it was obvious to her they did not know who she was - that is, their mother - and she felt it would be unfair to the children to disclose such information to them at this stage. This was particularly painful for her as it was obvious from comments the boys made that they had regular access to their father in Paremoremo prison.[159]

Difficulties associated with contact

As mentioned previously, the type of contact that the women had with their children had generally not changed in the intervening period between the two interviews. Similarly, the difficulties that the women felt were associated with maintaining contact with their children had not changed during this period (i.e. the cost, the distance, and the nature of the mother's relationship with the caregivers). However, for those who maintained contact by phone, the situation had worsened. In addition to their use of the phone being limited by their ability to purchase phone cards and having to obtain staff permission to make collect calls[160] to their families, a new phone system[161] had been initiated which further limited the women's contact with the outside world.[162]

---

158 One of these women had three sons with whom CYPFA was involved. After her transfer, she had had semi-regular contact with her youngest child, who lived with her sister, until CYPFA had curtailed this approximately five months before. She continued to write to two of her sons although she was not sure if they were getting the letters as she did not receive replies. These letters had to be sent via her sons' social worker so that she could approve them. Ironically, this woman had voluntarily transferred to a prison with fewer resources in terms of programming and industry so as to be closer to her children.

159 These two brothers will have been apart from their mother for approximately 10 years by the time she is eligible for release and will be teenagers. At the time of the interviews she was not having any contact with them and so her chances of re-establishing a relationship with them were minimal, unless she was successful in gaining some form of court mandated contact.

160 At the time of the first interviews, the women at Mount Eden and Arohata had been able to call their families collect.

161 Progressively from May 1995 all prisons in New Zealand were subjected to a new system. Existing pay-phones are now computer-controlled; prisoners pre-select up to 10 telephone numbers that are vetted by the prison before being approved. Those contacted have the option of declining to remain on a prisoner's list. When the calls are put through, those called are greeted with a pre-recorded message advising them that a prisoner is calling and that they have the option at this stage of refusing to accept the call. The rationale behind the new system is that it prevents the intimidation of witnesses, and the incurring of debts by prisoner's families for collect calls.

162 The women talked about hearing that the new phone system was a result of male prisoners phoning their partners collect and thus having the women incurring large debts as they were scared of the consequences

How visiting conditions have changed over time

The women were evenly divided on whether or not they thought that visiting conditions had changed within the prison since they had first been interviewed. Half felt that conditions were still the same, that is confining, stressful, lacking in privacy and having few facilities for their children (e.g. toys or play equipment). The other half had mixed opinions. Some felt conditions were worse and others felt conditions had improved over time.

Christchurch Women's Prison could probably be described as having the best visiting conditions of all the women's prisons and Mount Eden the worst and so those women who had been transferred from Christchurch compared their current situations to those previously experienced and found them lacking. For example, they pointed to the confined nature of the conditions at Mount Eden and the poor facilities at Arohata (for example, the smaller gym, the lack of access to the outside, the lack of play area for the children, and the general run-down environment).

Yet, even at Christchurch Women's Prison, adverse changes in visiting conditions were referred to by two of the women. Half of the visiting area in the gymnasium had been blocked off, leaving only a small area for the children to play in and the women were no longer allowed access to the children's outside playground.[163] One woman described how this affected her visits with her family:

> *My family spend most of their time running after the children to make sure they're not hurting other children or falling off the swings ... They (staff) said it's the drugs, of course the women that get the drugs in don't have children, or if they have children they don't know where they are - you know what I mean ... (and they're) not likely to be playing out there with them either.*

Another of the women, who had an adult family and a good support network of friends who often visited, felt that visiting conditions had improved. When she had first come into prison, she had had to sit opposite her visitors, whereas now she could give them a hug and sit next to them. However, she was unsure whether or not this depended on the staff who were supervising the visits rather than on changes in policy.

Changes in effects on women of contact (or lack of contact) with their children

Eight women[164] experienced some sort of ongoing contact with their children; 75% of these women had noticed changes over time in how they were affected. However, these appeared to be more related to the women's adaptation to prison, rather than to the level, and type, of contact they had with their children. One woman commented about how she now viewed the visiting experience with her family.

---

if they refused to accept the calls; whether this was true or not, the general feeling was, as one woman succinctly expressed it: *"Like I say, a man stuffed it up - women are penalised. Get used to it!"*

[163] See Footnote 36 in Chapter 1 for the basis for this policy.

[164] The three women who are not included in this analysis had little or no contact with their children at the time of the interviews.

Like in some ways I suppose it's become routine, it's become easier, but I do feel I'm getting more distant from them emotionally ...

For others, contact with their children was still hard to cope with, possibly even more upsetting than before. This was especially so for those who did not have any physical contact with their children through visits.

Ah it's just a very long time ... I came here and my youngest one was just a little kid - (now) she's a mother.

Oh yeah, it still upsets me as much. But I mean at the moment I'm powerless to do anything about it ... Well it's worse in a way, because I aren't (sic) able to say to them (kids) I'm going to see you soon ...

Changes in effects on children of contact (or lack of contact) with their mothers

Nearly two-fifths (38%) of the women had also observed changes in the effects of contact on their children, including both those whose contact was regular and those whose contact was only limited. These changes were not always negative. One woman, who had regular weekly visits from her young children, stated that it was less distressing for them now than it had been, even for the youngest who was 4 years old. They were:

Yeah, pretty much taking it in their stride ... pretty much routine now.

Another woman felt that contact was less stressful for her adult children now as she had been dealing with issues of familial abuse within the course of counselling and was, for the first time, able to be open with them and they with her.

The woman who had been transferred to a prison further from her family considered that her son was becoming more upset and withdrawn as time went on. She had spent a lot of time in prison and felt that he was angry and disappointed with her due to this fact.

Yeah, he's just quiet. Oh he talks to me n'that, but like when it comes to leaving he just looks back at me, you know, and I know he doesn't want to leave me.

One of the women, who had an adult family and grandchildren, talked about how they all put a great deal of effort into not becoming emotional or upsetting each other. This enabled her to feel that her family were coping without her and her children to feel that she was coping with imprisonment. This woman talked about not wanting her family to be upset when they left her after a visit. Her adult children and partner had a four hour drive home and she did not want them driving this distance while stressed out about her.

It depends on me - if they leave and I'm stressed, then of course, they're going to stress. But when they leave (if) I'm happy that I've had a visit and I'm happy to let them go ... they see that (and) even though they might be, like me, masking it ... I let them go.

Other women, who felt that there had not been any change in the effects of contact, were of the opinion that, for their children, contact with their mother was pretty much a routine exercise, in that she was just a voice on the end of the phone or that they had adapted well to the prison visiting experience.

> *(Daughter) treats this place like a bloody marae (laughs) and the staff all like aunties because they were really, really good with her over the years ... She just breezes in here, not a problem, and chats away.*

> *We have quite good conversations on the phone and he tells me about his school ... and he's doing this and he's doing that ... he's quite happy to talk to me.*

Mothers' concerns

As mentioned in relation to the first interviews conducted with these women, they had concerns about all their children, not just those who were under the age of 18. Table 5.4 lists the issues most commonly referred to in the second interview.

Table 5.4   Mothers' concerns: numbers and percentages

	Women (n=11)	
Concerns	**n**	**%**
They can't be there when their families need them	6	55
Child/ren getting negative messages about them (caregivers and/or community)	5	46
Behaviour - delinquency, acting out at school or at home	4	36
Growing apart from loved ones - children or partner	4	36
Little or no knowledge of children	3	27
Fighting for access to child/ren (visiting/contact)	3	27
Child/ren being angry with them	3	27
Child/ren bonding with others	3	27
Re-establishing relationships with child/ren	3	27
Trying to fulfil parenting role from prison	3	27
That they can't share special times with their child/ren	3	27
Other maternal family members not having access to child/ren	2	18
Child/ren's health problems	1	18
Problems for children at school/academic	2	18
Caregivers alienating child/ren from them	2	18
Children suppressing feelings	2	18

Note: Percentages do not add up to 100 as women often had several concerns

As with the initial interviews, the most commonly voiced concern for women with adult children was that they could not be there for their families when they needed them. A range of problems that had been experienced by the women's adult children since I had last talked with them included: unwanted pregnancies and/or abortions, eating disorders, breaking the law, grandchildren going into care, and illness in the family. In addition, missing happy events, such as sharing special times like the birth of a grandchild, were mentioned.

> *Oh that was horrible. I actually broke down that day, when I heard that she'd (daughter) had the baby and it was so tiny. I stood out in the corridor there howling for the baby and it's really freaky for me because I don't cry very much and when I do I feel like I'm losing control.*

It was believed that problems being experienced by families could have been dealt with more efficiently or even averted if the women had been at home with them.

> *I would've said, "Look we can manage." But I can't say "we" because "we" are in here.*

The paradox here is that it was not unusual for comments such as this to be made by women whose lifestyles were chaotic, to put it mildly, before they came to prison. It seems likely that these women had a romanticized notion of how they would have coped with these situations.

> *Well I was a fucked up addicted mess when I came to jail too, but given where I'm at now, if I was out there I'm quite sure (daughter's) bulimia and addiction wouldn't keep progressing.*

> *I think if I hadn't come to jail, I'd be dead ... drugs, violence, driving, violent home, violent partner ... yeah I was an accident waiting to happen ... it was like getting crazier and it was getting faster and faster like the craziness was coming closer and closer.*

Generally, the types of concerns that the women said they had at the first interviews were re-iterated when I talked to them again. The women's concerns centred around: the sorts of messages their children were getting about them from those in the community;[165] the health and well-being of their children; their children bonding with others; having little knowledge of children in long term care; and still trying to be a mother in prison.

That they and their loved ones, children and partners, might become more distant with each other also worried over one third of the women. One woman said she could feel herself becoming more emotionally detached from her children, the oldest of whom was 12, even though she had regular visits from them.[166] Another had fears that her adult children thought she was distancing herself from them, when in fact she did not feel that she was, but rather that she was only concentrating on her personal needs more.

As with the first interviews, issues related to the re-establishment of relationships with their children were frequently talked about by the women.

---

[165] Nearly half of the women expressed related anxieties. Worries such as this were more commonly talked about by women who had younger children living with caregivers, especially if there was not a good relationship with the caregiver and the woman did not have visits from her children.

[166] This woman was serving a long term of imprisonment which had only just begun when I first talked with her.

He doesn't say it (that he's angry) he shows it ... he just pulls, I know he really wants to hit me ... he's stroppy.

I killed the only father he knew. So you got a boy that sat in court and said what he was told to say ... Can you imagine how he must be feeling? ... And with that guilt comes anger for me I would say.

The reason I (was transferred) was ... my transition period to reunite the family ... so my kids and my mother and my sister can get to know me again.

Another factor which had remained stable was that women still felt that their families were keeping things from them. Again, this was primarily thought to be so that they would not worry when they were not in a position to be able to help.

They come to visits and they're all happy n'smiling and you know if anything is happening I'm not going to know about it ... I've said to them, "Why don't you tell me?" - "Oh we didn't want to worry you."

Although the women appreciated the intentions behind their families' actions, the result was that they felt they were not part of the family any more, as this meant sharing the good and bad times with their children. In the case of those with young children, such a situation could lead to children being questioned by the mother in an attempt to find out what was happening with them and their carers.

Support systems

The women were asked about their support systems, that is, whether or not they thought they had anyone they could share their concerns with about their children or families. Two women responded *"No"* though mentioned someone who had supported them or whom they discussed their problems with. The majority of women, therefore, seemed to have some form of support. Those referred to by the women are listed in Table 5.5 below.

Table 5.5   Women's support systems: numbers and percentages

	Women (n=11)	
Support	**n**	**%**
Prison staff	9	82
Family/whānau	4	36
Other prisoners	3	27
Friends	2	18
PARS[167]	2	18

Note: Percentages do not total 100 as some women mentioned more than one source of support.

The main source of support for the women had not changed and came from within the prison itself; over 80% cited prison staff. Those most often referred to, in order of frequency, were: the social worker, custodial staff (e.g. Unit Manager), and the chaplain. Family also played an

---

[167]   Prisoners' Aid and Rehabilitation Society.

important role in supporting the women and this was mentioned by nearly two-fifths of the women. The women also relied on each other and their friends in times of crisis. Two of the women had utilised the services and support offered by PARS fieldworkers and said that these were useful. However, clearly some women felt that field workers did not always live up to their promises, and that disappointment or uncertainty was the last thing they needed in their situation.

> *Since I've been up here I've asked them about paying for my boys to come and visit me right? Now I asked two different people from PARS they were gonna get back to me ...*

> *I've watched PARS telling other people that they would help and I've thought no, I don't think I'll ever ask them ... (Why?) ... Oh, I've sort of watched one woman being promised every week that they'd bring her children out and she didn't get to see them for five months ... I just thought it was a bit disgusting how they kept saying, "Yes, yes, we're sorting it out," and nothing ever got sorted out.*

Generally, almost three-quarters of the women (73%) felt that if they had a family related problem they could get the help they needed to sort things out, which was important since most of these women had been (or would be) in prison for some time. Two women considered that their children's care situations were such that any problems could only be sorted out by a lawyer and neither had the money to afford legal representation. Indeed, one remarked that if she had that sort of money she would not be in prison in the first place.

Changes for the women as mothers

The women's perceptions of how things had changed for them as a mother since the last time I spoke with them indicated that for many the prison experience had been positive. Nearly half of them (46%) said that for the first time they had the luxury of being able to concentrate on their own needs, which they felt had enabled them to be a better parent. They talked about dealing with: addictions, healing processes related to past abuse, and personal growth and development.

> *Just at the moment I'm working on myself and dealing with my addiction and things like that and I'm also working on being a parent too ...*

> *I feel better ... I really do, I feel better ... and I've got a lot of support ... from in here ... and I've talked very openly about my wrongs as a mother ... women have asked me certain things and I just tell them it's part of self-healing and that you've gotta want to do it ... I wanted to do it, I saw the damage that my family had gone through ... and I honestly wish I could turn back the clock ...*

For two of the women, this had had identifiable benefits. One said that she felt that she had gone full circle and was back to the time before things went wrong for her and her children; another indicated that, for her, the time had come to make changes, such as dealing with a long standing drug addiction and making up for years spent in prison away from her son. Sadly, however, this woman also did not think she would ever feel like a mother to her 11 year old son:

I don't think I'd be able to feel like a mother, I'd probably feel more like a sister (a) friend, than his mum ... (Why do you think that is?) ... I don't know because I look at him as being my little brother ... (I've) only had him in dribs and drabs during his whole upbringing ... all told I've had him for two years ... yeah, I'd say about two years.

Although almost half (46%) of the women still felt like they were mothers, being in prison meant that they could not actually perform that role in relation to their children. Fifty percent [168] of the women with young children said this.

I feel that I'm a surrogate mother. I'm a mother who can't be a mother. I'm a very torn up mother (crying) and the years lost can never be replaced.

I ... still feel the same feelings for my kids as I always have ... it's hard to explain. I suppose I get really frustrated that I'm not there, especially if something goes wrong ...

One woman who had just become a grandmother expressed similar sentiments.

Yeah ... because I'm a grandmother too, it's a different role, and it's not a role that I've lost it's a role that I ... should have that I've never had ... Yeah, I feel like it (a mother and a grandmother) I just can't act it out. I want to do stuff like baby-sit while they go out for dinner.

Another woman, when asked if things had changed for her, replied:

Well they've gotta have - I don't even remember seeing you. ... Um well they haven't changed a lot but ... at least I'm not totally wasted this time ... (You feel you've got more control over things?) ... Well I wouldn't say that either, but I'm more aware of what's going on ...

Relationship changes

Approximately one-quarter (27%) of the women felt that their relationship with their families had not changed since I last spoke with them. One of the women who was of this opinion had had little or no contact with her adult children and grandchildren, so her perceptions were based solely on limited contact through letters. Another was the woman with three teenage children whom she tended not to worry about a great deal, and the other had a large family who visited her often. Two mothers reported that they did not have a relationship with their children. Neither of these women had had contact with their children due to the care situations. One woman felt that the personal growth she had experienced during her time in prison had resulted in her children being unsure of how this would affect their relationship.

We love each other you know but I think it's more a fear for them than it is for me ... they've noticed that I've changed and they worry that I might not be the mum that I was when I come home, they worry about that ...

---

[168]   Three out of six women responded in this manner.

She tried to alleviate these anxieties by writing to her family and telling them constantly that she loved them and by spending her time in the prison sewing room making gifts for them. But she still felt that her children and partner thought she had become more self-assured and so more distant from them and that they were scared by this fact. She seemed to be building a life for herself which did not include them.

The two women who considered that their relationship with their children was worse than it had been at the time of my first interview with them referred to their becoming more distant from each other. Although one of these women only had contact with her sons over the phone, the other had regular, sometimes twice weekly, visits from her four children.

> *Like they're always really rapt to see me and all that sort of thing ... (we're) more emotionally detached or something - I don't know ...*

Three of the women considered their relationships with their children had improved. All of these women had healed rifts between themselves and their children. Children had been angry with their mother for reasons such as going to prison and deserting them, and abuse that had occurred within their family. Opening the lines of communication between themselves and their children, which was often made possible through undergoing counselling or having help to deal with long standing personal problems, had played a big part in these reconciliations.

> *I think it's got better with my older daughter ... she was very angry with me and she thought that I'd made choices that led me here because I didn't love her. But we talked it through and she knows that I made the choices because I lacked the skills to make good choices it wasn't because I didn't love her.*

> *Yes ... I'm able to stand up ... they can ask me anything and they do ... but it's part of all this healing ... it's healing for the family because the whole family they suffer, not just because I've been in jail either, before I even come into jail.*

> *He's getting older now he's starting to ask some questions ... (like) "Who's my dad?" Why I am the way I am ... I prepared myself for that.*

How things have changed for the children

Children whose mother had gone into prison when they were babies usually had no conception of who she was, even though one child was reported to refer to his imprisoned mother as his 'real mother' and to call her by her Christian name. For these children, a mother was the person who cared for you day-to-day, not someone you spoke to on the phone or visited maybe once or twice.

> *So he calls my sister Mummy and he calls me (name) ... or he says my real mummy ... I mean reality is I would assume he thinks (sister) is his mother ... with regards to me it's, "I have to call her my real mummy because (I've) been told that she is my real mummy ..." He doesn't know me ... but I knew to expect that, you know ... because after all I'd come in jail when they were only babies so I knew to expect that ... (but still) .... I was like - well where do I come in all this?*

For those children whose contact with their mother was limited to letters and phone calls, 'Mum' became just a voice on the phone.

Well to them I'm just a person on the end of the phone ...

Situations such as this added to the pains of imprisonment for these women.

Effects of changes on women

Not all of the women had views on how any changes that had taken place for them and their children, in the intervening period since the first interviews, might affect them. However, eight of them (73%) raised issues relating to how their imprisonment had had an impact on their lives: this was not always negative.

One woman indicated that, for her, prison had provided the first stable environment that she had experienced in her life. Although not directly referred to by others, it was apparent, from the issues that they discussed, that imprisonment had served this function for several of the women. Thus a term of imprisonment, especially one longer than twelve months, gave them time to assess where they were at, and to address issues related to chronic addictions and histories of violence and abuse.

I've gotta say in the four years I've done though I've learnt a lot and I've grown, if anything I've grown. I can look at the situation I was in and step back ... look at it now and realise how totally stuffed my life really was ...

Several women who had left a baby or a very young child when they came to prison expressed how aware they were that they would have missed an important part of their child's life. None of these women were serving a sentence of less than 10 years.[169]

I was really enjoying being with my youngest one ... and I see her getting bigger and bigger and think: Hell!

The three women who had limited, or no contact, with their children envisaged difficulties for them in re-establishing relationships with their children upon release. All of these women were serving lengthy sentences for violent crimes, which meant their children would have spent quite some time - at least six years and in some cases 10 years - away from their mother. These mothers were very aware that any future relationship they may have with their children depended heavily on how their absence was being explained to the children by the caregivers. Each of these women expressed concerns that this was not being done in a positive manner.

Effects of changes on children

Four women saw changes that had taken place as having had a positive effect for their families. Those women with younger children mentioned, for example, children getting older and therefore more able to ask questions about their mother's lifestyle and her offence. Others with older families talked about their own healing processes impinging upon their children. As a consequence, lines of communication had been opened which enabled the women to talk to their children about the past and why certain things had happened. This had

---

[169]   One woman had a sentence of 9 years 11 months but she had spent a month on remand.

resulted in relationships being healed between three of the women and their adult children who had been blaming them for childhoods of abuse, neglect and often perceived abandonment. There was often a great deal of hurt involved on both sides.

> *I made that mistake of telling my daughters to lie about what went down when (ex-husband) sexually abused them ... but the thing was they still wanted to go back to their father even though I made the ground rule that they weren't to be visiting him by themselves - and he abused my babies ... my children have suffered a lot, they really have ... that's why I say okay, they've done drugs, they've done burgs, they've done theft, they've done bank robberies and that, but nobody knew what was going round, nobody.*

If a woman had no contact with her children she was likely to believe that she would not have a relationship with them on her release from prison, that they would not know, nor want to know, who she was. One woman felt that her children were being given a biased account of events that it was not appropriate for them to know about and that this would have a detrimental effect not only upon how they (particularly one) perceived themselves but also on how they viewed her.

> *My mother told (10 year old son) after I come to prison that his father had molested my daughter (stepsister) and that's why we separated. I had no intentions of telling him that ... because I didn't think he needed to know and I still don't think he needed to know. ... And so you've got a boy that's been told his father's a child molester and his mother's a killer, now how the hell is that for his self-esteem?*

Summary

Although the number of women re-interviewed in prison was small, their problems and concerns are not dissimilar to those of women overseas who are serving either life sentences or several years in prison (Genders & Player, 1988; Howard League, 1999b; Woodrow, 1992b; Shaw et al, 1990). The main finding which has emerged from this chapter is that the majority of women who are serving long terms of imprisonment have limited or no contact with their children and in fact often lose touch with them. This was especially true where the women's crimes were seen as a justification by either the caregivers or the State to curtail contact between the woman and her children. These findings are consistent with those of Fuller (1993) who conducted a study of visitors to women's prisons in California. She concluded that children may be more likely to visit their mothers during the first year of imprisonment as 57% of the mothers visited by their children had been in prison for less than 1 year. However, Fuller cautions that this may be due to the fact that these mothers have shorter sentences, have committed 'lesser crimes' (p 46), and thus have a better relationship with their families and children than the mothers serving longer sentences. These findings parallel those of Woodrow (1992b) who also commented that, for over half the women in her sample serving life sentences or sentences over 10 years, contact with their children had usually tapered off after the first year of their sentence. Koban (1983) reported similarly that for the imprisoned mothers in her sample the frequency of parent-child visits decreased after the first year. Therefore, she concluded that the women prisoners in her study experienced a significant disadvantage compared to male prisoners[170] in attempting to maintain consistent contact with their children and the caregivers of these children - a factor that was found to be associated with problems during post-release reunification of mothers and children.

Women who had children under the age of 18 living with caregivers seldom had detailed knowledge of the caregivers who were not family members, especially in the situations where there was not an ongoing relationship between the carers and the mother or between the mother and her child/ren. However, the mothers were generally satisfied with how their children were being cared for even if their relationship with the caregiver was not good. Where a woman had more than one child they were rarely living with the same caregiver. This added to the difficulties of trying to maintain contact for the women. For the most part the children's care placements had remained stable; only three had had changes of caregivers. All of these new placements broke down resulting in one teenager ending up in prison, another living independently in Australia and the third younger child being placed with yet another caregiver. Such situations clearly caused stress for the imprisoned mothers. Similarly, Woodrow (1992b) noted that care placements had a 50% likelihood of breaking down if mothers had been in prison for 18 months or more. In addition, Larman and Aungles (1991) concluded that the children of women imprisoned for more than 12 months are most at risk of being placed in permanent foster care or of becoming wards of the State until they are 18. They added that this risk increases if the child is less than five years of age when the mother is first imprisoned.

The concerns that these women expressed when re-interviewed were primarily the same as those that had been talked about by the women during the initial interviews. The women were concerned about: the sorts of messages their children were getting about them from caregivers and/or others in the community; the health and safety of their children; their children growing closer to others; having limited knowledge of their children in long-term care; and still trying to fulfil the mothering role from within prison. Women with adult children were mainly concerned that they could not be there for their families when they needed them, and felt that a lot of the problems that their children and grandchildren had experienced could have been avoided if they had been at home with them. One study of women sentenced to life imprisonment in England (Genders & Player, 1988) came to a similar conclusion; over time, imprisoned mothers became increasingly unable to maintain close relationships with their family and friends even if they received visits. The women thus became powerless to provide support and reassurance when their families needed them and were said to have suffered a loss of self-identity as *"... it became easy to define themselves as failures in their roles as women"* (p 153).

More than a third of the women were worried about the breakdown of close relationships with their children and/or their partners; all parties were seen to in danger of becoming emotionally detached over time, especially if contact was limited to letters or phone calls. These findings are similar to those of other studies (Genders & Player, 1988; Howard League, 1999b; Woodrow, 1992b) which have found that women in prison for any length of time have concerns about their ongoing relationships with their partners and/or children. Woodrow (1992b) particularly noted how women quickly became dislocated from their outside lives relatively early in their sentences and tended to forget their own ages and their children's ages when asked. Furthermore, Shaw and her colleagues (1990) added that the longer women are

---

[170]   Due to the larger numbers of men in prison, they are less likely than women to be imprisoned great distances from their homes and families and consequently tend to receive more visits from their children.

in prison the more they feel that they have less and less in common with their children, families and the outside world.

Consequently, issues of concern surrounding their reunification their with children were often talked about by the women in my sample. Other researchers have made similar observations (Genders & Player, 1988; Woodrow, 1992b). Whereas, for some women, their time in prison had healed rifts between themselves and older children, those women who did not have contact with their children and who would be apart from them for several years viewed their prospects of re-establishing relationships with them pessimistically. In all such cases, the children would be teenagers/young adults by the time their mothers were released from prison. These findings are similar to those of Woodrow (1992b) who also commented on how many of the children of women serving long terms of imprisonment will have grown up by the time their mothers are released.

As with the first interviews, the women I re-interviewed felt that their families were keeping things from them so that they would not worry unnecessarily. However, although this was appreciated by the women, it had almost the effect of a double-edged sword in that it had the result of making them feel isolated from their families and children; for these women being a mother meant sharing in their children's sorrows as well as their joys.

The main source of support for the women had not changed over time and still came from prison staff. The women also relied on each other, their families and friends to support them through tough times. These findings are consistent with those of Genders & Players (1988) who reported that although the women in their study did not share problems with other women they derived comfort their supportive families yet did not want to worry them with their anxieties and problems. Thus, the women that Genders & Player (1988) interviewed said that their method of coping was repression; this was their tool for survival. To express emotional vulnerability was to become a victim of the system: *"If you let things touch you personally, then the system has moved in and you're done for"* (p 156).

In summary, the needs of women who are serving longer terms of imprisonment do not differ greatly from those of women serving shorter sentences. Their primary concern is to be able to maintain their relationships with their children and families. However, over time, the problems that they have keeping in contact with their children and families are exacerbated; children grow up and become more distant, and relationships which may have been fragmented before the women went to prison are, at the least, severely tested and, at the worst, destroyed. Furthermore, changes in prison policies which impinge upon the women's ability to contact their children (e.g. the new phone system introduced in New Zealand prisons in 1995) or which restrict the level of interaction that those women who do have visits can have with their children, have a greater cumulative effect on those women in prison trying to maintain relationships over a number of years. The next chapter discusses the post-release experiences of, and the problems faced by, the women who were re-interviewed in the community.

CHAPTER 6   LIFE AFTER PRISON

Introduction:

Twenty-six women were re-interviewed in the community:[171] interviews were conducted between mid November, 1995 and early December, 1996. Approximately 90% of the women were re-interviewed within 2 years of the initial contact. Interviews took place throughout New Zealand: from Whangarei in the far north of the North Island, to Invercargill, the southern-most city in the South Island and from the East Coast to the West Coast of the North Island. Eighty percent (21) of the women were living in the North Island; the largest number (10) lived in Auckland and Whangarei. Five women lived in the South Island, three of them in Christchurch. Five of the women (19%) were not living in the same area as they had been when they were sent to prison.

Length of time spent in prison

As indicated in Table 6.1, over two-thirds of the women (69%) had spent a period of less than 12 months in prison and only one-eighth (12%) served more than 18 months, including remand.[172]

Table 6.1   Length of time in prison: numbers and percentages

	Women (n=26)	
Months in prison	**n**	**%**
< 1 month	1	4
1 month and < 3 months	4	15
3 months and < 6 months	7	27
6 months and < 12 months	6	23
12 months and < 18 months	5	19
18 months and < 24 months	2	8
24 months and < 36 months	1	4

Of the eight women who had spent 12 months or longer in prison, 63% had served sentences for drug related offences and 25% for violent offences.

Length of time since release

Nearly two-thirds (65%) of the women had been out of prison for more than 1 year at the time they were re-interviewed. Only two women (8%) had been released less than 6 months previously.

---

[171]   Eleven (42%) of the women were Māori, 10 (39%) New Zealand European (Pakeha) and five (19%) were of Pacific Island origin. One woman described herself as 'Pakeha' when asked to identify her ethnicity, yet prison records identified her as Māori. As mentioned previously, for the purposes of this research I have used the women's own identification rather than that of the prison.

[172]   The only other woman who had spent more than 12 months in prison had been imprisoned for embezzling money from her employer, in an attempt to meet family obligations.

Release from prison

Most women (85%) were met by someone on their release from prison; this was usually either a current partner or some other family member. One woman was met by her lawyer, and three were met by friends. PARS fieldworkers met two women and took one woman home and the other to the bus station. Four women were not met by anyone when they left prison and were taken to public transport by prison staff. The most common method of travel home for the women was by private motor vehicle (65%); the next most common was bus (19%), followed by train (12%); one woman caught a plane home.

Living situation

On release, less than one-third of the women went back to where they had been living prior to their imprisonment. At the time of the follow-up interviews, these women, plus another two - making a total of nearly two-fifths (39%) of the sample - were the only ones who were still living in the same house they had been in since their release from prison. By far the majority of the women (69%) had moved at least once during this period of time. If a woman owned her own home, lived with relatives, or had a current partner who stayed in the family home while she was in prison, she was more likely to have had her home and possessions kept intact whilst she was in prison. However, one woman was not so lucky. Although she only spent a total of 29 days in prison, she came home to find that her home had been broken into and almost everything of value she owned (plus items of personal value) had been taken - allegedly by her ex-partner.

At the time they were interviewed, 38% of the women who were not presently living in the same house where they had been prior to going to prison (including one woman whose husband and daughter had moved during that time) were living, or sharing, with family or friends. The rest were living in rental accommodation that they had sourced either through a letting agency, the newspaper or with the help of family. One woman and her husband had saved enough money to buy their own home since they had both been released from prison.

Economic Situation

On leaving prison

For practically two-thirds (62%) of the women, the only money they had on release from prison was their re-establishment grant.[173] Four women reported that they still had money in their prison accounts, ranging from a few cents to sixty dollars for one woman who had earned money from knitting. This was deducted from the total amount they received. Three women mentioned that they had money invested with lawyers and so received their full entitlement yet had access to extra money on their release. Two of these women had been sentenced for drug-related offences and one had some money left from the proceeds of the sale of her house. Another woman had been working in the community for some time before her release and so went home minus her grant but with approximately $2000 in earnings. One

---

[173] Upon release, every prisoner is entitled to receive a lump sum re-establishment payment if they have served a minimum of one month (31 days) in prison. This payment is known as "Steps to Freedom" and is $350.00. It is a means-tested grant and is reduced by the total sum of money held in a prisoner's trust/earnings accounts. If money held in credit is more than the amount of the grant it is not received. Prisoners very rarely accrue significant amounts in their personal accounts and most ensure what money they do have is expended before their release date falls due.

of the women did not meet the criteria which entitled her to receive the lump sum payment[174] and so she did not have any money when she was released from prison.

Over two-thirds of the women had a regular income within 2 weeks of their release from prison. This number included four women whose partners were already on a benefit and this was just upgraded on the women's release from prison. Of the two women who reported that it was more than 1 month before they had a regular source of income, one had trouble getting a bank account and another had to get her previous partner to verify that their children had been living with her since the day she had been released. The majority of the women (85%) did not have any problems in obtaining a benefit from Work and Income New Zealand.[175]

Approximately two-fifths (39%) of the women had difficulties surviving financially until they had a regular income and many borrowed from family or friends to tide them over. Women often came home to outstanding debts incurred before, or whilst they were in, prison. Examples of this included two women who had left family members living in their homes and came home to find unpaid rent and utility accounts. When released from prison, women also often came home owing child support to the Inland Revenue Department for their children who had been in care.[176]

At the time of the interviews

Eighty-one percent of the women were welfare dependent,[177] 15% were employed and one woman was supported by her husband, who owned his own business. The source of income for 85% of the women had not changed since before they were imprisoned[178] although one woman commented that in one sense it had, since she no longer had an illegal source of income. The above percentage also includes two women who had been on a benefit for the period immediately prior to their sentencing, as their offence had been related to their place of employment. However, at the time they were interviewed, both of these women were again in full-time employment. Also included are three women who were supplementing their benefit with part-time employment.

Five women reported that they had problems finding, or attempting to find, work. This figure includes half of the women who were working full-time. Problems arose from the women telling prospective employers that they had been in prison. One example was a woman who described herself as applying for at least 150 jobs and undergoing dozens of interviews before she found work:

---

[174] She only served 29 days of a two month sentence. Situations such as this can arise if a prisoner's due date of release falls on a weekend as there is usually a set weekly day for releases at each prison.

[175] Those women who did mention such issues as: not having the required number of pieces of identification (e.g. the children's birth certificates and personal ID) and not having a bank account.

[176] A liable parent is not exempt from this on imprisonment unless they have spent the full tax year (i.e. from the 1st of April one year to the 31st of March the next year) in prison. Even if one does not have an income (i.e. a beneficiary) one must pay the minimum amount of $10 per week.

[177] Those who were welfare dependent included three women who were supplementing their benefits by working part-time and three women who were on the married rate of the unemployment benefit with their current partners. It was not unusual for women who had a current partner to report that they were receiving the Domestic Purposes benefit. Several women were receiving sickness benefits.

[178] Those who had been working tended to have found a job and those who had been on benefits tended to be still on them.

Every interview I went for I told them that I'd been to prison and some of them wanted to know all the ins and outs, all the details, all the gory details - a couple went "Ohhh" (gasped with horror) ... and only two, no sorry three, three places I interviewed said, "It doesn't matter, we don't want to know about it"

Three of the women said that employers, or prospective employers, were often "warned" about their past by people in the community.

Well, the first job I got was just a two hour a day job and those employers had an anonymous letter written to them about me. They knew about me because I'd told them and they'd employed (me) regardless ...

This place being such a small place you find a lot of the older people, the ones that don't understand about drugs and alcohol and going to jail, they'll snigger behind your back ... "Don't give her a job." It's very hard for me to get a job out here, I've been trying.

(People) were ringing them up saying, "Oh (she's) been in jail did you know that?" They made me lose three job interviews because of it, it's just unbelievable.

One woman who had been supplementing her benefit with part-time work before she was sent to prison was told she could not have her job back when she was released. She had subsequently moved to another area and at the interview asked me if I thought she should lie about being in prison when she applied for a job. I did not know what to tell her. I just agreed that it was a difficult problem. Another woman had solved this dilemma in her own way:

While I was working out there in a rest home I just really felt like with that new privacy law I didn't have to tell them that I'd been to jail n'that ... it wasn't asked so I didn't say anything. You know I was quite honest ... I said I'd come from a broken marriage and I was up here you know and my son was still down south and I was having a bit of time out to get my life back together.

However, even though she got the part-time job in a rest home for the elderly, the fact that she had not been totally upfront with her employers meant that she was always in fear that she would be "discovered" and so left the job of her own accord.

And then all of a sudden I just, you know, lost all of my confidence and thought ... what's gonna happen if ... something happens out here to one of my residents and you know, they do an investigation or something and find out I've been in prison ... how am I gonna deal with that?

Trying to deal with this stigmatisation and rejection by the community, and on occasion by their families, was a source of stress leading to depression for at least three of these women.

I felt like I was heading for a nervous breakdown. I started going into depression ... I withdrew for a long time.

One of these women felt that her probation officer could have been of assistance in helping her to find work.

> *I was really actually quite pissed off about their part of the system (in) that there was no offer to help me find employment. You know if you're going to rehabilitate someone and make them a worthwhile member of society again ... I mean surely they (probation officers) have got avenues where they can help people get back into gainful employment. They must have contacts ... in the areas where they live.*

Only four (15%) of the women did not consider they were having financial problems at the time they were interviewed. Most of the women indicated that they were either "just managing" (42%) or not managing very well at all (39%). This included those women who had current partners. It was evident that a significant number of the women (one-third) had come home to outstanding debts. This may have contributed to their poor financial situation.

Women's relationship status

At the time of the interviews, almost a third (31%) of the women were still living with the partner that they had been involved with before they were sent to prison.[179] Two were still involved in the same relationship that they had had prior to their imprisonment, but neither were living with their partners.[180] One woman had just (within the week before the interview) left her former partner of 12 years and another woman was sharing a house with a partner she had broken up with since coming home from prison. Information was not available for two of the woman.[181] More than two-fifths (11) of the women did not have a current partner.

Almost two-fifths (10) of the women in this sample had a current (or now previous) partner who had also been sent to prison either at the same time as, or prior to, the women themselves. The partner of a further woman had been sent to prison for an attack on her since her release. Three of the four women who still had a partner in prison stated that they no longer had a relationship with these men. Indeed, two of these women had concerns relating to their former partner's future release from prison.

Women often had problems resuming a relationship on their release from prison. They talked about partners being unfaithful to them, which had sometimes resulted in the eventual breakdown of the relationship, or about how they had had difficulty re-adjusting to considering the needs of a partner, after only having to consider themselves in prison.

---

[179] It was not unusual for women to disclose that they had been living with a partner at the time they went to prison when at the first interviews they had said they had a current partner but did not live with them. This anomaly may have been due to issues relating to trust between the women and myself; they were often noticeably more relaxed with me at the second interview. Being outside of the prison environment may have also contributed to the women's willingness to disclose.

[180] Only one of these women was in a relationship with the father of her children. Both she and her partner had been jointly sentenced to imprisonment.

[181] One was interviewed over the phone and was no longer with her previous partner, yet said she was pregnant and it was not clear whether or not she had gone back to an earlier relationship. The other woman was interviewed in a situation where two men were also present drinking, and so it was not considered appropriate to ask her that particular question, as one of those present may have been her current partner.

And then he had an affair while I was inside and that I couldn't live with, even though we tried to stay together for the sake of the kids.

Well I had doubts about his faithfulness although he'd gone to great measures to make sure I couldn't prove anything but it's all since fallen around my ears and all my suspicions were true.

You get too used to your own ways inside eh? You know, and you come out here and you got to compromise pretty hard ... you've done it alone for so long it's pretty hard ...

I got too independent for him in the sense that I'll have an argument with him now. Once upon a time I'd have walked away, but now I won't I'll stand there (and have) a bloody good go with my tongue.

However, even women who did not think there had been problems in resuming their particular relationships spoke about being stressed and "needing space" or time to themselves when they came home.

Well I ... wasn't used to having (partner) around. I was used to being in my room all by myself ... yeah I always had my own space sort of thing (in prison)

I probably had strange behaviour when I came home that (partner) had to put up with (he) puts up with a lot ... just my withdrawal ... I withdrew for a long time and having to go through my moods when I was job hunting and coping with society.

Out of the 10 women who were still in a relationship with the partner they had prior to prison, half felt that the nature of this relationship was the same as (assuming that this was alright) or better than before their imprisonment. The partners of three of these women had also been imprisoned. Of the two who felt things had improved, one had married her partner and they had done extremely well for themselves since both being released from prison; both were employed[182] and they had bought their own home. The other couple were both drug addicted. Since their release from prison they had both been accepted on the methadone programme which had enabled them to stabilise their lives.[183]

Women who had been pregnant when they went to prison

Three of the women who were interviewed after their release had been pregnant when they were sent to prison. Only one delivered her baby whilst she was still in prison. She was allowed to remain with the child in the hospital for three days after the birth and then had to make provision for the child to be cared for. She said she 'gave' the boy to her cousin and her partner as they did not have any children of their own. The arrangement was fairly informal and the natural mother and father of the boy visited often. All seemed happy with this situation. The other two women had their babies after they were released from prison. One

---

[182] The husband was self-employed, having started his own business.

[183] At the time of the interviews both were working full time.

96

kept her baby, and there was no information on what had happened to the baby of the other woman.[184]

The children

Slightly more than three-quarters of the women (19)[185] said that they had had all of their children living with them at the time they were sent to prison. This number includes one woman who reported all her children were living with her, when in fact some spent more time with their grandmother than with their mother.[186] All except two of the six women who reported that their children had not been living with them before they went to prison had children who were in long-term care with family/whānau often with Social Welfare (CYPFA) involvement. The children of the other two women were under CYPFA care with foster parents.

All of the women, except one,[187] had at least one child under the age of 18 at the time of the interviews. Two women were pregnant and one woman had had another baby since her release from prison. All of these women had children still in care. One had two children in CYPFA foster care and was working towards them coming home; the mother of one woman had adopted her son; and the other woman had four children living with various members of her family. She was only interested in regaining the custody of one of these children.

Women who had children living with them

As mentioned previously, 19 of the women had had their children living with them alone, or with them and a partner, before their imprisonment. At the time of the interviews the majority of these women (17) had all of these children living with them again.[188] Another woman who had not had the care of any of her children at the time she went to prison now had two out of the three living with her, plus a new baby. She was attempting to gain custody of the son who was not living with her and who was living with his father, her ex-partner. One woman had given birth to a baby whilst she was in prison. This child was "given"[189] to a cousin of the woman who did not have any children of her own. At the time of her interview, this woman had two of her children living with her (as they had been before she went to prison) and the youngest was still with her cousin. The natural mother and father still had full involvement in the boy's life and fully expected him to return to them at some stage.

---

[184]   It was not clear at the time of the interview whether or not she had kept the baby, I subsequently wrote to her and asked her directly but did not receive a reply. The woman's mother, who was interviewed as part of the caregivers' sample, seemed to think at that time that the baby may be given to its natural father when born.

[185]   This number does not include the woman who only had one adult child.

[186]   However, this was not unusual in extended family/whānau situations involving women who were Māori or of Pacific Island origin. Examples of this were three of the women reported having 'given' at least one child, and in the case of one woman three, to a whānau member to rear, usually a maternal grandmother. Another woman had also 'adopted' two of her young whānau.

[187]   This woman had an adult daughter and grandchildren.

[188]   However, it should be noted that one woman had become estranged from an 18 year old daughter who had been living at home before her mother's imprisonment.

[189]   This notion of ownership of children was not unusual. As indicated previously in Footnote 195 above, women often spoke of giving children to another family member, formal adoption processes were not considered necessary.

Women whose children were in care

There were seven women who reported that their children were not living with them at the time of the interviews. The children of all but one of these women had been in care prior to their mothers' imprisonment. There were diverse reasons why these children could not live with their mothers. The children of two of the women were in CYPFA foster care; the son of another woman had been adopted by her mother; another woman had just left her partner and did not have her children living with her at that stage; the ex-partner of one woman was temporarily caring for their teenage children as she was having financial difficulties; and the last two women both had children in long-term care with family/whanau. One of these women had four children in various care situations. One was with a family member in another area; one was with their father (one of her ex-partners) and two were with her mother. She was fighting to regain the custody of one of her sons. This is an indication of how complicated the lives of these women and their children often were.

How soon mothers saw their children and regained custody after their release from prison

As has been mentioned, at the time of the interviews, 18 (72%)[190] women were living with at least some of their children. However, this was not the case when the women first left prison. At the time they first arrived home after their release, 20 (85%) women had been living with one or more of their children.

Almost all of these women (85%) saw at least one of their children the same day that they were released from prison. Two of the remaining three women saw at least one of their children within 2 days; only one woman did not have physical contact with her son until 2 months after her release. However, she had spoken to him on the phone shortly after her release from prison.

Table 6.2 describes how long it was after the women were released from prison before they got their children back to live with them.

Table 6.2: Length of time from mothers' release to regaining custody of child/ren: numbers and percentages

	Women (n=20)	
Length of time	n	%
The same day	16	80
Within 2 days	1	5
Within 1 week	1	5
Within 2 weeks	2	10
Over 2 weeks	3	15
Not at all	2	10

Note: Some women did not get all their children back at the same time. This table records this and so percentages do not total to 100% nor the numbers to 20. These numbers mainly relate to women who had their children living with them before they went to prison but include one woman who had not, yet got her children back after her release.

---

[190] These percentages are based on the 25 women who had children under the age of 18.

Ninety percent[191] of the women who had their children living with them at this stage had at least one of their children back within a week of their release. For most of the women (64%), this happened the day they came home from prison. Where the children in one family had been separated and were living with different caregivers this sometimes took a little longer. For one woman, whose children had been taken from her and placed in whanau care[192] before she was imprisoned, it was about two months before she got them back, although she had access to them every weekend. This woman was attempting to regain custody of another of her children who was living with his father, and had given birth to another baby since her release from prison. The son of the only other woman who did not get her child back within a month had been living with his aunt in Australia. He also came home within two months. The 18 year old daughter of one of the women did not come back to live with her mother, as did her brother and sister. This young woman stayed with the caregivers until she left school and then went flatting. This was the result of an irreconcilable breakdown in the relationship between her and her mother.

Only one woman said that she had had trouble getting her children back into her care and this was the woman whose children had been placed by CYPFA with whanau before she went to prison.

Children still in care

Six of the women still had children, under the age of 18 years, being cared for by others. These children had been in care before the women were sent to prison. The children in one family were not always living with the same caregiver. These numbers do not include the woman whose ex-partner was caring for her three teenagers on a temporary basis and the woman who had just left her partner without taking her children: there was some indication during the interview that she might return to get her children at some stage, and she was still very emotional about the situation. Also excluded is the woman who had her baby in prison and whose family had 'adopted' the baby three days after his birth.

Two women had one child each in care with family.[193] The mother of one of these women had legally adopted her son. One woman had two sons living together in a professional foster care situation,[194] and she had had another baby. Another woman, who had spent several terms in prison, had two children who had been in CYPFA care for some time. Her son and daughter both lived with different caregivers. The last woman had four children who were not living with her; she was, at the time of the interviews, pregnant. Two of her children had gone to live with separate family members at an early age and she did not speak of them. The two youngest boys were with her mother. She had 'given' the baby (then 3) to her mother virtually at birth and was only concerned with getting the four year old back into her care. There were problems with this as the family did not think she was capable of caring for the child,[195] and there was a great deal of animosity on both sides. The sixth woman had three of

---

[191]   These 18 women had had their children living with them prior to their imprisonment.

[192]   This was carried out by CYPFA.

[193]   There had been CYPFA involvement in both cases.

[194]   Again CYPFA were involved.

[195]   This was due to the woman's long history of drug addiction, prostitution and offending.

her young children living with her[196] and was attempting to regain custody of a fourth child from his father, with whom he had been living for some time.

Changes of caregiver for those children not living with their mother

The only children who had changes of caregiver since I first interviewed the women back in 1994 were those in CYPFA related foster care who were not living with whanau/family. The two sons, aged five and four, of one woman had had three changes of caregiver since that time, and had had two prior to that. Thus these boys had had six different caregivers in the space of approximately three years. The reasons for moving them all related to the children's safety. One caregiver was allegedly involved in incest with his daughter; another neglected the children to the extent that one had lead poisoning, was undernourished and had received physical injuries such as a cauliflower ear and the loss of the tips of his toes due to an infection which was neglected.[197] Initially, these children had been voluntarily placed into care by the mother. The children had at first been placed with Catholic Social Services as the parents were having difficulties in their relationship and both were due to go to prison. At some stage, CYPFA got involved and the children had had a number of caregivers, including Maatua Whangai.[198]

Another woman had two children in separate CYPFA foster care placements and one had had a change of caregiver since her mother's release from prison. These two children[199] had also had numerous care placements during the time they had been living away from their mother. They were first taken into care in 1990 at a young age when their mother (a chronic drug user) had gone to jail for the third time. During the next five years these children had six different caregivers before they were separated. Reasons for them being moved included: being beaten in one placement, caregivers who did not get on with one or other of the children, or caregivers who could not care for them any longer. Since that time, the daughter had changed caregiver again so she had had a total of eight different carers in seven years. Both of the women discussed in this section were, at the time of the interviews, on the methadone maintenance programme and both had access to their children, although in one case it was limited (supervised).

It was obvious that children involved with CYPFA not only were at risk of multiple placements but also did not have a continuity of social workers. This was often mentioned by concerned mothers and will be discussed more fully in the section relating to the women's concerns.

> *I think they're ... really confused. Like they've had so many different placements and every placement something's happened and which is not due to them or our fault and I think it's just starting now to have a bit of a detrimental effect on them actually.*

---

[196] This was the woman mentioned previously who had not had any of her children living with her at the time she went to prison and who, after her release, had given birth to a baby that she had been pregnant with whilst in prison.

[197] His mother showed me photographs of his injuries; they were horrific.

[198] This is a Māori social services agency.

[199] These children were a boy of 10 years of age and his eight year old sister.

Contact between the mother and those children not living with her

There were a total of nine women who did not have at least one of their children under the age of 18 living with them.[200] Of these, four expressed experiencing difficulties in maintaining contact with, or getting access to, their children. This was more often than not due to the relationship between the mother and the caregiver.

All of the women expected to live with these children at some stage, including those who had adopted their children out to family/whanau. For six of the women there were criteria that had to be fulfilled before they could get their children back home. These included: remaining alcohol and drug free; meeting CYPFA requirements;[201] applying to the court for custody; or maintaining a stable environment/providing a suitable home. At least four of the women had to meet several of these requirements.

Only two women expressed concerns related to the quality of care their children were receiving. Both had reservations about the health and emotional state of their children and also concerns about their children being alienated from them by the caregivers (one of whom was the children's maternal grandmother).

Difficulties women experienced when they first came home

During the interview process, it became obvious that on their release from prison the women had faced numerous difficulties related to their enforced isolation from society and the dependency fostered by the controlled institutional setting of the prison. I consequently decided to ask the women directly what difficulties they had faced when they were back in the community with their families and Table 6.3 lists their responses.

---

[200]   This number includes all those women omitted from the analysis in the section on children still in care - i.e. the two women who were temporarily away from their children and another two women whose children had been adopted by others (either formally or informally).

[201]   Some women felt that these requirements continually changed so that it was difficult for them to know where they stood in relation to getting their children back.

Table 6.3   Difficulties women experienced on release: numbers and percentages

	Women (n=26)	
Difficulties experienced	**n**	**%**
Being amongst people again	11	42
Shopping - going to the supermarket	9	35
Meeting people they knew or who knew they had been to prison	9	35
Leaving the prison routine behind	9	35
Everything - life in general	6	23
Paying bills - being responsible for yourself /others again	6	23
Dealing with reputation in the community	5	19
Adjusting to the children	5	19
Coping with freedom	5	19
Drug/alcohol relapse	5	19
Not giving in to peer pressure to take drugs/offend e	3	12
Settling down to normality	3	12
Trusting people	3	12
Preparing meals	3	12
Crossing the street	2	8
Going outside the house	2	8
Unrealistic expectations of being perfect mother	2	8

Note: Percentages do not add up to 100 as women often talked about several areas of concern

Only two women[202] did not think they had encountered any difficulties when they first came home. However, these women still talked about anxieties they had had at some stage.

Nothing - (I've) done too many lags ... the first time I did (I was) too scared to cross the road.

The stress of encountering crowds of people

Clearly, those activities that posed difficulties for the women, or caused them anxiety, when they were first released from prison were related to just being out in society amongst people again. Forty-two percent of the women talked about being amongst crowds of people as threatening or stressful.

I don't like going to town very often since I've been out of jail ... I find it too crowded for me there.

Oh, so many people. Oh, my head just was (spinning).

I found it difficult, I didn't like going out. I just hated being around a lot of people.

---

[202]   One of these women had spent time outside of the prison on work parole and the other had an extensive history of institutionalisation spanning over 20 years from the age of 17.

I had to walk out (of a shop), it was just all too much, there was people everywhere and I still sometimes feel like that. But if I just, you know, breathe and just tell myself to relax - yeah, it's okay.

Stigmatisation

The fear of meeting people they knew, or those who knew they had been to prison, also caused some women anxiety, as did having to deal with their reputation in the community as "someone who had been to prison".

I had a speech all planned for people who said, "Oh, you're out, what was it like?" And I had this big speech that went, "None of your fucking business! You want to know? Try it!" ... But of course it didn't work and everybody wanted to know and what do you say? There is no explaining it.

Difficulties adjusting to freedom

Nearly two-fifths of the women found going shopping (to the supermarket) very stressful. For many, this had been a routine task which had now become alien, unfamiliar and thus time consuming. It was not uncommon for the women to ask a family member or one of their children to go shopping with them until they became re-oriented. Finding it difficult to get back into routines such as paying bills, preparing meals and adjusting to the children were also factors discussed by many of the women.

The effects of the prison regime were not easy to discard. Thirty-five percent of the women talked about the difficulties they had readjusting to the freedom to come and go, and talked about following a pseudo-prison routine for some time after they came home.

I mean when I first came home ... I'd be in the bedroom, sitting on the bed ... because we were just used to being in one room ... I used to just take myself off to the bedroom and I know some of them, you know that I spoke to, that they'd quite often stand at the door waiting for someone to unlock it - in their own homes, once they went home - depending on how long they'd been in.

Being released from prison was often just as frightening as being sent there.

They open that bloody door, they push you out, they shut it and lock it behind you. Like you've been locked in and now all of a sudden you're locked out. The first thing I wanted to do when they shut that door and locked it behind me, was ring the bell and get back in ... it's the same as going in. One minute you're a person, part of the world and the next you're nowhere, you're nothing – it's like dying without dying, almost ... the whole world carries on without you. You see how unimportant you are.

Mothers' post-release/current concerns regarding their children

The majority of the women felt that their imprisonment and related separation from their families had had an adverse effect on their children, either by causing problems or by aggravating problems that may have occurred anyway: for example, the rebelliousness of adolescents. All of the mothers, not just those whose children lived with them, had concerns about their children and their relationship with them. Table 6.4 lists these concerns.

Table 6.4   Women's post-release/current concerns: numbers and percentages[203]

Concerns	Women (n=25)	
	n	%
Children still suffering from effects of separation	13	52
Children's behaviour - delinquency, acting out	8	32
Children having grown closer to/bonded with others	7	28
Problems for children at school/academic	2	20
Children suffering from effects of mother's/family's previous lifestyle	5	20
Relationships irreparably damaged	5	20
Children being angry with them	5	20
That children now have no respect for/afraid of the police	4	16
Children have lost respect for them/feel they have lost control over children	4	16
Trying to explain to children why they went to prison and what it was like	3	12
Stopping children getting into trouble: they feel they have lost the right/children don't think they have the right	3	12

Note: Percentages do not add up to 100 as women often voiced several concerns

Over half of the women indicated that they considered that their children exhibited behaviours or attitudes that were attributable to the separation due to their imprisonment. These included children (particularly the younger ones) displaying signs of insecurity by not wanting their mother to go anywhere without them. Quite often, the prison sentence was the first time the mother and her child(ren) had been separated for any length of time.

> *You could see she (five year old) was stressed out because I wasn't allowed to go out the door without her, or even if I went up the back of the house she'd be screaming and looking for me.*

> *I was supposed to go ... and work with some girlfriends, stripping wallpaper from some houses and she (teenage daughter) packed such a wally (tantrum) that I wouldn't go ... she thought I was going and never coming back again and I thought, "Oh no, I can't do this to her."*

One woman had gone to court promising her children that she would be home that afternoon.[204]

---

[203]   This table does not include the woman who only had one adult daughter and grandchildren.

[204]   She had been told by both her lawyer and a probation officer that she was unlikely to receive a custodial sentence.

For a few weeks there I couldn't go anywhere without them wanting to come because I think they thought that I might not come back again ... because when I got sentenced, when I went to court, I said I'd be back that same day - but I wasn't.

However, women often reported that the severity of this behaviour lessened over time, quite often only lasting a few weeks. Nevertheless, some children still exhibited signs of that insecurity at the time of the interviews.

Oh shit yeah, if it didn't affect somebody there'd be something wrong with them ... like I'm not allowed to go anywhere a lot by myself, (she's) very clingy, sleeps with me most of the time ... yeah, that's why she doesn't go to school that often at the moment - she just likes to stay home with me.

Concerns about the effects of the children's contact with the police

Several of the women (4) were concerned that their children were now either afraid or distrustful of the police due to the part they played in taking their mother away. Younger children could not understand why someone they thought had been there to protect them was responsible for taking their mother away.

Well she doesn't trust cops full stop: because she had to see me being dragged downstairs, you know, they didn't even let me say goodbye to her or anything ... you know she was wondering, "Why did (detective) do that to you Mum?" Well at that stage and time I don't think I put it across very well at all. I tell her that they're (the police) there to help her but ...

As soon as he saw a police car he asked, "Are they coming to get you?"

The loss of respect for the police by teenagers was considered to be partially due to experiences related to the mother's offending.

Both of my daughters were strip searched by the police - they still have nightmares about that.

She doesn't like the cops in any sense for what they put her through ... she's got no time at all for the police since I've been away - none at all and that all stems back to when they locked her in a room up at the high school with the police (to answer) questions ... before my trial ... she was five hours locked in a room with them ... she was 13 at the time.

Issues of safety and trust were also mentioned. Who was left to protect you and your children if you no longer trusted the police?

They hate the system. They hate the police; they have no respect for them.

Concerns related to teenagers' schooling

Problems related to their teenagers' schooling were not uncommonly seen by the women to be attributable to the effects of the separation due to imprisonment.

My 14 year old girl she got affected pretty badly because she's still not in school today ... she's 15 next month.

Yeah I got home on a Wednesday, (daughter) had been suspended from school on the Monday of that same week but she didn't tell me, when I walked in the door she was still in her school uniform ...

Well my eldest dropped out ... she hasn't really been there this year at all.

Well, she's still going to school but when she gets a mid-term report to bring home to me I don't get it (laughs) it gets lost between school and home ... she was doing really well, her ambition was to bring home reports with the attendances full - not even half a day taken off. Now if they have a sports' day she won't go.

Concerns about the behaviour of children

Concerns related to their children's behaviour (when she was first home or ongoing) were voiced by close to one-third (32%) of the women.[205] Younger children were frequently difficult to control when their mother first came home from prison. It was often expressed by the women that they felt that this behaviour had developed whilst they were in prison.

They were wild, I mean they just ran around everywhere ... they weren't like how they used to be ... they just can't sit down in one place.

I'm getting aggro (angry) talking to him and he's standing in front of me and ignoring me.

Women with teenage children were willing to admit that this acting out or rebelliousness was probably mainly due to the testing of boundaries inherent in adolescence. Some mothers were having difficulties setting the limits of acceptable and unacceptable behaviour for their teenagers, who were often quick to point out the fact that their mother had been to jail and why. Children were seen as having lost the trust and respect that they once had for their mother.

Oh just trying to keep them (sons) on the right track and telling them and they keep using my jail sentence (saying) "Oh what about you? You went to jail for drugs." And I'm trying to keep them off it ...

I do believe that a hell of a lot of it (daughter's rebellion) is the age and the phase ... (But) she (daughter) says, "How can you talk? You lead such a bloody good life that they locked you up." And I say, "Well you know I got locked up for smoking dope." And she says, "Yeah, that's all they caught you for."

Clearly not all young people who get into trouble when their mother is away in prison react in the same way. Two of the women[206] whose children acted up whilst they were in prison were convinced that this behaviour was directly related to their absence.

---

[205] This includes both women whose children's behaviour was problematic when they first came home and those who were still having problems.

[206] Including the woman mentioned previously whose eldest son was sent to prison for 12 months.

I would swear that it was because I wasn't there because they did a lot of things that were sort of just not them you know? My kids were big in sports and that was their life ... They hated smoking, because they used to hate me smoking. My kids used to actually hide (cigarettes) in the rubbish from me to stop me smoking and that was the attitude before I went away. When I came back two of my kids were smoking ... they had all been into trouble with the law - the four big ones anyway.

I used to hear all these stories about how teenagers ... always get into trouble and they get into dope and do this and run away and my kids weren't doing that you know, and I was thanking my lucky stars that they hadn't started. But when I went away oh no, all Hell broke loose.

As soon as one of these women was able to get transferred to a prison closer to her family and could see her children, the trouble died down.

It's because I wasn't there ...when the trouble started (ex-partner) said to me, "You better hurry up and come home because I'm on the verge of letting these kids on the street, I've had enough." ... I got transferred up here, I rung him and told him, "I'm up in (prison) bring the kids around I want to see them." And (from then on) they're fine ...

Concerns about children's anger

Children also gave indications that they felt let down by their mother and were angry with the fact that she had not been there when they needed her. Issues related to this were talked about by one-fifth of the women.

At times I still feel that there's a little bit of anger there aimed towards me ... it's more in her behaviour you know, the things she doesn't say.

I've let him down ... because I've gone back to jail ... even before that when I started using drugs again.

She has lost a lot of respect for me and in losing it for me it's followed on to her teachers and anybody and everybody that's authority.

She has belted it out a couple of times you know, "Piss off, go on holiday again" sort of thing; you know, if she gets really angry with me ... she does (still) remember it.

(Daughter) doesn't want to be part of the family unit ... she's angry at me ... I wasn't here when she needed me ... she thought I should have been here at that stage of her life (and) it was my fault that I was't ...

Concerns about children having bonded with others

Children were often perceived as having bonded with, or grown closer to, those who had been caring for them and it required a concentrated effort on the part of the mother to re-establish a closeness with her child(ren). This effect was more common when the child concerned was either a baby or toddler;[207] someone else had become 'Mum'.

> My son he was young when I left him so I had to adjust to him and he had to adjust to me ... just trying to be a mother to him, you know, trying to be close to him and because it was different he always ran to his grandmother and his aunties and then it was hard.

> My babies didn't know me, that took a long time.

> (Son - was) stand offish for about a week, nearly two weeks after I got out. No we had to rebuild our bond and trust in each other eh? And that's been the hardest part of my being out of prison is winning him back.

Concerns about the effects of imprisonment on relationships with either a partner or a child

The effects of imprisonment had been devastating for some of the women; at least 20% considered that it had been responsible for the destruction of at least one of their intimate relationships - either with a partner or a child.

> Actually I would say it was because I went inside that we are separated now. We have split up five times since I came home and this time I made it final.

> Yes, well me and mine have split - he couldn't cope with the separation, he found himself someone else. Going in there's (prison) one bloody shock on its own; coming out's another one!

> He (son) goes back to stay with them (caregivers) during the holidays and frets when they go home. He said he wanted to go and live with them, I said, "What about me?" He said, "I can come and stay with you during the holidays." I just feel like we lost something in that four months.

> No ... my eldest won't have anything to do with me. She's out flatting, she stayed with the carer who was looking after her while I was in prison ... she's only just left her and gone flatting three weeks ago, so she's been with her all this time.

> Yeah, I feel like I'm not a mother any more. I feel like I'm struggling to be their friend at best and half the time, from their point of view, I feel that it's forced. They learned to get along without me, it was almost like they'd buried me and they learned to live without me and now here I am back in their lives trying to resume the role I had before I went away, but it's not there any more it's been filled. They filled it themselves.

Women's individual post-release concerns

Adjusting to their release from prison and becoming a mother again also caused problems for many of the women, Table 6.5 describes those they most frequently talked about.

---

[207]   That is, mainly pre-school children.

Table 6.5   Women's individual post-release concerns: numbers and percentages

Concerns	Women (n=26)	
	n	%
General financial concerns	7	27
Finding it difficult to get over the effects of imprisonment	6	23
Coping with being a parent again	5	19
Being continually judged on their past (re children etc)	4	15
Coping with their addictions	4	15
Coping with the loss of a family member	2	8
Ex-partner (children's father) being released from prison	2	8

Note: Percentages do not add up to 100 as women often voiced several concerns

Coping with being a parent again was often problematic for these women, especially adjusting to caring for babies.

> *Yeah, (I was) slow at everything, because he used to cry for everything and I had to work out what cry is for what ...*

> *I found it hard to adjust to the baby ... oh, you know, getting back into a mother routine. I just sort of just stared at her for a while (and thought) oh, shit I've gotta snap out of this, I've gotta get my act together.*

In an attempt to mend relationships and alleviate some of the hurt that children had experienced when their mothers went to prison, some women tried to explain to their children why they had gone away. In the manner of all parents, these women did not want their children making the same mistakes that they had: going to prison was not "cool".

> *(He - son) asked me why I went there, I think he was upset that I left. I tried to explain to him that I'd done something wrong and that was why I had to stay there.*

> *When I came (home) they had a lot of questions about being inside and that and I said, "You must think it's a nice cool place but it's not. It's good, like they look after you in a way, but you get stuck in there: no friends, no families ..."*

> *Like you know, I been there, done that, and I don't want them to do it and you try and tell them and that kind of bullshit you know; they don't want to listen to you.*

Coping with addictions outside of prison

Women who had serious long term addictions, in this case related to drugs, talked about trying to keep these under control. One woman talked about being incredibly lonely for the first three months she was out of prison because she was straight (drug free). Such women often did not cope well with their first experience of freedom. One woman in particular, who had little or no contact with her son for over 18 months as he was being cared for by her sister in Australia, came out of prison determined to be the perfect mother. She was not going to use drugs and she was going to get a job and make up for being separated from her son for so long; in hindsight, she admitted that she had set herself an unrealistic task. Her son arrived back in New Zealand two months after her release and after what she described as a 'magic' first month at home with him he became withdrawn and very unsettled. He would not fully communicate; he had tantrums at home and at school would withdraw into a corner and curl into a foetal position or alternatively refuse to do as he was told. Understandably, this was an extremely stressful time for his mother who coped in the only way she knew how - she started using again and was very aware of the danger she had placed her son in by doing so. This lapse lasted for six months.

> *I wasn't coping (I remember) feeling so relaxed and comfortable and thinking, "Oh God, the relief." ... When I was stoned I could be the perfect mother.*

The prognosis for this mother and son, at the time of the interviews, seemed positive; she felt she was keeping on top of her addiction, her son was undergoing counselling and he had settled down both at home and at school.

Nearly a quarter (24%) of the women spoke in terms of how they were still finding it difficult to leave the prison experience behind them. They talked about issues such as: coping with their reputations in the community; finding work; dealing with damaged family relationships; and trying to re-establish control over their lives. Added stressors for some of the women included: coping with the death of a parent and worrying about how they would cope with the release of an ex-partner (their children's father) from prison.

Specific concerns related to children not living with the mother

Those women who still had children in care[208] also had anxieties which reflected the nature or quality of the care situations and the process of attempting to have their children live with them again. Table 6.6 lists the most commonly mentioned concerns that women had.

Table 6.6   Women's concerns about children not living with them: numbers and percentages

	Women (n=6)	
Concerns	n	%
Welfare (health/safety) of children in care	4	67
Regaining custody	4	67
High turnover of social workers	3	50
Children in care not understanding why they can't go back home -	3	50
Children in care bonding with others	3	50
CYPFA not taking into account parents' concerns/opinions	2	33
Finding it difficult to relate/talk to social workers	2	33
Instability of care arrangements for children in CYPFA care	2	33
Getting regular access to children still in care	2	33

Note: Percentages do not add up to 100 as women often voiced several concerns

---

[208]   This includes the woman whose mother had legally adopted her son as she talked about the boy coming to live with her at some stage in the future when his grandmother was too old to care for him.

Women spoke about the hopelessness they often felt with regard to regaining the custody of their children. They spoke about the constantly changing criteria[209] which they had to fulfil before their children would be allowed to come and live with them.

When you're up to their standard they put up a hoop and we have to jump through it and when we jump through it they put another hoop up ... (initially we had to) attend counselling (and) have clear urines, it was just that - but then it'll be something else ...

These women felt that no matter what they did they were continually being judged on their past.

And because I am just a drug addict and I've been in jail you get this label put on you.

Since I've been to prison the chances of me ever sort of getting him back (are slim). Because like if Mum fell ill and I wanted him back they (CYPFA) just look at my past history and I think they'd rather turn him over to someone else than me. They just look at the past history, not at the present, and I find that really hard to deal with.

Difficulties with relating to social workers

The instability of placements and the high turnover of social workers for children under CYPFA care caused the mothers concern and exacerbated the problems these women had communicating with and relating to social workers. It was not unusual for mothers with children in long term care to have concerns about the well-being of their children. Two of the women felt quite strongly that any concerns they might have about their children's placements were discounted out of hand and their opinions were brushed aside as worthless.

I find it hard to talk to the social worker - I mean she's okay but she never listens to what we've got to say ... I kept on insisting with the social worker there's something going on but she didn't bloody follow up ... (then) she went round there and realised. They (CYPFA) moved her (daughter) within a week because they knew it wasn't right - and I was really pissed off ... she really get's up my nose she's quite patronising.

It was felt that social workers had preconceived ideas of what these women were like and how they lived their lives. They were subjected to naive questioning about facets of their addictions particularly relating to the methadone maintenance programme e.g. they were questioned about levels of doses, method of ingestion and so on. One woman described an incident where she was meeting her son's social worker for the first time. The social worker seemed quite taken aback when she was first told that this was the woman she had come to see. It was obvious to the woman that from reading case histories she had conjured up a negative image in her mind of how a woman who was involved in drug importing and who had a child who had been removed from her care due to suspected abuse, should look. The fact that this was what was happening was easily picked up on by the woman in question.

---

[209]   Particularly with regard to those children under the guardianship of CYPFA.

Growing distant from children in care

Women also spoke of becoming more distant from children who were not living with them and this was a source of distress, but seen as inevitable. If children became unwilling to see their mother this often raised concerns about what they were being told by the caregivers. Sometimes children would ask why they could not come home or why they had been placed with different caregivers and the women were very aware that they had to be careful what they said to their children. It was not uncommon for mothers to be taken to task by social workers if it was felt that they had been discussing 'inappropriate' matters with their children.

> *They (sons) ask a lot of questions. I don't know what to tell them because I don't want to be blamed for telling them conflicting stories. I don't know what they're being told by the foster parents. I don't know what they're being told by the social workers.*

> *Yeah, he (son) talks about coming up here all the time but I can't say anything to him because I got into trouble in the past by saying things that I shouldn't have said to him ... basically just telling him fact and what was going on ... And they (CYPFA) just said stuff like that is inappropriate.*

Admittedly though, where the women and the caregivers did not see eye to eye, volatile situations could often arise, which were stressful for all concerned: mother, child and carer.

> *I just go there and I let her (children's grandmother) ring the police. I just want to go there and see him and have a cup of tea. When the police come I just talk to them and at least I can see him while it's all going on.*

Along with issues related to their children and being a parent, the other problem commonly referred to by nearly 30% of the women was the difficulty they were having managing financially.

Children's reactions to mother on her release

Over half of the women[210] said that their children expressed pleasure at having their mother home again or seeing at her for the first time after a long period. Even those children who later presented problems were glad to have their mother back initially.

> *Oh they were rapt ... it was wonderful but embarrassing because ... when we got home they (daughters) had used all the lunch wrap roll and they Sellotaped from one end of the fence ... right down to the other. They had to use two rolls of greaseproof paper and they'd written all over it: "Mum's coming home today" and "Welcome home Mum" and all this and it was hanging all over the property it was really beautiful but it told all of (the town) ...*

One woman, who was unsure of the reception she would get, found her fears were unnecessary.

---

[210]   This section only deals with those women who had children under the age of 18 - n=25.

No, they were alright when I first came home. I thought they would react in a different way ... I was expecting them to say, "Oh we don't want her any more, she's a criminal." ... Yeah, they were alright, they were happy to see me come back home.

Those children who were either withdrawn or insecure when they first encountered their mother were more likely to be pre-schoolers, babies or younger children. Only two women with teenagers said their children reacted in this way.

She wasn't angry ... yeah she did cling to me for about a month, every time I turned round to do something she was there.

They were pretty reserved ... it was a strange feeling.

One woman could not remember her first encounter with her son after her release from prison.[211]

That's a question I can't answer because when I got out of prison I spent nearly every day drunk or off my face ... for months and months and I can't actually really remember seeing him.

Despite children being rapt to have their mother out of prison, homecomings were not always as joyous for the women.

I saw (daughter) and the two little ones the minute I got home. They came running out to me ... the car pulled up, I got out of the car got my stuff out of the boot and I heard the kids go), "Our Mummy's home, our Mummy's home," and I thought, "Oh choice," because I hadn't seen them. And they come running out and they gave me a hug and a kiss and they didn't say hello or anything, they just says, "Mummy we've got nothing to eat," and that put me down straight away.

Problems experienced by children due to mother being home again

Slightly more than two-fifths (44%) of the women thought that their being home had caused problems for their children. Those most commonly mentioned were: young children being unsure of them and continuing to go to the caregiver for assurance and nurturing; children exhibiting insecurity by not wanting to let their mother out of their sight; and behavioural problems, such as being disobedient or withdrawn. The majority of women considered that things had settled down over time, after the children and their mother had adapted to each other again. However, although for some this readjustment period only took a few weeks for others it took some months and there were those who felt that things would never be the same between them and their children.

To some extent yeah, I think I've got them back to as normal as possible, but I don't think I could ever get them back exactly the same as it was before I went away.

However, in some cases problems encountered were wider ranging and longer lasting.

---

[211] This was the young woman whose mother had legally adopted her son.

Well (daughter) said to me last week she's got this new boyfriend on the scene and he said to her, "I'm a bit scared of your mother," and she said, "Why?" And he said all the things (that he had been told) about me.

In one extreme situation, a teenage girl ran away rather than face her mother.

He (partner) said, "(daughter) ran away on Saturday because she knew you were coming home this week." Because she knew she was doing a lot of things that she shouldn't be doing you know, and I knew about these things; like when nobody was home she'd bring her mates home for a party n'stuff like that.

How mother coped and helped her children cope with the problems

The most common method used by women to address problems and help themselves and their children cope was just to give the children time to settle down.

Oh I tried bribing him and all that, to ... come to me. But I just took my time and just treated him the way I treated my daughter and we're alright now.

The women tried to deal with issues by talking to their children, both about what had happened and their current behaviour.

(I) just spoke to her about what I'd done and why I'd done it you know, and things just happened and I won't go back again if I can help it.

It was not always easy for the women to try to explain things to their children and at least one had been unable to accomplish this.

I always thought when I came home I was going to, you know, sit down and have this great big discussion with them but it's something I can't do. I think ... I'm probably waiting for the time and the need to arise before I have to do it.

One woman was having real problems controlling her frustration with her 6 year old son who was continually disobedient. She talked about how angry she got with him and how she used to hit him, but was aware that this was not appropriate so she now just yelled at him. It was clear that this woman was really hurting; her relationship with her son had not regained its previous closeness and she was sure that at some time in the future he would want to go and live with his caregivers.

The only method of professional help solicited by the women to help them address their post prison problems was counselling. Six of the women were, or had been, undergoing counselling to help them with problems not related to their children. This process was ongoing and had either started in prison or before then if the women had been dealing with personal issues relating to abuse (normally sexual) or addictions. If a woman had a counsellor it was not unusual for her to seek this sort of aid for her children. The children of four of these women had undergone counselling.

Although at least 14[212] of the women were released from prison on parole, they tended to talk about their probation officers (either voluntarily or when I asked them) in terms of being generally approachable and helpful, rather than as being able to help them deal with specific problems related to their children. The women mostly viewed visiting Community Corrections as a condition of their parole, rather than a means of assistance when they had problems.

> *I had this really nice Community Corrections Officer, a nice Māori lady, and I just used to go in there and we just used to talk. She'd talk about her family and I'd talk about mine and what we were doing and that was it. ... I mean I could have gone in there and said, "You help me with this and you help me with that," but I really didn't want to have anything to do with them. I mean I was only going in there because it was part of my early release conditions.*

Even when assistance was offered it was not always welcomed. For example, in one case, when a probation officer was proactive in offering help to one woman and her children it was seen as coming too late: the children needed it when their mother was still in prison.

> *She (probation officer) came around, she insisted on meeting the kids and whatnot, she said she had to, it was her duty. She said to them any time they had a problem they could go and see her at the probation office and my eldest daughter said, "Well it's a bit bloody late for that: Mum's home."*

Forty-four percent of the women said that they had experienced difficulties resuming the day to day care of their children again. Factors most frequently mentioned were: coping with freedom, getting back into household routines, taking control; disciplining children again; and being responsible for others, as well as for themselves.

> *I found it was hard to ... take on the responsibility again, I found it a little bit hard to sort of handle when you've gone so long without it. And I have to admit that I did enjoy having no responsibility ...*

Remarks such as this are in some ways easy to empathise with, as for at least half[213] of these women the time they spent in prison may have been the first chance they had had to focus on their own needs.

Nature of current relationship between mother and child/ren

At the time they were interviewed, two-thirds of the women felt positive about their relationship with their children. That is, they considered that it was as good as, or better than, it had been before they were imprisoned. Women talked about not taking their children for granted any more and having more patience with them. As their children got older, the women found that it was easier to explain things to them and so their relationship became closer, more open and more honest. They felt that the children appreciated them more too.

Nearly a quarter (24%) thought that their relationship with their children was different somehow - not worse, not the same, and not better. These women mentioned issues such as

---

212   Information was not available for seven of the women.

213   From what the women said there were indications that this was so for at least 14 (53%) of the women.

children not valuing or heeding their advice and a loss of closeness with their teenage children.

> *Oh I've lost their respect and admiration ...they trusted me, they trusted my opinion, they valued my advice ...*

Consequently, although they said that the relationship was "just different", it appeared to be, in fact, worse. However, the women were prepared to admit that this may not have been wholly due to their separation from the children but a function of their children's age or developmental stage. Nevertheless, in the situations where relationships had irretrievably broken down (or might take some time to mend) teenagers were invariably involved.

> *You find the teenagers are the hardest ones to repair the damage with when you come out ...*

Only three (12%) of the mothers considered that their relationship with their children was worse than it had been. One could not cope with her son's continued disobedience and felt her relationship with him would never be the same as before her prison sentence. He was still fretting for his caregivers nearly 18 months after her release. The other two women both had children in care and were having difficulty maintaining contact with them.

CYPFA involvement with families

Approximately one-fifth of the women had dealings with CYPFA relating to their children, that is, either through the children being in foster care or in counselling, or their own attempts to regain custody of their children. The common consensus was that this relationship was a "necessary evil" rather than of assistance to them. Only two of the women not already involved with CYPFA felt that they would have appreciated some help from the Department of Social Welfare and that help related to financial assistance rather than input with their children. The general feeling was:

> *No, I don't want them poking their bloody nose in!*

During one of the interviews, a young woman voiced concerns related to the release of her ex-partner, her children's father, from prison. She was worried that he would try to take the children from her and I suggested that talking to someone at CYPFA may ease her fears. She did not seem to realise that because the children were living with her and she was receiving a benefit for them that she, in fact, had custody of them.

Support systems

Over 80% of the women answered *"Yes"* when asked if they had anyone that they could share their concerns with about their children or families and whether or not they could obtain the help they needed to sort out any problems. Five of the women answered in the negative. As only one of these five did not have any immediate family/whanau living in New Zealand, their reply to this question may have been more an indication of their state of mind at the time of the interview, than the fact that they were bereft of support systems. None of these women were satisfied with their relationships with their children and two had broken up with their partners of long standing.

Oh what I normally do is go in the room and have a damn good cry ... and I sit
there for a couple of hours and do nothing but think about it and then if I find a
solution, I go sort it ... But I sort my problems out by myself!

This particular woman felt that she could not rely on her family/whanau for support as her
mother had recently died and her siblings now looked upon her as a mother-figure.

Nature of women's support systems

As indicated in Table 6.7, family was the main source of support for nearly three-fifths (57%)
of those women who answered in the affirmative in relation to support systems. Only two of
the women said that they talked their problems out with their partner, and another five had
friends who were supportive.

Table 6.7   Women's support systems: numbers and percentages

Women (n=21)		
Support	n	%
Family/whānau	12	57
Friends	5	24
Partner	2	10
Other	11	52

Note: Percentages do not total as some women referred to more than one source of support.   The Other
category includes those who found PARS, DSW, probation officers or counsellors, helpful.

Those outside the family/whānau who most often provided the women with support were
counsellors (either current or past). Two women spoke of the help they had received from
their probation officers,[214] who had expressed their willingness to support the women after
they were no longer officially required to do so; these women spoke appreciatively of this.
Two other women mentioned support systems related to their church.

Changes for the women as mothers

The perceptions of those women who still had children under the age of 18[215] as to how
things had changed for them in their role as a mother since I last spoke with them indicated
the paradoxical nature of the prison experience for them: a negative experience such as this
could often result in positive outcomes. Almost two-fifths of the women thought they had
become, or were becoming, a better parent. Reasons for this mentioned related to self
development issues, changes in attitude, increases in self esteem and confidence. Being in
prison had enabled women to access counselling which was often beneficial in dealing with
unresolved personal issues and changing attitudes. One woman who had gone directly from

---

[214]   One other woman had had the same probation officer as her husband and had said that he had been
helpful to them both, but of course this support was not ongoing as their period of parole was over by the
time I talked to her. However, another woman said she would have appreciated a probation officer that
she could just talk to over a cup of tea and a cigarette - this was not the case. She told me she felt she just
had pressure applied to her to get herself together and get on with her life, rather than the help she needed
to adjust to society again.

[215]   That is, 25 out of the 26 women interviewed.

prison to a drug rehabilitation centre expressed sentiments which were indicative of how a lot of these women felt:

> *I think more about myself, I've got a lot more self-esteem, heaps more confidence than I've ever had.*

As she felt better about herself she was sure she could be a better mother.

A similar percentage of women (36%) expressed how they now appreciated things that they had taken for granted before, such as their children and their freedom.

> *I appreciate a lot of things more ... everything, just everything ... yeah, the kids, being home, life itself, just being free ... you gotta appreciate that, after being in there ...*

A number of these women felt that they were actually being a mother now, instead of relying on others to fill that role for their children.

Conversely, there were some women who talked about concerns relating to their role as a mother. Almost one-fifth (16%) felt that they were not as close to their children as they had been previously. Those with children in care found it difficult to feel like a mother; yet two of these women talked about how they now had a more realistic view of whether or not they could cope with the full-time care of their children.

> *I've always wanted to get my kids back straight away basically and I can't do it this time ... Because back then I think (it) was just some of my maternal (feelings) saying this is what I should be doing and this is what's expected of me - right? But it's not like that I can't ...*

Effects of changes on women

Nearly half (46%) of the women had opinions on how their lives might be affected by any changes that had taken place due to their imprisonment. Although for two-fifths of these women changes had been positive, a similar number felt that they would always be aware of how they had let their families down.

> *Oh yeah, I'm sure (problems) will always be there and I'm sure there will come a day when it's thrown back in my face at some time, I'm sure of that ... plus it's something that I've got to live with for the rest of my life as well ... no, it'll never go away.*

Effects of changes on children

Although, as discussed previously, most children adapted to having their mothers home again after an initial period of readjustment, 31% (8) of the women talked about how they thought their children might be affected in the long term by their experience of having a mother in prison. Almost all of them talked in terms of negative outcomes. Only two women thought that their imprisonment would not have any future effect on their children.

I don't think so because I've asked them about things like that you know, and they said, "No, people make mistakes ... and we('re) not all perfect, I mean you never know, we might be doing things too."

Summary

The findings in this chapter indicate that on leaving prison most women experience a disorientation; coping with the freedom thrust upon them was difficult for many to adjust to. Simple tasks which had been routine before they went to prison, were now insurmountable: the cause of trepidation. This was evident from how the women described the difficulties they encountered when they first left prison. Being amongst crowds of people caused many anxiety and they often felt they lacked the capacity to manage their own lives. Women who had addictions often struggled to stay drug or alcohol free in the face of many temptations, as do their contemporaries in other countries (Fabb, 1995; Hampton, 1993; Morris et al, 1995; Eaton, 1993). The women in Eaton's (1993)[216] research also spoke of the fear they felt on first leaving prison. The outside world was perceived as strange and unaccommodating. The words of one woman parallel the general feeling: *"You can never leave prison because prison never leaves you."* (Eaton, 1993: p 58).

Women talked about dealing with stigmatisation in the community, especially when trying to find work. Several women talked about how they agonised whether or not to tell prospective employers of their prison record. However, generally, those who had been employed before they went to prison again found employment, even though it was difficult. Also, those who had been welfare dependent on entering prison, were again receiving benefits. Most of the women spoke of the difficulties they were having financially. These findings are similar to those of Eaton (1993) who noted the stigmatisation ex-prisoners were subjected to, especially on disclosing their status when job hunting. Researchers in other countries such as the United States (Johnston, 1991 cited in Johnston, 1995c; Stanton, 1980)[217] and England (Wilkinson, 1988;[218] Morris et al, 1995) have also found that one of the biggest problems women have on their release from prison is coping financially. Considering the number of women who come into contact with the criminal justice system for offences related to their economic marginalization, this raises concerns about the likelihood of re-offending. For example, in their Canadian study, Bonta et al (1995) found dependence on welfare and illegal sources of income to be predictive of re-offending in a sample of women who had been released from prison. In addition, Morris et al (1995)[219] found that women ex-prisoners who re-offended were more likely to be having financial difficulties and lack paid employment than those who did not re-offend.

---

[216]   Eaton (1993) explored the prison and post-release experiences of 34 English women, the majority of whom (30) had been out of prison for over two years.

[217]   Stanton (1980) compared the effects on children of separation from their mothers due to imprisonment against the general effects of the mother's criminal lifestyle. To accomplish this she compared children whose mothers were in prison with those whose mothers were on probation. Both mothers and children were interviewed twice, while the mother was serving her sentence and one month after her release.

[218]   Wilkinson (1988) conducted a study to determine the effects of imprisonment on women by examining their post-release experiences. Interviews were carried out between 1982 and 1984 with 123 imprisoned women. Interviews were conducted 1 month prior to release and again up to six months after release.

[219]   Morris et al (1995) interviewed 200 women prisoners both pre- and post-release as part of a project to determine what these women saw as their needs and assess the extent to which the Prison Service was meeting those needs.

The majority of women were reunited fairly quickly with their children on their release from prison. This was especially true where the children had been living with family/whanau, or with friends of their mother. These findings coincide with those from other studies, both in New Zealand (Aikman, 1981) and overseas (Butler, 1994; Stanton, 1980; Wilkinson, 1988). There were, of course, exceptions to this, notably those women whose children had not been living with them before they were sent to prison. Women with children mainly in CYPFA care had little contact with them and voiced concerns relating to regaining custody of the children and the lack of continuity of both caregivers and social workers. This lack of contact between imprisoned mothers and their children in foster care has also been commented on by overseas researchers (Beckerman, 1991; Johnston, 1995a; Kampfner, 1995). Moreover, as discussed in Chapter 4, women frequently have difficulties interacting with their children's social workers and indeed may not receive any communications at all, either written or verbal, a situation which leaves mothers ill-informed of their rights and obligations under the law; this has implications for the reunification of mother and child/ren (Beckerman, 1991, 1994; Henriques, 1982; McGowan & Blumenthal, 1978). Wilkinson (1988) also found that on the mother's release from prison reunification of mother and child/ren was a relatively hassle-free process where children had been in the care of friends or relatives.

For those women with children in local authority care it was another matter; regaining the custody of these children was a slow process based on the criteria set by the local authority in question. That is, the women had to prove themselves as stable and responsible and so often felt at a disadvantage in these proceedings (Eaton, 1993; Wilkinson, 1988). These issues were also discussed by the women that I talked to. They felt that the criteria were continually being changed as they reached each goal (e.g. staying drug free) another was imposed making the task virtually impossible. As Carlen and others (1987) noted, regaining custody virtually can become a battle during which ex-prisoners fight to prove themselves to be 'fit mothers'.

Concerns the women had about their children were felt to be related to the effects of the separation. For many of these women, as with those in Caddle & Crisp's 1994 study (1997),[220] it was the first time they had been away from their children. Young children often exhibited insecurity they became clingy and were worried about their mother leaving them again. Children were seen to be angry with their mother and often difficult to control. Similar experiences have been documented elsewhere (McGowan & Blumenthal, 1976; Fritsch & Burkhead, 1981). Wilkinson (1988) reported that the mothers in her study had said that after their release their children were sometimes more clinging and often difficult to control. Children are frequently angry and hurt because their mothers have been away (Butler, 1994; Henriques, 1996; McGowan & Blumenthal, 1978, Michigan Women's Commission, 1993). Stanton (1980) also found that the children whose mother had been in prison repeatedly expressed fear of future separation and exhibited some behavioural problems, including less obedience to their mother. Some even said that they had lost trust in their mothers. Women in my sample also felt that they had lost the respect and trust of their children. Those women with teenage children felt that problems they had experienced with them were not so clear cut; they may have been just a function of the young person's developmental stage. Women with younger children or those in care talked about a loss of closeness in their relationship with their children due to lack of contact and children bonding with their caregivers.

---

[220] For 85% of the children in this study, their mothers' current term of imprisonment was the first time they had been apart for any length of time.

Overseas research has also found that when a woman leaves prison she often finds she has lost the ability to relate to her children and no longer occupies the place that she once had in their lives. Children had come to see others as their mother (Butler, 1994; Catan, 1989; Eaton, 1993). Moreover, Morris et al (1995) found that more than a third of the mothers in their study living with their children post-release said that their children had problems which they were unaware of during their imprisonment. However, only a minority (19%) felt that their children were experiencing these problems as a result of their release.[221] The group which had been categorised by Morris and her colleagues as having high child-care problems[222] were found to be more likely than the medium problem group[223] to say that they were having problems caring for their children, that their children had problems during their imprisonment which they were unaware of and that their children were still having problems after being reunited with them. These women were also more likely to report the involvement of social services with their children.

The findings in this chapter indicate that women were concerned about the attitudes of their children towards the police and the implications of this. Younger children were said to be afraid and distrustful, whereas older children had lost respect. Similarly, Stanton (1980) found that children who had had negative experiences with the police through their mother's offending were reportedly more reluctant to call them for assistance and had less confidence in them. As the children had more exposure to the police and the legal system, they developed more negative attitudes toward both. The Michigan Women's Commission (1993) also reported that many children who were present at their mother's arrest said that they hated the police.

What has clearly emerged is that women leave prison to encounter a range of problems that they are poorly equipped to deal with. Most go back to the same, or in some cases worse, social and economic situation that they were living in prior to their imprisonment and which often contributed to their offending. That is, they return to: poverty, welfare dependence, rented accommodation, dealing with addictions, the responsibilities of single parenthood, and/or the worries of children in State care. Additionally, they have the task of trying to mend, or renew, relationships with children, families and often partners, which have been damaged by the separation caused by the women's imprisonment. The findings from this research of the negative consequences that the women's imprisonment often had on their relationships with their partners has been replicated in other studies (Caddle & Crisp, 1997; Hadley, 1981; Morris et al 1995; Wilkinson, 1988). The women face all of this on top of trying to overcome the effects of being confined within a regimented, controlled, hierarchical environment, which has fostered their dependency for at least some months but possibly for some years. Carlen (1985, 1988) has also commented on the general debilitating effects of imprisonment upon women. Furthermore, the release of the mother from prison not only creates problems of readjustment for her but also for her children; both have to adjust

---

[221]   Morris et al (1995) note that this is likely to be an under-estimate. They felt it was more likely that women would admit to having problems with substance abuse/misuse rather than take the risk of admitting to a situation where they may be perceived as an 'inadequate' mother.

[222]   This group was comprised of all mothers who had reported that their relationship with their children had been affected as a result of their imprisonment, that their children were experiencing problems or that they were not planning to reunite with their children. This category included all those who were single mothers.

[223]   This group included all other mothers with dependent and non-dependent children at the time of their sentence, who were not in the care of the local authority, fostered or adopted, and who were not reporting any of the conditions of the high problem group.

individually and in their relationship to each other. The women's suggestions as to what would have helped their post-release experience are discussed further in Chapter 8.

CHAPTER 7   THE EXPERIENCE OF CAREGIVERS

Introduction

This chapter presents data from the interviews carried out with caregivers. Women were asked to provide contact details of the carers of their children if they felt it would be appropriate for me to talk to them about their experiences as caregivers.[224] Fourteen women in total provided contact details for those who were caring for their children and, of these, only the caregivers of one woman's children refused to see me.[225] Eleven interviews with caregivers were carried out.[226] These provided information on 12 caregivers[227] who were caring for the children of 11[228] imprisoned women. The majority of the interviews were carried out between July and December 1994 and October 1995.[229]

---

[224] Not all women in the sample were asked for this information. Ultimately I asked 19 women based on how I perceived the situation. I did not consider it appropriate to contact caregivers where children had been in long term care situations or where they were in CYPFA or other professional foster care situations. I was primarily interested in how caregivers coped with children who were normally cared for their mother who was now in prison, on the assumption that she would regain custody of her child(ren) on her release. There were 38 women who were caring for children under the age of 18 before their imprisonment who had children living with caregivers at the time of the interviews. This exercise was not as straightforward as I anticipated it would be since a number of women were visibly distressed during interviews. Therefore, women were not asked for permission if I felt it would be too distressing for them to have me contact the caregiver, especially if they themselves did not have contact with their children (19 women) or if English was not their first language (2). If a woman was suspicious or nervous of the interview situation, as was the case with three women, I did not pursue caregiver contact with them. Not all women who were asked (i.e. five out of 19) were keen to have the caregivers contacted and stated reasons which were usually grounded in them not wanting to upset tenuous or stressed care situations. One of these women whose husband was caring for several young children felt that it would be a waste of my time as her husband was a man of few words. As the number of caregivers I was given contact information on was small I included two women whose children were in long term care with maternal grandmothers, and who were keen for me to contact the caregivers and to talk to them.

[225] This woman had two young sons who were living with separate caregivers: her sister and a friend of her sister. She had doubted that they would agree to talk with me as her relationship with them was not good and the Family Court had decreed that she should not have contact with her sons as it was upsetting them although the only contact she said she had had whilst in prison was infrequent phone calls and letters that were not answered. This attempt at contacting the carers took place after my second interview with the mother as, at the time of the first interview I considered it would be too distressing for her to ask her for these details. She had not been in prison for very long at that stage.

[226] Most interviews were carried out in the homes of the caregivers, with the exception of one which was conducted over the phone and another which was conducted at the interviewee's place of work.

[227] One interview was carried out with a support person to the caregivers' of one woman's five children, who was also one of two guardians who had been appointed for the children. She gave me details regarding the children's caregivers. Another interview was carried out with a woman's sister who had close contact with and provided support to the caregiver, who was also a family member.

[228] Two of the mothers who had provided caregivers' details had been on remand and were subsequently released and so I did not contact their children's caregivers.

[229] This last interview was with a caregiver who had had long term care of the son of a woman who had spent numerous terms in prison. Although originally I had only asked some of the women for permission to contact the caregivers for the reasons mentioned in Footnote 1, by the stage of the follow up interviews I had decided to ask women who were still in prison and whose children were still living with caregivers for permission to contact these carers. The only exceptions were two women who were experiencing difficulties in contacting their children.

Characteristics of caregivers

The 12 caregivers were looking after the children of 11 of the women in the sample; 10 caregivers were female and two were male. One of the care situations might be best described as 'communal', since two women were joint caregivers and they shared a house with their children and another woman and her children. For the purposes of analysis I have categorised this arrangement as one 'caregiver'.

Of the carers who were women, seven (58%) were members of the imprisoned women's families - i.e. mother, aunt, sister or niece. One male was a woman's current partner - although not the child's father; the other was a woman's ex-husband who had custody of their child. The remaining three carers (including the joint care situation) comprised one friend and two who were "a friend of a friend."

Eighty-three percent of the caregivers were welfare dependent,[230] one was self-employed and another was supported by an employed partner.[231] Three-quarters of the carers indicated that they were either living in rental accommodation or sharing with friends or relatives. The majority of the caregivers were either single or single parents. Only two were living with a current partner and one was involved in a relationship but lived separately from her partner. All caregivers considered themselves to be in good health, although in one case it was obvious that the family member present did not agree with this assessment.[232]

The caregivers' children

Over half (58% or 7) of the caregivers had their own dependent children and 86% (6) of these had sole financial responsibility for the children who were living with them. The partner of one of the imprisoned women, who was caring for her baby, had a child of his own, but the child lived with her mother (his ex-partner).

Between them, the caregivers had a total of 17 children ranging in age from 2 to 19 years of age. Included in this figure are two teenagers who were receiving welfare assistance and still living at home. One of these was a 16 year old girl who was attending a work skills course and the other was a 19 year old with her own baby. Although not totally financially responsible for these two young women, their mothers - who were single parents - still gave them emotional and practical support.

Children of imprisoned mothers

The 12 caregivers were caring for a total of 19 children whose mothers were in prison. The ages of these children ranged from nine months to 15 years, including one 15 year old boy

---

[230] Of the ten caregivers who were receiving welfare benefits, three supplemented this with part time work. One of these was a father who had custody of his daughter and therefore received the domestic purposes benefit; another was a woman who received a benefit for her own dependent children and who had not received any welfare assistance for the two grandchildren in her care; the third also received welfare assistance for her own dependent children and the boy she was caring for.

[231] The one caregiver who was employed owned a business with her partner. The caregiver who was supported by her partner also received an unsupported child allowance for the child in her care.

[232] This woman had said that 'others' (presumably doctors) 'reckoned' she had a heart problem, but she dismissed this diagnosis. However, it was obvious that her daughter who was present at the interview had concerns for her mother's health.

who was at boarding school.[233] At the time the interviews took place there had been a change of caregiver since their mother had been imprisoned for eight of these children. However, it is important to note here that only six[234] out of the 19 children had experienced an upheaval in their living arrangements when their mother went to prison. By far the majority had already been living with the caregiver either with or without their mother before she went to prison.

Also, by the time the interviews took place, two caregivers no longer had any of the children they had previously been caring for. A brother and sister had gone from living with their maternal grandmother to live with their father and one boy had gone to live with his maternal grandmother, whom he had had little or no contact with previously.

The caregiver of this five year old boy related to me the circumstances surrounding the child leaving her care.

> *The mother rang collect from prison at 2.00 pm on a Friday afternoon to say her son was to go to his grandmother's the following Tuesday. He had only just started school four weeks previously and the caregiver asked if they could wait until the term finished, as it was only a matter of a few weeks until the Christmas holiday. The mother refused. On being told he was to go and live with someone else the boy was very upset, he started to cry and demanded, "What have I done? What have I done now?" It took the caregiver three hours to reassure him that they all still cared about him and that they would always be there for him, all he had to do was phone. He asked, "Well, how will I find you?" The caregiver wrote the phone number on a piece of paper for him and they hid it amongst his possessions. He was taken to his grandfather's house on that Friday where he would be collected by his grandmother the following Tuesday. By the evening on the day he arrived at his grandmother's, the caregiver had received 11 phone calls from him - six within two hours - then the phone calls stopped. The caregiver said she was convinced that the phone number had been taken from him. She did not know how to contact his grandmother to see if he was all right.*

Five siblings had also had a change of caregiver; they had gone from being cared for in their home by a former flatmate of their mother's to being separated - three went to their maternal grandmother and the other two to the two women joint caregivers mentioned previously, whom the children had not met before. However, all of these children stayed in the city where they had been living and still had contact with each other.

For 14 of the children, the situation in which they were living was expected to last until their mother was released from prison. However, for the five siblings mentioned above, this would be for some time as their mother was serving a lengthy sentence. The caregivers of another five of the children reported that, for these particular children, the care situation was long term, that is, it was intended to last beyond the release of the mother. One of these children was under the guardianship of the State (CYPFA); another was in the custody of her father; and two were in the unofficial custody of their maternal grandmother - the youngest having been 'given' to her by the mother when he was born. It was intended that another child would

---

[233]   Almost half (47% or 9) of these children were under five years of age and the majority (79% or 15) were under the age of 11. All of the children, except the five who were under the age of three, knew that their mother was in prison.

[234]   Five of these were siblings.

also stay with the extended family until his mother, who had a long history of criminal offending and drug abuse, felt that she was able to resume his care. Indeed, all the mothers of the children in long-term care had problems relating to addictions.

Caregivers said that all those children who were old enough to understand knew that their mother was in prison.[235] In relation to the younger children, caregivers tried to explain to them why their mother had gone away in terms that they could understand.

> *I've explained it to him - it's a place where ... you go if you've been naughty. So he knows Mummy's been a naughty girl, that's why she's been in there.*

> *I told him Mummy's in jail. Because when she comes out she's probably gonna tell him, so I want to tell him now. I don't think he understands, (I said) ... it's more or less a holiday.*

One woman had told the five year old boy in her care that: *"Mum's made a mistake."* She did not want him to feel he was in any way to blame for his mother going away or that she had left him because he had done something wrong; she described living with a caregiver as something special: *"A foster mum is like a Fairy Godmother."*

Contact between mother and child/ren

As has been discussed previously, contact between mothers in prison and their children is infrequent and often limited by the nature of the relationship between the mother and the caregiver. All of the caregivers interviewed said how important it was for the children to have contact with their mothers, even if in some cases it was distressing for the children or caused problems for the caregivers themselves.[236]

Siblings did not necessarily have the same amount of contact with their mother. One example concerns two teenage brothers and their baby sister. The 15 year old boy was at boarding school and his 13 year old brother and one year old sister were being cared for by a family member. Of the three, the youngest had the most regular contact with their mother in that she was taken to visit when other family members visited, almost every week.

From what caregivers said, it was obvious that most (84%) of the children in their care had what could be described as regular or semi-regular contact with their imprisoned mothers.[237] The most common type of contact was through letters; 95% of the children received mail from their mothers.[238] I was told that one five year old boy would quite often carry a letter from his mother around with him. Eighty percent of the children spoke to their mother on the

---

[235] This was 12 out of the 19 children.

[236] An example of this was one young woman, who had no children of her own, but who was caring for the nine month old baby boy of a friend. She took the baby regularly to visit his mother in prison and realised the mother needed to have some input into her child's life. However, the caregiver felt that her input as the child's day to day carer, was not being valued or appreciated by his mother.

[237] Two of the three children whom caregivers regarded as having irregular contact with their mothers were in possible long term care situations.

[238] This number includes all those mothers who wrote to their children even if the child was too young to read the letter or write back.

phone[239] and nearly four-fifths visited her in prison.[240] In fact, there were only four children who had not visited their mother in the prison where she was serving her sentence at the time of the interview.

As has been discussed previously, data on the number of children who visit their mother in prison may be misleading. Of the children who had visited their mother, two had only visited once: one had visited just after the mother was sentenced; one had visited on a special family day and one who was normally at boarding school some distance from the prison had only visited during the school holidays. One girl only visited her mother in prison occasionally, when her father could get someone else to take her.[241] Other children visited regularly (weekly) or semi-regularly (fortnightly). Half of these consisted of the five siblings whose mother had very good support systems and the others were being cared for by supportive families/whanau or friends of the mothers who lived within an hour's travelling distance of the prison. One brother and sister had visited their mother only once after she had been sentenced. This took place in the police cells where she was being held awaiting transfer from Rotorua (near their home) to Mount Eden Women's Division to serve her sentence.

Two of the mothers had had contact with their children during home leave visits. Although the visit itself was beneficial for the children of one woman, the carer said they were upset when their mother had to go back to prison, especially her 15 year old son.

> *He was upset, I didn't think he would be, but the moment we took her into the prison and said goodbye n'that he just broke down.*

The five year old son of the other woman hardly saw his mother at all. After a visit with her he told the caregiver, *"She was here for this many days (he held up his fingers) and I saw her (one day)."* She spent the rest of the time out with her friends.

Visiting and associated difficulties

Not all of the children were able to visit their mothers regularly, or even at all. Over half of the carers (58%) expressed feeling sorry for those children. They considered it important that the children should be able to visit their mothers regularly in prison for the wellbeing of all concerned.[242]

> *Well, I worry because you see it's been too long since he's seen her and I do worry about that, because usually he looks forward to going and seeing his mother.*

---

[239] Obviously this was limited depending on whether or not the mother could afford to make calls or whether or not the caregivers could afford to accept collect calls. At the time of the majority of the interviews, women at Mount Eden and Arohata were still able to make collect calls to family. Policy has since changed.

[240] This number does not include one boy who did not now visit his mother regularly as she had been transferred to another prison, although he had visited her once.

[241] This was the ex-partner of one of the women who had custody of their daughter. He found the prison environment depressing yet did not want to stop the child from what limited contact she had with her mother who had spent numerous terms in prison primarily due to her drug use.

[242] Half of the caregivers said that they thought that visits to the mother were important for both the women and their families.

The system is so unfair. They're (women) getting punished and they've done something wrong but we shouldn't be punished as well, because they're depriving us (families) of seeing her.

Caregivers generally expressed their willingness to take children to visit their mother in prison, even those who had been unable to do so. There was only one exception to this.

Basically I just don't like going out there myself. It's sort of a downer seeing the ex (partner) locked up once again ... because I still think of her as (daughter)'s mum - you know.

However, as discussed earlier, there were difficulties associated with visiting the women in prison. Table 7.1 lists these in order of those most frequently mentioned by caregivers.

Table 7.1   Difficulties with visiting mothers in prison: numbers and percentages

	Caregivers (n=12)	
Difficulties	**n**	**%**
Distance	9	75
Money	9	75
Transport	2	17
Work commitments	1	8
Accommodation	1	8
Relationship with child's mother	1	8

Note: Percentages do not add up to 100 as caregivers often voiced several difficulties

The two problems that were most frequently cited by caregivers were the distance they had to travel to the prison and the cost of doing so.

I'd really love to go and see her and take the boys but it's just money. If I won a lotto I'd be gone tomorrow.

I was supposed to take him last week and I couldn't get any money ... for petrol.

I really wish that I could take the boys to see her but I haven't got that money and I haven't got anyone to stay with down there, I can't afford a hotel or anything like that ... The whole family probably would've loved to go down.

Caregivers said that although the mothers seemed relaxed when their children visited them it was often difficult for caregivers themselves and the children to feel comfortable in the prison environment. Those who felt uncomfortable cited such reasons as: the environment was artificial, hating to see the women in prison and, for one caregiver who had been imprisoned herself during the 1980s; the prison evoked unpleasant memories.[243] None of those who had visited the prison felt that visiting areas catered to the needs of any of the parties involved: the women, their children or the caregivers. Facilities were lacking and children often got bored.

---

[243]   Two of the female caregivers interviewed had spent time in prison themselves.

128

(It's) like Fort Knox to get in - overpowering - three locked doors to get to (the) small rooms where special visits are.

It sucks - it's grubby, it's dirty and he crawls all over the place and we got to strip him down ... every Tom, Dick and Harry goes through that place and you want to see some of the people, gosh!

Well he gets bored (visits are) too long for him you know? He just likes to know how she is - I like to know how she is.

Despite the inadequate facilities and the artificial environment, the experience of visiting their mothers was seen to be beneficial to the children, even for those children who were upset to leave their mother behind.

Sometimes they've been upset (but) I think in the long-term the stability of being able to see their mum is really good.

Sometimes it sort of disturbs her and sometimes she's just that wee bit happier to know that Mum's still there.

Caregivers' concerns

When a mother is imprisoned the focus of research is usually on the concerns she has for her children. However, it became obvious during the research that those who are caring for the children in their mother's absence also have concerns, not only about the children, but, for those who were related to the mother, about her as well. Caregivers were usually willing to involve mothers in any decision-making relating to their children[244] by discussing with them, not necessarily the day to day concerns but any important decisions that had to be made. The main reason cited for not keeping mothers fully informed of what was going on with their children was so they would not worry.

I mean we don't tell her everything that's going on over here, we just tell her the kids are fine. I think that when she's good, we're good - you know, we're okay.

Table 7.2 lists concerns that caregivers had about the children in their care, in order of those they most frequently mentioned.

---

[244]   Nearly two-thirds (58%) of caregivers indicated this.

Table 7.2   Caregivers concerns about the children: numbers and percentages

Concerns	Caregivers (n=12)	
	n	%
Feeling sorry for the child/ren	7	58
Child/ren's health problems	7	58
Behaviour - delinquency, acting out	5	42
Child/ren being negatively affected by mother's lifestyle	4	33
Child/ren missing or fretting for their mother	4	33
Child/ren not able to have regular contact with their mother	3	25
Young child/ren forgetting who biological mother is	3	25
Child/ren being angry with mother/carer	3	25
Child/ren trying to settle into new routine with carer	3	25
Child/ren not seeing their mother for a long time	2	17
Problems for children at school / academic	2	17
Child/ren distressed at changes of care situation	2	17

Note: Percentages do not add up to 100 as caregivers often voiced several concerns

The children being looked after by caregivers often had health problems (those most commonly mentioned were asthma and eczema). These were of concern to caregivers in terms of managing these conditions and meeting medical expenses.

> *They have lots of different medical problems ... eczema, asthma, they've all got asthma except for (six year old) ... all typical signs not only tied in with the separation from their mum but also the fact that their mum was abused by her partner and also they were abused (by him) as well.*

Concerns about the effects of the mother's lifestyle on her child/ren

A significant number of the concerns the caregivers had about the children were related to the mother's lifestyle. Caregivers were concerned at what children may have been exposed to prior to their mother's imprisonment as a result of such factors as her criminal offending, transient lifestyle or drug addiction. One example of this was cited by a father who now had custody of his five year old daughter.

> *In the past, in her bad stage, she didn't like going to her mother's at all. If I wanted to go out or something myself and I'd take her round there she just used to pack a fit and just start kicking and then she'd run into the car and lock the doors n'that and she just basically didn't want to stay there at all. I've heard so many disturbing stories about the care that was given when she was in (mother's) care, needles getting left around, really degrading, I don't want to mention too much. Real disgusting care giving, that's what it was, but I blame it fully on the drugs.*

A woman who had her two small grandsons in her care was convinced that the temper tantrums exhibited by one were due to his mother's addiction to tranquillisers. His younger brother had gone through a detoxification process at birth as their mother had overdosed on Valium a few days previously, but this had not been the case for the older boy.

Some children were reported to be unable to express emotions such as anger or sadness. Examples of this were one child who did not cry at all for the first 10 months his mother was in prison and another who did not exhibit any distress when his mother went away.

> *When we were at the courthouse and he was being separated from his mum he didn't cry, that happened twice. When she went to the High Court he didn't cry, it's like he's got no emotion towards her, just nothing close. I think he's come not to rely on her because me and my older sister, we've had him between us since when (mother) went walkabout for a month ... he's just used to not being with her.*

Yet all of the children, except those who were two years of age or younger, were said to talk about their mother, particularly when they missed her or when they were angry with her.

> *When's Mummy coming back from her holiday?*

> *Mummy's gone to jail - doesn't Mummy love me?*

> *My mummy's in jail, she's not coming home till next year.*

Other children were seen to be insecure or over-familiar with the drug culture - for example, they knew how drugs were administered, what implements were used and so on.

> *"Oh, there's a spoon in there with filters on it." And I looked at him and I said, "A what?" He said "A spoon with filters, you know, to cook."*

In fact, one caregiver related how the imprisoned mother, who was her niece, was always trying to persuade the family to either bring drugs into the prison for her, or send them in with her 11 year old son, when he came to visit. Not surprisingly, this worried the carer, especially when the boy expressed his willingness to do this for his mum - to make her happy. Another child would freeze when he saw the police and say, *"Uh oh, busted!"* Two of his mother's friends had died in the three months before her imprisonment, one from a drug overdose and the other was murdered.

Concerns that children should not forget their mother

Those caring for babies were aware that quite often when a mother and child are separated small children forget who their biological mother is. And those who were related to the children discussed how painful it was for them as a family to see something like this happening.

> *He classes me more as his mother than he does his mother, but I try not to let him do that, you know?*

Caregivers frequently said how they talked to young children, for example toddlers or those just at school, about their mothers so that they would not forget them.

In his mind I think he is wondering where his mum is, because when the phone rings and I say, "It's Mummy (name)," he'll look at the door to see if she's coming and I'll say, "No it's the phone (boy's name)," ... He doesn't cry he just gives me the phone back and he'll look and then he'll go off and play. And then at night time I'll just give him a kiss, say, " Goodnight boy ... kiss your mummy nyny," and he'll (pretend to) kiss her ... every day I'll talk to him about her.

Concerns related to the child/ren leaving the carer

Two young women who did not have children of their own had become very attached to those they were caring for and were worried about how they would deal with giving the child back to his/her mother.

The way I see it is that I think she's just gonna come out and take him off me ... yeah, it's gonna be hard to just hand him over.

One maternal grandmother was worried that the father of the children in her care would try to take the two boys from her when he was released from prison. He frequently phoned her making such threats.

"Oh, when I get out of jail," he said, "I'll knock on (the) door and ask for my boys." I said, "Like hell you will, it won't be that easy ... the kids are mine." He just wants them to take them into his whanau, that's all. I'll swear on the bible - he'd never get the kids off me ... I mean he could go a bit of a mean way if he liked, but no - bugger it - I'd kidnap those boys and take off. It used to get me down ... now if the phone rings ... I'm not in, I can't be bothered talking to him .

Concerns about the behaviour of older children

It was also mentioned that older children were quite often angry - with their mother, with the carer, with the police or with anyone who could be considered responsible for their separation from their mother. Such anger often resulted in these children getting into trouble at school, becoming involved in friendships with similar angry or anti-social young people, or even refusing to have anything to do with their mother. However, it is important to remember here that we are talking about the caregivers' perceptions of the situations. It is possible that these young people were just displaying the characteristics of "normal" teenagers.

Caregivers' feelings towards children

Almost three-fifths of the caregivers said that they felt sorry for the children in their care for reasons such as not being able see their mothers regularly or for what they had experienced due to their mother's lifestyle.

I get a bit sorry for the boys because they're doing all sorts of things that she's (mother) missing out on.

I feel sorry for him ... I bought him up with my twins since the time (mother) first went to prison, he was only little. And then she came and took him but every time she goes in (to prison) she brings him back here to me.

Children's adaptation to living away from their mothers

Sometimes it was difficult for the children to settle into a routine in their new home, three caregivers said that this was so for the children they were caring for. In two cases this was perceived to be as a result of the disorganised lifestyle of the children's mothers. In the third situation the children were missing the way their mother had looked after them and the routine that they were used to.

Yeah, we had some complications to start with, it was just because (4 year old) wasn't in no routine. Like he was going to bed 10 o'clock and sleeping late, and he goes to Kohanga (kindergarten) so yes, it was real difficult to get him into a 8:30 bed, 7:00 o'clock get up, get ready for Kohanga and then off you go ...

Like if ... (caregiver) does something different they'll say, "Oh, my mum says this ...," or whatever or you know. ... "Mum does this ..." or whatever, "Mum says I have to do ... ," and all that kind of stuff.

However, most children responded well over time to a stable, loving environment and, understandably, another change of caregiver was distressing to those children who had experienced this during their mother's imprisonment.

A lot of people have said to me that he's (four year old) changed for the better and ... like to be honest with you ... I get offended when they say that to me cause it's like they're running down my sister ... (but) he's real good now.

It was really stressful when they changed care-givers and really it's only the beginning stages of them getting settled (now). (Boy) who's 10, has found the change in caregiver (and) the separation from his mum really hard, he's been really upset and then he('s) ... been angry and all of that, yeah.

From the information I received from caregivers, it was obvious there was no one uniform response by children to their separation from their mother. Some fretted; others did not. Of course, this effect was often dependent on the relationship between the child and his/her mother and on the prior relationship between the child and his/her caregiver. However, it was not unusual for young children to cry for their mother if they were being reprimanded by a caregiver, even if, as in one case, the child had virtually lived for the past three years with her father.

Well, 90 to 95% of the time she's fine (but) there's other 5 or 10% ... like if I tell her off and send her to her room she'll go, "Oh, Mummy, I want my mummy," and she might start crying n'that - apart from that everything's just normal.

I'd say he's coping fine ... the only time he'll cry for her is when I've scolded him or I smack his bum cause he's been naughty (laughs) ...

For other children their mother's imprisonment was the first time that they had been away from her for any length of time and this caused them distress, no matter what age they were.

I think that it's been really hard on them, really hard on them ...

I know one visit I took her out to and then that night she woke up saying, "(Mum)!" And that was really horrible.

Caregivers' financial concerns

Most carers had financial problems and talked about not being able to afford counselling, medical care, special dietary needs (for a hyperactive child), new clothes or treats such as toys for the children in their care.

I'd like to take the boys out and get them what I want, it wouldn't be expensive ... something new, instead of second-hands or hand-me-downs.

We manage ... it's difficult but we get along. We struggle now and then, but at least we've got food in our cupboards to feed ... the kids.

Why don't they (mothers) think? They've got kids - think of the kids. See there's lots of things these kids want at the moment (that) I can't get, I can't, it's impossible.

One particular caregiver spoke of having borrowed a $400 advance on her welfare benefit in an attempt to meet her commitments and $1500 from a private loan company to buy bicycles for her two sons and the child she was caring for. The $1500 loan had fortnightly instalments of $200 which, as a single mother on welfare, added to her financial worries.

Concerns about the imprisoned mothers

As mentioned previously, those carers who were family members - which was by far the majority - often had concerns about the imprisoned mothers themselves. They were worried about how they were actually coping in prison: about not being able to afford to send the imprisoned women money (for example, for phone cards); and how the mothers would cope with their children on release from prison.

She used to ask me for money and I can't afford to give her any money and I feel so terrible - you know?

If I could afford it I'd send it to her, I'd send money up if I could. I know that she needs things ... you've got to have money (in prison) alright.

At least six of the 11 mothers had a considerable, usually long term, problem with drugs and/or alcohol and three of these women had served several terms of imprisonment before the current term. Caregivers were worried about the possibility that the mother's drug taking and general criminal lifestyle would resume on her release.

I said, "You know, if Mum don't change her ways you're not going back to her until she does ... because I think you don't want to go through all that again."

Yeah, basically it gets down to her friends, as soon as she gets out she's alright for a while and then as soon as she starts mingling with her friends again she's away with the fairies and just gets in exactly the same situation.

It's the people she gets amongst, she's sort of always been like this but I told her when you've got children they come first, before good times. Until (she) does get her act together and gets really settled down and off these bloody drugs I don't want the kids going into that environment because they're in a stable condition here.

Those caregivers who were related to the mothers spoke in terms which were not only supportive of the children in their care, but also of the women in prison. This was despite the fact that, from what the caregivers said, they had often been angry with the women. It was clear that many women had caused their families a great deal of pain, especially if they were drug dependent. This had sometimes led to their families being unable to trust them.

I don't need any bullshit from (child's mother). I don't need her coming around squawking and screaming at me saying that she's all better ... because she tries that a lot. She tries to tell me that everything's fine, she's gonna be good for the rest of her life, that upsets me because I don't trust her any more. If she gave up on that and really got herself together before she tried to get (daughter) back, I'd be happy.

Oh sometimes I break down in the room you know cause I think of (name) all the time, I know that's she's been a real bitch but you just can't wash them away ...

"Mum went through heaps at your age," I said, "She bought herself up more or less ... you can't really blame her for anything that she's going through at the moment ... because that's what she saw all her life."

Caregivers' support systems

For the caregivers, the day to day care of the children along with the attempts to make sure that they had some sort of contact with their mothers and that the women in prison had support from them as a family was often a stressful, exhausting experience. The only support many had was where a strong extended family network existed.

There should be some kind of support for people, you know caregivers like me. Because now and then we need time out and like it's alright in my situation because I've got heaps of whanau who will take him just so I get my time out ... because when you're looking after a kid it's stressful especially if you're not getting away from them and getting time by yourself.

These comments were made by one of the two young women caregivers who did not have any children of their own.

Although the carers said that their own children were coping with well having others sharing their home and their mother, it was obvious that many of these caregivers did not have "time out" or someone to discuss their problems with.

Well, I'm always busy, very busy. I don't get much time for myself - no I don't.

I'm one to keep things inside me ... when you do try and open up to someone, it's like they don't want to know, or it's the wrong person ... so basically that's why I keep it to myself.

Some nights when I go to bed and I've got the boys in there I get really sad but no-one knows because I don't tell them.

What clearly emerged from these interviews with caregivers was that, however disappointed, abandoned, or angry the children were, they still loved their mothers.

He knows his mum, he loves his mum. Probably sometimes he wishes he could be with his mum or see her - that's what I honestly think.

She still knows about her mum, she knows she's there (prison) - I guess she still loves her (mother).

Caregivers plainly thought that the women were not the only ones being punished for their crimes: their children were also victims. Consequently, not only the day-to-day, but the future needs of the children were uppermost in the minds of carers.

There's always one thing I said and it's in my heart, that I'd never let her (mother) hurt the boys - never!

"You know, if Mum don't change her ways you're not going back to her until she does," and he (boy) nodded his head. "Because I think you don't want to go through all that again," I said.

Yeah, because the kids are punished in all of this you know, and it's tragic - it's such a tragedy!

Summary

Only a few studies have included talking to, or surveying, the caregivers of the children of women in prison and most of these have had small samples. Carers of the children of women in prison are a population which is not easily accessed[245] and might be easily forgotten about. However, the findings from this New Zealand study seem generally to mirror what we know from studies overseas about the concerns and problems faced by those who care for the children of imprisoned women.

The findings in this chapter reflect the profile of caregivers and their relationship with the children in their care provided by researchers in the United States (Bloom & Steinhart; 1993; Henriques, 1982; Hungerford, 1993) and in England (Woodrow, 1992b). That is, caregivers are invariably women from the imprisoned women's families and, as noted by Woodrow (1992b), this usually means that the children know their caregivers well and may have spent some time living with them in the past. The fact that some children may have been in care previously as a result of their mother's addictions or lifestyle has also been remarked upon by

---

[245]   Bloom and Steinhart (1993) note that correctional system confidentiality rules may impede attempts to access caregiver details. In addition, mothers in prison may not want to disclose details of who is caring for their children for fear of welfare agency intervention and possible loss of custody of their child/ren (Woodrow, 1992a, 1992b).

Woodrow (1992b). Other findings which have been validated by Woodrow's (1992b) research are that care placements often broke down for children[246] and it was not unusual for siblings to be separated when their mother went to prison.

Hungerford (1993) found that caregivers, all of whom were family members, were disappointed and angry with the imprisoned mother;[247] indeed, they were ashamed of her. Although in part this is true of the findings from this research, in that caregivers were quite often angry or disappointed with the mothers, they were more often than not still supportive of them. Caregivers spoke in terms of feeling sorry for the imprisoned women, rather than of being ashamed of them.

Caregivers generally felt that contact between the mother and her child/ren was beneficial and actively encouraged this. These findings are similar to overseas research (Bloom & Steinhart, 1993; Woodrow, 1992b). Along with Henriques (1982), these researchers also discuss the problems faced by caregivers when taking the children to visit their mothers such as: having to travel long distances; the cost involved; and the unfriendly nature of the environment due to the rules and regulations of the prison regime. Consequently, few children visited their mothers regularly, and others not at all. In the majority of cases, children kept in contact with their mother mainly by letter; only a few could afford to keep in regular contact by phone.

Caregivers generally said they had concerns about the behaviour and emotional state of the children in their care and the adjustment of these children to the separation from their mothers. Children were reported as being angry, insecure, distressed and/or experiencing problems at school. Again this finding reflects previous research (Henriques, 1982; Woodrow, 1992b). However, Woodrow (1992b) cautions that mothers and caregivers had both reported that a few of these children[248] had exhibited behavioural problems **before** the separation. Researchers also note that the children's problems could have either worsened or improved during the mother's imprisonment. Again, as I found, there was no one uniform response by children to their separation from their mother. Some coped well,[249] particularly those who had been living with the caregiver (e.g. a grandparent) and the mother before her imprisonment. However, several caregivers in my sample expressed concerns about the chronic poor health of children in their care (citing complaints such as asthma and eczema) which replicated the concerns of caregivers in Woodrow's (1992b) research. In both these studies the children had been in ill-health before their mother's imprisonment and caregivers reported that these conditions had deteriorated.[250]

Caregivers said they did not generally have adequate financial support to meet the needs of children in their care and, indeed, were usually poor and often welfare dependent, themselves. Overseas researchers have reported caregivers' financial concerns which are not dissimilar to those the caregivers related in this research. Caregivers invariably said that they were

---

[246] This was so for 42% (8 out of 19) of the children discussed in this chapter.

[247] Woodrow (1992b) found that caregivers *'in a few cases'* were repulsed, shocked and upset by the mother's crime.

[248] This was the case for 10% of the 34 children living with the caregivers interviewed.

[249] Just under one-third of the children in Woodrow's (1992b) sample.

[250] Woodrow (1992b) further commented that three of the children in her study were said to have developed these conditions (i.e. asthma or eczema) during their mother's sentence.

suffering financial hardship and that welfare payments[251] did not cover the cost of supporting the children in their care (Bloom & Steinhart, 1993; Henriques, 1982; Woodrow, 1992b).[252] The findings in this chapter indicate that there is little respite for those who take on the responsibility of caring for the children of imprisoned women. Caregivers often have to make sacrifices and adjust their lifestyles to take these children into their homes. Frequently, caregivers felt that their efforts were not appreciated. These sentiments have been echoed by caregivers in other studies (Henriques, 1984; Woodrow, 1992b).

I asked the caregivers I interviewed for their ideas on how their needs and those of the imprisoned women and their children could be better met. Their suggestions for improvements in policy and practice are discussed in the next chapter along with the suggestions made by the mothers themselves.

---

[251] Woodrow (1992b) noted that only a fifth of the carers in her sample received additional benefits for the children in their care.

[252] However, Hungerford (1993) noted that none of the caregivers in his sample (made up entirely of the family members of the imprisoned mothers) had any pressing financial concerns. This would seem to be at odds with the majority of findings.

CHAPTER 8   MOTHERS' AND CAREGIVERS' IDEAS FOR IMPROVEMENTS

Introduction

I asked the women (both initially in the prison[253] and at a later date again in the prison or out in the community) and the caregivers how they thought things could be improved for them and their families. In the case of the women, I asked them specifically what sorts of initiatives would facilitate contact with their children and how caregivers could be aided. The caregivers were also asked what would make their task easier.[254]

The data from all of the interviews with the women have been integrated, where appropriate, in this chapter for two main reasons. First, in the main, the same themes were repeated at the two interview points. Where issues were raised only in the second interview this is made clear. Second, the women were quite often more forthcoming at the second interview and elaborated on these earlier themes. They appeared to be either more at ease with me the second time around or to be more likely to speak freely if they were interviewed outside of the prison. With this in mind, women who had been released were asked in retrospect how they thought their situation as long distance mothers could have been improved whilst they were in prison.[255] I did not ask this question again because I doubted the validity of their first responses, but because, at the time of the first interviews, many of them had only been in prison for a short time and I felt that, as time went on and as the experience of imprisonment impinged upon them and their children, new problems might have arisen for them that they had not envisaged earlier. Also, it was obvious at the first interviews that some women were still in shock at being imprisoned and were quite emotional. Consequently, I thought they might be able to assess their needs in a more detached manner in retrospect. In the same manner, the women re-interviewed in prison were only asked what they thought would assist mothers in prison to maintain their relationships with their children and how caregivers could be aided; they were not asked how the plight of mothers recently released from prison could be improved as the majority of them had not yet been through this process.[256] Indeed, it became obvious that a number of issues raised for the first time by women in the community were as a result of problems that the women were currently experiencing or problems which their children and/or caregivers had experienced that the women had not been aware of until their release.

Furthermore, at the time of the second interviews, the women appeared to have stronger opinions on how their various situations could be improved and consequently I did not ask

---

253   At the first interviews, the women were asked how contact could be improved or facilitated between them and their children. I asked them specifically what they though about enhanced visiting initiatives such as mother and baby units, all day/holiday special visits and whether or not they thought that their families should be assisted to enable them to bring children to visit. In addition, the women were asked for their opinions on mixed prisons, regional prisons for women and non-custodial sentences for low-risk female offenders with dependent children.

254   Caregivers were asked how they thought their situation could be improved as caregivers e.g. financially, emotionally and/or practically, and how the needs of the children in their care might be better served.

255   Women re-interviewed in the community were asked what sort of assistance they would like to see made available for mothers in prison and their children, the caregivers of these children and mothers newly released from prison.

256   Mothers re-interviewed in prison were asked how they thought the situation could be improved for them, their children and the children's caregivers.

them directly about specific initiatives (e.g. mother and baby units, enhanced visiting, mixed prisons), or prompt them as I had during the first interviews. Therefore, if some women did not suggest a particular initiative during the follow-up interviews, this did not necessarily mean that they were not in favour of it or had changed their minds since the first interviews; this also applies where initiatives are only discussed by one particular group of women (e.g. women post-release).

Women's ideas for improvements

The following section presents the main themes that emerged from the interviews with the women.

Assistance to solve urgent problems

When I first interviewed them, the women stated that there was a real need for some mechanism by which they could solve urgent problems regarding their families, as social workers in the prison were invariably seen to be too busy or to be absent for one reason or another.

> *To see her ... it might take two or three days. I mean if there was a real major disaster you wouldn't get to see her. because I've even writ that it's urgent ....*

> *You put in a request slip and you know several times I've wanted to see her about something urgent when all that was coming up (was): "She's off today." "She's sick." "She's at a course." "She's on holidays." "She's somewhere else." I think they need to have one here all the time, every day.*

> *I've noticed she's never here most of the time when things do crop up for a lot of the women ...*

> *Yeah, well she's on holiday now for a month and there's no-one to replace her ... and it wasn't just me, I've spoken to other women that have been waiting with urgent problems ... someone told me that they waited a week for her to giver them five minutes. Now when she comes back from her month's holiday how much backlog is there for her to deal with?*

Consequently, most of the women said that they had already solved the problem or it had gone away by the time they were able to see someone. For example, one woman described a situation where an opportunity arose for her to arrange for her father to bring her son up to visit her when he was passing through Christchurch on his way to Wellington. A work colleague of his had arranged to provide him with accommodation in Christchurch for a few days. However, this could not be arranged as the prison social worker was away and she normally let women make toll calls from her office when they could not afford to use the payphone. The following is another illustration of the frustration many women experienced when attempting to get 'urgent' assistance to deal with family problems.

> *She (social worker) called me into her office last week because she'd received a form that I'd written on the 19th of September (three weeks before) and I said, "Well it's all sorted out now." And I mean it was urgent, and I'd written on it that it was urgent and I ended up sorting it out with the Unit Manager, which*

didn't please her very much because it's not her job to sort things out with the kids.

One woman's comment summed up the general opinion:

We need access to someone ... you know, they should have a reliever to take over when she's (social worker) not here or whatever ... I mean when you need to see a social worker you need to see her now - not in ten days time.

Mother and baby units

At the first interview, a large percentage (91%)[257] of the women indicated that they thought that there should be mother and baby units available for women in prisons and were familiar with this concept:[258]

I think that's what they need, to get up a base where mothers can have their children with them.

If you've just had a baby just before y'come in here ... that baby sorta doesn't know the mother ... sometimes they're breastfeeding y'know ... I think there should be a special unit here for especially breast-feeding mothers.

The bonding, that's the most important - bonding, isn't it? ... I'd have hated it for my babies to be taken off me.

I think they are really a necessity ... I think one mother with a young child warrants it.

Even the woman who was pregnant with her first child had a comment to make regarding the provision of mother and baby units in women's prisons.

I wish that they had these sorts of things here so that I didn't have to worry about when I give birth if I'm allowed to go home with my child or not y'know? ... I want to be with my child.

One young woman, whose parents were also in prison, added that she thought facilities should be provided for mothers to have children up to the age of 12 or 13 years living with them.

Another of the women, who had been brought up in foster-care, said that if it was a choice between the baby going into foster-care or staying with the mother in prison, then she was in favour of the latter option. However, in principle she did not think that babies belonged in prison.

Enhanced visiting programmes

---

[257] The percentages relating to the first interviews are based on the total sample of 56 women.

[258] Two women who were in favour of mother and baby units had previously been in Australian prisons where similar facilities were available and so had actually seen them in practice. However, one admitted that not all women wanted their children *"growing up behind bars"*.

141

At the first interviews, all of the women were in favour of enhanced visiting programmes that is, all day (family days) or extended visiting for children during the holidays. In practice, as discussed in previous chapters,[259] few women and children experienced these. One of the mothers described family days as a 'privilege' as whether or not they took place depended on the women's behaviour and approval from unit management. Other women talked about how they felt that extended visits and having a place where children could stay would help ameliorate the effects of the separation for both mothers and children.

> *Even if they had one wing where once a month, it wouldn't matter how old the kid was - even my daughter of 16 could come down here and have a weekend at the jail with the mother they wouldn't have half the problems they've got with the children.*

> *I think it's really important not just for those kids but I think it's also important for the mother. Because I mean seeing how people can get hardened I think it would help keep them (mothers) mellow ... There are circumstances why people offend and I think it's important to still keep that family unit together as much as you can, if that's what the family wants - some don't want it.*

Five (50%) of the women re-interviewed in prison raised these issues again. They thought that enhanced visiting programmes such as all day visits, overnight stays and school holiday programmes would help them maintain family relationships.

> *I would like it, like in that documentary I saw on (Bedford Hills prison in New York) ... American prisons for mothers where they (children) spend a week of the school holidays ... I would really like to see that in place for mothers in place of family day really ... where they have that involvement with their children for a whole week, they (children) just don't sleep at the prison.*

These issues were elaborated on during the second interviews with the women in prison.[260] Only one of the women thought that facilities and resources to help the women maintain their family relationships were as good as they could be. She considered that the opportunities were there if a woman wanted to take advantage of them, especially for those with younger children.

However, it was apparent that the other women did not share this view. They all stressed how important they thought visiting was and how this exercise, even if only in a small way, enabled them to feel part of their children's lives.

> *That's all I want ... I'm happy with where they're at and how they're being looked after but hey, I just want to say to (caregivers) don't cut me out fully because they're my kids too (crying) ... and I want to have something to do with them. If I can't have them with me then let me be a part of them in some way. If I can't be with them on a daily basis ... let me at least be able to sit there and give them a piece of me.*

---

[259] See Chapters 1 and 5.

[260] The percentages relating to the follow-up interviews with women in prison are based on the number of women who had ideas for improvements (10).

Almost two-fifths (39%) of the women re-interviewed in the community[261] talked about the importance of enhanced visiting programmes such as family days and special school holiday visiting. Again, the programmes available at prisons overseas were mentioned by one of the women.

> *I've seen some of the prison systems over in, is it America or somewhere? Where they let the children come and spend time during the day, I mean if they could set up something like that in New Zealand ... because people who go to prison n'leave their children behind and the children are too far away to visit - you do lose something, you do lose you know ....*

Three-quarters (73%) of the women re-interviewed in the community saw improved contact with families as an essential ingredient in maintaining relationships and reducing the trauma suffered by children.

> *Oh just ways of the women seeing their children a lot ... so that when they get out then their children know who they are and the children know that their mother didn't (just) leave them.*

> *I think the children definitely need to be able to keep in contact, I think that has to be a priority, for the children's sake.*

> *Too many women lose contact with their kids - and that's not on!*

Sharing food with visitors

A new issue which emerged at the follow up interviews with women in prison, and which was related to enhanced visiting, was the importance that four (40%) of the women attached to being able to a share a meal with their families. One woman, in particular, considered that meal times had been some of the special times that they had shared as a family.

> *But I find that at home when the girls were growing up, the time that we spent - you know, the most intimate times - have been when we've been eating ... it's the sharing ... it's the one time that they'll say things to you that they might not say while they're playing, or while we're watching the grandchildren.*

The sharing of food had particular significance for these women; for another, just the common courtesy of being able to offer a visitor a cup of tea during visiting hours (which was also a suggestion made by many of the women during the first interviews) would have been appreciated.[262]

---

[261] Percentages relating to the follow-up interviews with women in the community are based on the number (26) of women re-interviewed in the community - unless otherwise stated.

[262] Deane (1988) noted the cultural importance of the sharing of food for Māori and Pacific Islanders especially in the welcoming of visitors and the breaking down of social barriers. Similar observations were made by Phillips (1992).

Assistance to families to visit

When first interviewed, the women were in favour of some form of assistance being offered to families so that carers could bring children to visit them. Suggestions made by the women were: financial assistance to enable families to visit; transport from main centres to the prisons for family days and the provision of accommodation where children or families could stay when visiting the prison.

> *I know it's a lot to ask for ... I know we put ourselves in here, but they (the criminal justice system) are locking us away from our children. They should take responsibility for that and pay half (of the fare) so our children can come and visit and set up a facility for them to visit.*

> *Yeah, definitely (some sort of assistance). Because most of the girls in prison they don't come from rich families - rich whānau (families) - and they're in here because they've done something to get themself in here through (lack of) money.*

> *Houses set up so that like they can come down (and have somewhere to stay) if they're coming from a long way and just to be funded would be nice ... like my Dad he came down and had to sleep in the car because he had nowhere else and he brought all his children.*

One woman who was serving a long term of imprisonment suggested that the women themselves could put on plays or concerts for the public to raise funds to assist families who could not afford to bring children to visit. She saw that this would serve a double purpose, it would help families and it would also allow the women a measure of independence from the 'system'.

During the follow-up interviews in prison, most of the women (70%) reiterated these concerns and suggested that unused buildings within the confines of the prison grounds could be utilised usefully in this way.

> *For families that are coming from a distance either (the) South Island or away from the Wellington region (they could) be together, like there's a kitchen up there in that little house ... or even if the families could stay there.*

> *Somewhere for them to come and stay, like somewhere cheap where they could come up and stay, you know, a house or something. Hey, there's no reason why they couldn't, look at the property here, look at the size of it ... Or what about those houses (prison staff houses that were empty) down there or something ... ?*

The availability of assistance, to those who wanted to visit, by way of financial supplements, was seen by 70% of the women re-interviewed in prison as a way to enhance their contact over time with their children and other loved ones.

> *Anything to help the families that find it especially hard.*

> *If we had enough money that they could come and visit me more regular.*

A significant number of women re-interviewed post-release agreed that there should be assistance to enable families to visit women in prison, particularly subsidised accommodation[263] and petrol money.[264] Even though most women knew funds were available from the Department of Social Welfare and PARS they were also aware of their limited nature.

> *I mean if you can get assistance for travel if you're doing a course or if you're on a sickness benefit you get assistance to travel to go see a doctor if the doctor's far away - I mean why can't they just do that for children?*

> *Some of them, they couldn't see their children, the people who were looking after them couldn't afford to bring their children a long distance ... I think it would be a great idea if they could get a subsidy.*

> *I've heard of (families) sleeping in vans, you know over night, so they could come and visit.*

Subsidised contact

The women also suggested at the first interviews, that some provision for subsidised contact (e.g. postage or telephone cards) with their families should be made available to those women whose families could not afford to assist them.

> *Money goes so quickly on the phone cards. I really feel that they (prison system) should do something for people with kids so that they can ring them a couple of times a week.*

During follow-up interviews, when asked how resources might be improved to facilitate contact between imprisoned women and their families, 50% (5) of the women in prison and 12% (3) of those in the community stressed that subsidised, or even free, phone calls should be made available.

> *If I could ring them say once a week, even if I rung one of them once a week and talked to them for ten minutes or so and not have to pay for it.*

> *Free phone calls would be great, even here in Christchurch we have to pay for our phone calls here and I think that's really mean. And I think they could make them cheaper, you know the weekend where it's the $5 and talk as long as you like - well we can't do that ... my family are the most important thing to me ...*

> *I mean there are times I'd love to ring my daughter but I can't afford to ring - I have to buy a phone card ...*

---

[263]   Two-fifths of the women talked about issues related to subsidised accommodation for visitors.

[264]   Sixty-two percent of the women thought that this kind of assistance would increase the number of caregivers who could bring children to visit.

Maybe even once a week or once every fortnight or something like that, a five minute call just to ring your kids, you know, that would make a hell of a difference ... I'm sure they could make arrangements with Telecom to have a cheaper rate or something.

Regional/mixed prisons for women

At the first interviews, 97% of the women thought that the establishment of regional prisons for women would be a good idea as it would enable them to maintain better contact with their families. When told that, due to the small number of women in prison, this would probably mean the establishment of a women's wing in what was essentially a men's prison, most (82%) of the women said that this would not bother them as long as they were kept separate from the men and had proper facilities. Improved contact was their first priority.

Who cares, as long as you got to see your kids ... If they could put me in a prison closer to my son ... I wouldn't give two shits (about the men) ... as long as I was seeing my son.

Well, that's not a problem is it? It wasn't a problem when they (men) were here (Arohata).[265] Well it wouldn't bother me, because as long as they're in another wing that's all that matters.

Yes, I don't think women would have a problem with that if they could be closer to their families ... and when women have had a terrible deal with men, it's "a man" it's not "men".

However, it was recognised by some women that the presence of men could pose a problem for other women.

It really depends on why you're in there in the first place, because if it's to do with men y'know, you don't want to be seeing them everyday ... When they (men) were here they used to call out and get smart to us through the windows, it's just for me that wasn't a problem I'd just get smart back ... but to some women who had been in there because of crimes with their husband, violent crimes, I just think it's no good at all.

A minority were adamant that shared-site facilities were not acceptable and could only lead to trouble for some women.

I didn't even like it when they had it here (I'm) dead against that. Gee, I don't know how many of our women got charged or threatened with incident reports because (they were) talking to the men. And yet you know this was our prison ... it was the principle of the thing. This was our prison - no way has it got on the sign down there: 'Arohata Women's and Men's Prison' They (men) were eggheads, they disrespected the women!

---

[265] See Chapter 1.

In one way it's good in that you're going to be close to your family. In the other way it's bad because at the most we're going to get a small wing of a male prison and it's going to cut out your habilitation options because it's going to cater to the majority. We're already the minority, we'd be even a smaller minority. ... And also ... being in a part of male prisons we'd all be held accountable for men's sexual behaviour and when they have men anywhere near women in prison it's like extra accountability ... It pisses me off that the attitude is that it's the women who are going to run after the men ... it's like "She asked for it" when she got raped ... no (it's) not practicable.

Two women re-interviewed in prison, who had no access to their children, thought that there should be more women's prisons, so that women could be closer to their families. These were both women who had fought for transfers, one on a temporary basis, so that they could be nearer to their children in an attempt to gain access. Neither had been successful. One felt that being closer to their families would enable women to have first-hand knowledge of how their children were, which would help relieve stressful situations for them.

I strongly suggest that at least another two women's prisons have to be built, it's essential ... I mean like there's a lot of women in here they get a letter from their family and it might say - oh, that their child is really sick or something, right? That stresses the mother out. How does the mother cope with the stress? Some become very violent, some become withdrawn.

Women re-interviewed in the community endorsed these ideas.

Community based alternatives to imprisonment

All of the women indicated at the first interview that they were in favour of non-custodial sentences for women who were non-violent offenders and who had dependent children.

Definitely - restorative justice I think has to be the aim for the future.

I think it's a much better idea ... especially treatment and things like that ... Sending you to jail just teaches you how to be more deviate, how to learn more crimes, how to do other things y'know - it's not exactly a positive attitude (that you learn).

I think that's what they should have (community based sanctions) ...(Women should be) put into counselling that they have to go to, someone coming (and) checking up on the family now and then that sort of thing, just to make sure that you are okay and that you are coping and not doing what you did before ... Yeah, I reckon that'd be good.

I think that would be excellent because then you're not breaking up the family and because you know like when you do break up the family the children are the ones that (suffer).

In addition, women who had addictions thought that it would be more effective, for them and their children, if they had been placed in a rehabilitation facility rather than a prison.

147

The thing is in all of this I'm not the only victim here so is my child and he's being punished for my crimes as are all the other children. I mean sending me to jail was really a waste of time, I mean I need to be in a rehab not in a jail.

However, there was a recognition that such programmes did not always work.

I know (a) few women in here who have gone to about four rehabs and just come back, so obviously they need something more ...

Two women expressed strong views relating to the imprisonment of pregnant women: they felt that prison was not the place for them.

I don't think they should go to jail - irrelevant of the crime ... I think there's other things that can be done ... I think they could be kept at home and if they stuff up again while they're under this home "whatever it is" (detention) then sure, maybe look at it (imprisonment). But I don't think pregnant women should have their children in jail, I really don't.

Those who are ready to have their babies ... they should be put into a home and if need be to have a fence around the building or some thing, but not here into the prison.

Another woman thought that, in principle, community based sentences were a good idea as long as they were only utilised as an alternative to imprisonment.

Yeah, except for the double-bind of net-widening ... I think they need to set firmer parameters to define it ... "this is instead of prison".

Two of the women re-interviewed in prison considered that prisons should only house women who were violent offenders and that other women who had broken the law could be dealt with more constructively in the community. Ironically, both of these women were serving prison sentences for violent offences. Women re-interviewed in the community agreed with this view.

(It's) stupid sending women to jail for minor offences -three months for social welfare fraud can disrupt the whole family.

I don't think that prison's appropriate for non-violent offences ... it's a supreme waste of time.

One woman felt strongly that women should be given time immediately after sentencing to make arrangements for their children's care, if they had not already done so.[266]

I think if the Judge is going to sentence you to jail he should at least tell you and give you two weeks or something to plan things ... I was told I wasn't going to jail

---

[266] It would appear that there is some inconsistency in practice here by criminal justice professionals. Other women reported being given extended periods of time to address family issues, which they found frustrating in that it only put off the inevitable term in prison.

by my probation officer and my lawyer because it was a first offence ... I hadn't sorted anything out.

Need for information

When re-interviewed, other suggestions included providing more information for the women on all of their entitlements and not just supplying information on the institutional rules and regulations. One woman, who was still in prison on follow-up and who had spent a large part of her life in institutions of one kind or another, had a thorough working knowledge of 'the system'. She said she thought that there was a need for women in prison to be provided with such information on their admittance to the facility. In the absence of this, she often found she ended up dealing informally with questions which women with less experience of prisons had. This woman also felt that staff often played 'head games' with the women in that they would not always fully inform them of their entitlements.

Not with me (laughs) ... but then they (staff) do play games with (women) ... first timers especially ...

Indeed, this woman also advocated that prisoner's children should be given information on their mother's living conditions and perhaps be able to see her cell during visiting times.

And like kids like to know how their mothers are living, especially in places like this. We should be allowed the right to show our children our slot (cell).

Women in the community also saw that the provision of information for children, describing their mother's living environment was important, especially for those children who could not visit. One woman described an aborted attempt by herself to provide such information, which resulted in her being accused of plotting an escape.

I actually drew a map of my wing and all the slots (cells) and I drew ... where my bed was and my bench and what-not and the exercise yard and sent it out so my girls had some idea of what I was living like. And (staff) bought (sic) it back to me in the middle of the night ... and stuck it under the door saying: "Fuckin' useless escape plan that was you stupid bitch. Try it again and you'll be in the pound!" And it was just my little map to show the girls what I was living like (laughs).

Prison programming

At the time of the initial interviews, only two of the women voluntarily raised issues related to the needs of imprisoned mothers that they thought could be addressed through the provision of programmes in prisons. One talked about how she thought most women could benefit from parenting courses (and from legal advice). The other woman, who was serving a long term of imprisonment, said that she felt that the women needed programmes to help them acquire cognitive skills and improve their levels of literacy.

Women re-interviewed in the community also raised issues relating to the types of programmes offered to women in prison which appeared to be based on their individual post-release experiences. They thought that prison programming should address such issues as positive parenting, relationships, pre-release preparation for family re-unification and community orientation/re-familiarisation. They thought programmes should also be available which would provide women with a chance to talk to someone about their problems and learn new skills. In addition, it was suggested that parent support groups run within the prison might help some of the women, especially long-termers, deal with issues relating to their families. These were clearly areas of concern which had not yet arisen for the women re-interviewed in prison.

Support for children/liaison between mothers and children

The need to provide support for children who have a mother in prison was also advocated by these interviewees, along with the suggestion that there should be a liaison service between mothers and their children to help rebuild relationships, or to let the mother know if everything was alright, where there was limited or no contact. Again, these were issues which had not yet arisen for women re-interviewed in prison.

> *I think there should be somewhere that children should be able to go. Some independent person that has authority to get in touch with the mother inside. Even if somebody went round and sort of saw the family and then came down and saw you ... and tried to put your mind at ease ... I mean when I was down there ... not knowing at all, killed me you know. I wasn't getting any information, nothing.*

Support for caregivers

Women re-interviewed in the community were asked how caregivers needs might be better met. Factors relating to the quality of care which children had received whilst their mothers were in prison and ameliorating the added stresses placed on caregivers were to the fore in the suggestions they made. More than two-thirds (70%) of the women thought that caregivers should receive adequate financial assistance to enable them to provide quality care for these children.

> *They got financial assistance while they had my kids, but that didn't even cover what my kids were eating.*

> *The lady who was looking after them ... she was on a benefit with one child and she was getting the benefit for the kids on top ... I think she did find it a little bit hard.*

Approximately three-fifths (61%) of these women felt that caregivers could also benefit from some kind of support system, to enable them to take time out or help them deal with problems.

> *I think they need extra support as well themselves ... not just money, because they have to deal with the children asking, "Where's Mummy?" And you know, "What's going on, why isn't Mummy here any more?"*

The provision of information, in booklet form, for caregivers and families was also seen to be important. It was felt they needed information about their welfare entitlements as caregivers and on prison regulations (e.g. on what they were allowed to bring women) as well as on how to contact prisoners in an emergency.

The fact that these issues were not discussed by women re-interviewed in prison might have been due to the fact that only five of these women had young children living with caregivers and three of them did not have a good relationship with the caregivers. Therefore, issues relating to contact with their children were more important to these women.

Assistance on release from prison

All of the women who were interviewed for the second time after their release were asked if it would have been helpful if there had been someone whose job it was to contact them on their release from prison, to provide support and advice if it was needed. Over 95%[267] of the women were in favour of such an initiative.[268] They suggested, however, that preferably it should involve someone who was familiar with the prison experience e.g. an ex-prisoner.

> *Yeah, because that doesn't happen eh? It would've been nice.*

Over three-quarters (77%) of the women saw a need for some sort of post-release support system for women who had been in prison where they could access practical and financial assistance or advice, and emotional support.

> *I think there's a lot of women that would just really appreciate something like that ... most definitely.*

Although more than half of the women were released from prison under parole conditions, which required them to report periodically to their local Community Corrections Office, women did not always find it easy to seek assistance from, or talk of personal matters with, their probation officer. Visits in such cases were limited to superficial discussions.

It was clear that the women saw a need for a support system that was less formal than that provided by Community Corrections Officers and which they could access as and when required. Two women thought a drop-in centre might facilitate this. Women quite often expressed a need for someone just to talk to; this was so even for those with family/whanau support. They said that if there had been someone they could have contacted for help they would have done so.

> *Yeah, because you know when I got out there was (sic) a lot of things that hit me too - that I started worrying about when I got out, just family things ... and it would be good just to talk to someone.*

> *I never got that kind of support but it would've been nice, yeah, to have received that support ... You need someone that will go in there and just sit down, have a cup of tea or a smoke with them and just ask them how they're feeling and for them to sort of have somebody to talk to - whereas I never got that and I still haven't ...*

---

[267] This figure includes one woman who approved in principle. She did not think she needed such a service but saw that it could be helpful for others.

[268] In fact, none of the women were completely opposed to this suggestion and there was just one woman who was unsure whether it was a good idea or not.

Caregivers' ideas for improvements[269]

The areas of assistance that were considered important by caregivers were identical to those talked about by the mothers themselves. As discussed in the introduction, the fact that not all caregivers talked about a particular issue does not mean that they were against it, rather that these issues were not raised by all of them. Not surprisingly, extra financial support or assistance for the caregivers of children whose mother is in prison was seen to be a priority by almost all (92%) the caregivers interviewed. It was also felt that assistance should be made available to those who wished to take children to visit their mother in prison - e.g. money, transport or accommodation - as very few of the children were living close to where their mother was imprisoned.[270] Some sort of community network or support system for caregivers and for the children of women in prison was advocated by slightly more than two-fifths of carers. A need for more information on prison procedures, such as visiting, and advice or information on their legal and welfare entitlements as caregivers was also seen to been needed by a third of caregivers.[271]

> *You know unless you actually know what to ask for you don't find out. Nobody's there volunteering the information ... it's terrible.*

Many caregivers mentioned the need to be able to take the children to visit their mother more often and were in favour of prisons implementing extended visiting programmes, such as family days, on a more regular basis. Maintaining contact between mother and child/ren and mother and family were seen as important for all concerned and to this end it was suggested by many that families should be able to contact the women in prison by phone if there was an emergency,[272] and that the women themselves should have easier/subsidised/free access to a phone so that they could keep in touch with their children regularly.

> *Even if it was, just say, one phone call allowed a week for three to five minutes ... yeah that'd be quite nice .*

Other suggestions made by individual caregivers which raised issues that had not been talked about by the mothers were: access to legal support for caregivers;[273] easier access to women in prison for those from out of town;[274] and custodial staff should not maintain such a visible presence during visits.

Summary

Despite the fact that interviews with the mothers took place over an extended period of time, the issues that were seen to be in need of redress remained for the most part constant. Women

---

[269]   Percentages are based on the number (11) of caregivers interviewed.

[270]   Three-quarters of caregivers were in favour of this.

[271]   For example, caregivers said they would like to know what they are allowed to bring the women when they come to visit.

[272]   More than two-thirds (67%) of caregivers suggested this.

[273]   This was mentioned by one caregiver who was having problems with the children's father and his family.

[274]   Currently, caregivers have to arrange special visits ahead of time. The caregiver who raised this issue had to arrange a special visit every week as he relied on public transport, which involved having to change trains and travel some distance to reach the prison. There were few trains on weekends when normal visiting times were scheduled.

in prison (and those released from prison) articulated a need for systems and facilities which would enable them to maintain their relationships with their children and their families during the time they were separated. Suggestions included: family oriented visiting programmes; mother and baby units; subsidised (or even free) phone calls; and assistance to families to visit. Caregivers also spoke of the need for regular contact between the imprisoned mothers and their children, reinforcing what the women had already said. These findings are similar to those of a national survey of imprisoned women in the United States (McGowan & Blumenthal, 1978) and a small study of the post-release experiences of Australian women prisoners (Butler, 1994). The researchers noted that most suggestions made by mothers were related to the provision of family-oriented programmes and services and their desire for increased contact with their children. Other studies of women prisoners, both in New Zealand (Young, 1993) and overseas, produced similar findings (Arias-Klein, 1984; Caddle & Crisp, 1997; Farrell, 1996; Hadley, 1981; Task Force on the Female Offender, 1990; Wine, 1992).

The women saw a need for prisons to provide them with comprehensive information on their rights and privileges as prisoners and to provide programmes which would prepare them for release into the community for living with their children again. These recommendations parallel those made by women in prisons overseas (Butler, 1994; McGowan & Blumenthal, 1978; Wine, 1992). The women in this sample agreed with those interviewed by Farrell (1996) that the imprisonment of mothers should be used as a last resort and that, if utilised, women should be placed in prisons close to their children and families. The majority (68%) of the women in Shaw's (1990) study also stressed the importance of being in a prison situated as near to their homes as possible to ameliorate the difficulties faced in coping with long-term separation from their children and families. The concept of mixed prisons did not concern the women I interviewed unduly, provided the sexes were segregated within such facilities. These findings parallel those of a survey of federally imprisoned women in Canada (Shaw et al, 1990) and a comparative study of community prisons for women in England and in the Netherlands (Hayman, 1996). Women held in "shared-site" prisons in both England and the Netherlands said that they did not experience any problems being detained in such a facility. One woman commented: *"Just like outside, you know, in normal life, you go everywhere, you see men"* (Hayman, 1996: p 36). However, some women acknowledged that others might have difficulties with such environments and Hayman cautions that she only talked to a small number of women.

Women re-interviewed in the community said that prison programming did not meet the needs of mothers and should address parenting and relationship issues as well as preparing women for release into the community and for reunification with their families. They also suggested that programmes should enable women to deal with their problems and learn new skills. Prison-based parent support groups were seen by the women as crucial, especially to help long-termers deal with family-related issues. Programmes to specifically prepare mothers for release from prison have also been advocated by imprisoned women in Australia (Farrell, 1996), Canada (Shaw et al, 1990), the United States (McGowan & Blumenthal, 1978) and England (Caddle & Crisp, 1997).

The women said that there was a need for post-release support systems for women who had been in prison where they could access practical and financial assistance or advice, and emotional support. This was seen to be especially important for those women whose only friends were involved in the drug or criminal lifestyle. Overseas research supports these findings (Butler, 1994; Fabb, 1995; Hampton, 1993). Although many of the women in this study had been released from prison on parole, they did not find that their probation officers provided this support for them. Indeed, Wilkinson (1988) noted that women were reluctant to approach their probation officers for post-release assistance. This was also true for the women in this sample, who saw visits to their probation officers as primarily a condition of their release rather than as a method of obtaining assistance with problems. It was suggested by the women that possibly this support role could be filled by ex-prisoners. Similarly, Morris et al (1995) recommended that post-release help or advice could be provided for women by means of resource centres in the community. These centres, they suggest, could be managed by either a voluntary agency or the probation service but could perhaps be staffed by ex-prisoners. The use of ex-prisoner based support networks to provide emotional support and for the dissemination of information is also advocated by Hampton (1993). Overseas researchers have also commented on the lack of post-release support for women prisoners (Farrell, 1996; Hampton, 1993; Johnston, 1995c; Wilkinson, 1988).

There was seen to be a need for more support for caregivers: financial, practical and emotional. This was suggested by both the mothers and the caregivers themselves. Other research has also highlighted the need for supportive services for families who are caring for the children of women in prison, to help them meet the increased demands of providing for these vulnerable children (Gaudin & Sutphen, 1993). The fact that general themes have arisen from the needs expressed by both the mothers and the carers would appear to indicate that related areas of policy and practice need to be addressed by welfare agencies and by the prison system. In the final chapter of this book, I will discuss these issues and make recommendations for changes in policy and practice. These will be based both on my observations and on the suggestions made by the mothers and caregivers that I talked to.

CHAPTER 9   OVERVIEW AND RECOMMENDATIONS

Introduction

The results of this research clearly confirm the findings from overseas studies which indicate the need for programmes and facilities to assist women in prison to maintain relationships with their children during their separation. Furthermore, the provision of assistance and support for the women post-release as well as assistance to their families, as caregivers, is also of importance if the impact of women's imprisonment upon their children is to be minimised as much as possible.

This chapter takes the ideas of the women and the carers for improvements and describes broadly where such initiatives have been implemented in overseas jurisdictions. Where research has been undertaken to assess the efficacy of each initiative this will also be discussed. Finally, after discussing whether or not the Department of Corrections are moving towards paying more heed to the plight of women and mothers in prison, I will make recommendations for changes in policy and practice which will address the needs of imprisoned mothers, children and their substitute caregivers.

Prison based family-centred programmes

As ion New Zealand, imprisoned women overseas usually maintain ties with their children by means of letters, phone calls,[275] and intermittent brief visits. However building on the recognition that the maintenance of a prisoner's family ties increases the likelihood of his/her successful reintegration into the community and decreases the likelihood of re-offending, there have been efforts to encourage the development and strengthening of such bonds for imprisoned parents and their children. In the case of imprisoned mothers there has also been much debate about the maintenance of bonds between mothers and children, particularly relating to the formation of an initial bond between a mother and a baby. Prison based programmes which are aimed at strengthening the mother-child bonds fall into three broad categories: enhanced visiting programmes, child development and/or parenting, and mother and baby units.

Enhanced visiting programmes

The bulk of the literature on family-centred correctional programmes emanates from the USA and Canada,[276] although some limited information is available relating to Australia and England.[277] The range of family-oriented visiting policies described which enable mothers to interact meaningfully with their children outside normal prison visiting hours include: furloughs or home leave and enhanced or extended visiting, parent child/family days,[278] camp

---

[275]   In recognition of the fact that many women rely on telephone calls for contact with their children, two Australian women's prisons (Brisbane Women's and Mulawa) allow mothers a limited number of free phone calls (four and two calls respectively) per week to their children (Farrell, 1996, 1998).

[276]   See Boudoris (1985, 1996), Giles (1995) and Cannings (1990) for surveys of available programmes in USA and Canada.

[277]   For example, Farrell (1996) provides a limited amount of information on Australian and English initiatives which aid imprisoned mothers to maintain family ties.

[278]   These incorporate longer than usual visiting hours and special activities during holiday periods. For example, Bedford Hills Women's Prison in New York State has a system where during the summer

retreats,[279] and overnight visits[280] (Cannings, 1990; Boudoris, 1985, 1996; Farrell, 1996). Programmes such as these not only give imprisoned women a chance to interact constructively and get better acquainted with their children; they help them reaffirm their role as mothers; and they reduce the anxiety of separation for both parent and child.

The majority of programmes are available in mixed or female only prisons. For example, Cannings (1990) noted that while supervised play areas or child care facilities may be found in a number of prisons generally, parent-child centres,[281] particularly those with extended programme options, appear to occur mainly in women's prisons. Visiting programmes where children may stay overnight in the prison,[282] are also more commonly found in women's than in men's prisons (Baunach, 1985; Boudoris, 1985, 1996; Neto & Banier, 1983). Although one mixed prison ran such a programme it was limited to children of imprisoned mothers due to a stated lack of appropriate sleeping quarters in the men's division, each woman had her own room (Cannings, 1990).

Do they work?

In the update of his 1985 survey into family-oriented facilities available in North American and Canadian correctional facilities, James Boudoris (1996) notes that the development and expansion of family support programmes have far outpaced the availability of research information on programme implementation and effectiveness. Formal evaluations of "what works" are few in number and are mainly subjective in nature; few are conducted by independent external evaluators/researchers (Giles, 1995). Cannings (1990) describes in detail the efforts made to assess the outcomes of the earliest programmes including their parent education components. She notes that, although these programmes made extensive

---

school holidays the children of imprisoned women stay with host families in the community for a week during which time they spend each day at the prison's children's centre with their mother (Boudoris, 1985, 1996; Cannings, 1990; Lord, 1995; Roulet, 1993). Other examples are the all day visits for children at Holloway women's prison in North London (Llyod, 1992) and full-day family visits allowed at six women's prisons in three Australian States (Queensland, New South Wales and Victoria) (Farrell, 1996).

[279] Cannings (1990) reported the availability of camp retreats at three women's prisons. Retreats for women and their children were commonly held at local church camps over a weekend

[280] These are usually where children may stay up to 48 hours in the prison with their mother. Examples are two low security women's prisons in Australia - Tarrengower in Victoria and Helena Jones in Queensland - where children may stay for limited periods usually during school holidays. At the former, there is a 'bunkhouse' to accommodate children and their carers which adjoins a farm where children can play with the animals. At the latter, prison facilities exist for older children to stay in their mothers' rooms and outings for both mothers and children can be negotiated with the prison management. In both of these prisons, mothers are expected to contribute to the costs of the visits (i.e. they pay for food and a nominal cost per visitor). Clearly whether or not a woman is reliant on her prison earnings to provide for her personal needs while she is in prison limits her ability to participate in such programmes.

[281] This term is used interchangeably with "children's center" in the literature. In some facilities, the designated space is exclusively for the use of children while parents spend time with their other visitors; in others, it is a place for inmate parents to interact with their children. All variations offer a designated space and adult supervision but the area set aside may range from specified and/or demarcated (e.g. roped off) locations within regular visiting areas, to separate rooms or buildings. Supervisors may be correctional staff, programme personnel, inmates and /or community volunteers. Training of supervisors and planning of activities for the children range from non-existent to comprehensive (Cannings, 1990).

[282] Programmes of this type are described at two women's prisons in Canada and several in the USA e.g. Kentucky Correctional Institution for Women, Nebraska Center for Women and the Arizona Center for Women. See also Footnote 5.

efforts at evaluation, they were focused on clients' and participants' satisfaction with services and neglected to measure objective outcomes such as improved parenting skills or improved relationships between parents and children. She also notes that the collection and analysis of relevant programme data are often thwarted by views that this is a luxury in an environment of limited resources. There is the understandable tendency to sacrifice information gathering in the interest of advancing programme delivery (Cannings, 1990). However, it is important to note that without data gathering and dissemination the principles of best practice cannot be identified, thus running the risk of channelling limited funding into poorly designed and implemented programmes.

There is evidence, however, (from both the United States and England) that extended visiting programmes do promote better relationships between mothers and their children and help to alleviate children's fears about their mothers' wellbeing (Jose-Kampfner, 1991; Lloyd, 1992; Tilbor, 1994) and mothers' fears about their children (Howard League for Penal Reform, 1993a, 1993b). The voiced concerns of prison staff about the safety of children in the prison environment and the possibility of the introduction of illegal contraband, such as drugs, into the prison has generally proved to be unfounded (Stumbo & Little, 1991; Hinson-Smith, 1990). Nevertheless, it is important to note that visitation programmes are rarely used by those prisoners whose families live a long way from the prison (Baunach, 1985; Faith, 1993; Neto & Banier, 1983). This finding is particularly relevant for women in prison where so many are geographically isolated from their children and families. In recognition of the fact that many prisoners (particularly women) are located far from their homes and families, the Prison Service in England set up the Assisted Prison Visited Unit in 1988 to financially assist families who had to travel long distances to visit. Relatives on low incomes can receive assistance for two visits every four weeks (Caddle & Crisp, 1997). However, considering the fact that many women have children living with separate caregivers – some of whom are not relatives – the efficacy of such a scheme is limited at best.

Not all prisoners are in favour of family-oriented programmes. This is generally in the case of extended visitation where some are uncertain whether they want their child/ren to visit in a prison setting (Neto & Banier, 1983), or where they are not parents and describe themselves as "just not into kids" (Baunach, 1985: p 83). Other prisoners feel that family issues are not the concern of the institution (Giles, 1995).

Enhanced visiting programmes clearly aid in the maintenance of family ties and play a part in reducing the separation-related anxieties of mothers and children. However, whether a mother can take advantage of these opportunities to spend quality time with her child/ren is dependent on: firstly, the ability of the caregivers to meet the cost of travelling to the prison and secondly, the nature of the relationship between the mother and the caregiver. Women with children in the care of the State are not likely to be able to participate in such occasions as they often do not know who is caring for their children and there is no funding to enable their children to visit the prison. In addition, few prisons are easily accessible by public transport and tired, cantankerous children may not always get the most benefit from time spent with their mothers.

Child development and/or parenting Programmes

The introduction of a parent-child visitation programme in a prison has often acted as a catalyst in the development of a wide variety of services including parenting programmes (Cannings, 1990). Approximately 97% of the eighty-six institutions responding to Boudoris'

(1996) survey offered classes on parenting and related subjects or were planning such courses. He reported that classes were diverse providing education on such issues as child development, parenting skills, prenatal care, first aid, nutrition, child rearing, job opportunities, child abuse and neglect.[283] Other American and Canadian researchers have noted that such programmes may be staffed in a variety of fashions: for example, by volunteers (Clements, 1993), dedicated programme staff or prison staff (Cannings, 1990).

Most programmes use participation in parenting skills/education courses by prisoners as a condition of being involved in special/extended visiting programmes (Cannings, 1990). Quite often, the rationale behind this is to use supervised visiting as a practical laboratory or evaluation setting, where parents have the opportunity to practise what they have learned while interacting/playing with their children and where programme staff can model desirable behaviours, provide feedback and relate interactions to material covered in the course (Cannings, 1990).[284]

Do they work?

Reactions of participants to parenting programmes are universally positive. Both male and female prisoners state that they benefit from involvement (Baunach, 1985; Caddle, 1991; Hairston, 1989). In fact, some even openly express gratitude for both the knowledge and skills they are learning, and, even more, welcome the opportunities to interact with their children during extended/special visits (Harris, 1996). Needs assessments undertaken with prisoners provide evidence that, where parenting programmes are not freely available prisoners state a need for them (Pollock et al, 1996; Hairston, 1995). Furthermore, programmes (especially those addressing parenting or substance abuse issues) invariably operate at full capacity with long waiting lists which prevent the participation of many (Owen & Bloom, 1995).

Most reports of parenting course evaluations indicate that participants learn the content. That is, those who successfully complete the courses exhibit increased: knowledge of child development and positive parenting techniques (Caddle, 1991; Hairston, 1992; Hairston & Lockett, 1985, 1987; Showers, 1993); empathy with their children (Harris, 1996); knowledge of healthy family relationships (Bayse et al, 1991); and they develop better communication skills (Marsh, 1983). A positive side-effect of this knowledge acquisition is that parenting information learned in prison is often shared with family members and other prisoners (Hairston & Lockett, 1987).

For example, Showers (1993: p 44) found that women prisoners' participation in a parent education programme, which included tactics for managing children's problem behaviour, resulted in 'very significant' gains in their knowledge of child development and non-violent

---

[283] Target populations are also diverse. In some prisons, programmes are for parents only; in others, all inmates are eligible (Cannings, 1990).

[284] Researchers have previously noted ineffective parenting, characterised by harsh or erratic parental discipline, cruel, passive, or neglecting parental attitude, inadequate supervision and rule enforcement and parental conflict, as being risk factors (criminogenic, psychological etc) for young people within such families (see Farrington, 1995; Fergusson et al, 1992, 1994). This situation may be exacerbated in the case of imprisoned parents as relationships between them and their children can be particularly difficult, both during the separation and upon reunification. For example, according to a study by Fritsch & Burkhead (1982), 62% of their sample of imprisoned mothers reported that on their imprisonment their children displayed behavioural problems. The researchers also noted that, on their release from prison, the majority of parents reported problems in disciplining their children.

behaviour management. Positive effects were noted for both African-American and white women. Furthermore, Browne (1989) examined the parent education project of The PROGRAM for Female Offenders.[285] She measured self-evaluation, parenting attitudes and knowledge (including scales for developmental expectations, empathetic awareness of children's needs, and belief in corporal punishment) in a sample of 29 women offenders.[286] Browne found only three areas of significant change among programme participants. Self-esteem was improved, but belief in corporal punishment and inappropriate parental expectations also increased. However, this study has limitations, particularly its relatively small sample size and the lack of a comparison group. In addition, Browne (1989) states that the suggestion that the programme was ineffective may be erroneous as there may be other possible explanations for her findings. For example, it is plausible to hypothesise that programme content or duration may not have met the women's needs.[287] Browne (1989) concludes that changes in behaviour may not be observed until these women have opportunities to practice or model the parenting practices, child management techniques, and problem solving skills they acquired. Johnston (1995b) adds the caveat that the primary effect of such courses may be to inculcate ideal parenting goals without providing either a realistic route to those goals or actual situations in which to apply newly learned parenting skills.

An assessment of a home furlough programme by McCarthy (1980) questions the efficacy of such initiatives as a forum for prisoners to practice skills learned in parenting classes. Women prisoners were found to enjoy their time away from the prison but rarely utilised the home visit as an opportunity to assert parental rights or to practice parenting skills. Nor, indeed, were they encouraged to do so by the caregivers of their children. McCarthy (1980) concludes that under these conditions home visits may serve to maintain the inmate mother's ties with her family and children but are unlikely to aid in her preparation for assumption of parental duties on release.

If we go back to consider the debate on whether or not participation in parent education programmes aid in the prevention of recidivism, there would seem to be limited support for this assertion. Clement (1993) notes that, although there is a lack of evaluation of the effects of parenting programmes, the experience in the state of Virginia has been that women prisoners who go through such programmes have a much lower rate of return to prison than the general population, although she does not provide supporting statistical data. Showers (1993) comes to the same conclusion and provides data to back up her assertion. Statistics from the Ohio Reformatory for Women reveal that the recidivism rate for women who complete the parenting programme is 1.5%, compared to 19% for those who do not. However, Showers (1993) does not provide any information on the criteria on which women were selected for the programme. Nor does she describe the characteristics of the women themselves, or those of the control group. Without such information statistics on re-offending are flawed. It may just be that the women who volunteer to take part in such programmes are

---

[285] The Program Center is an alternative to incarceration at the Allegheny County Jail in Pittsburgh. This is a structured community treatment programme for female offenders. The average length of stay at the facility is six months.

[286] These women had initially been in jail but had either requested or been assigned by judges to the Program Center.

[287] Parenting classes may not have provided sufficient information to help women change their expectations, knowledge and attitudes about parenting. Also, it may be unrealistic to expect change to occur in attitudes and behaviours that have taken a lifetime to acquire, after only 24 weeks - the duration of the programme.

those who are more motivated to modify their behaviour and are therefore less likely to re-offend on their release.

An important point made by several authors is the absence of research determining whether knowledge gains experienced by prisoners completing and parenting education/skills programme are sustained over time (post-release) and whether knowledge about child development and behaviour management changes actual parenting behaviour (Baunach, 1985; Hairston, 1988; 1990; Showers, 1993). Once back in their home environments the gains in parenting knowledge exhibited by the women in the artificial environment of the prison may very possibly be difficult for them to put into practice as they deal with the stresses of day-to-day living.

Mother and baby units

Facilities which allow babies to reside with their mothers in prison are to be found in the United States, England and Australia as well as several European countries.[288] The age limits for the children to be accommodated with their mothers vary from prison to prison, and country to country; however, practice is usually for babies to be able to stay with their mothers until approximately 18 months of age

Four English prisons have Mother and Baby Units providing a total of 66 places for babies to live with their mothers up until a certain age.[289] Admission to one of these units rests partly on the expectation that the mother will continue to look after the baby after release from custody. Prison Service policy is that on reception all eligible women,[290] whether sentenced or remanded, should be advised of the limited number of places in Mother and Baby Units and that it may be possible for them to have their baby with them in prison. Women within such units are also expected to take responsibility for, and to make day to day decisions concerning, their children (Caddle & Crisp, 1997).

By comparison three prisons in the United States and one in Canada have facilities and policies which enable women to keep their babies with them in prison (Boudoris, 1996). The Nebraska Center for Women allows a woman who gives birth whilst in prison,[291] and who is within 18 months of her release date, to live in a special unit with her baby until her release. One condition of this is that the mother must attend special child development/parenting classes. The Bedford Hills women's prison in New York State has had a prison nursery since 1901 and in 1990 another was established at the adjacent Taconic women's prison. These

---

[288] Boudoris (1996) cites West Germany and France as examples of European countries where children, usually infants, may reside with their mothers in prison. Similarly, Holland has provision for women who give birth whilst in custody to keep their babies with them until the age of nine months (Hayman, 1996).

[289] For example, Holloway and New Hall prisons accommodate babies up to the age of nine months and Askham Grange and Styal prison allow children up to the age of 18 months.

[290] That is, those women who have a baby or who are pregnant. Every prison with a Mother and Baby Unit has a multi-disciplinary team responsible for assessing each application from a mother to have her baby with her in the unit. These teams are usually chaired by a prison governor and include a prison officer, a probation officer, a prison medical officer and a liaison social worker. Other specialists previously or currently involved in the care of the mother or child (e.g. health visitor, paediatrician and/or psychiatrist) may also be invited to participate. See Appendix 5 for a list of the criteria on which decisions are based (HM Prison Service, 1995). The final decision about whether a place should be offered rests with the Governor of the prison with the available Mother and Baby Unit place. The mother has no say as to which unit she is placed in (Howard League, 1999a).

[291] The woman must also meet certain criteria.

facilities provide a total of 48 places for women and their children up to the age of one year, and in some cases 18 months, of age.

Some Australia States also make provision for women prisoners to be accommodated with their children (Farrell, 1996, 1998).[292] Examples of these are the Brisbane Women's Prison and the Helena Jones facility. There is no fixed upper age limit for the children. However, in practice, the majority of the children are young, having either been born during the mother's imprisonment or entering the facilities during the early months of infancy. At both Fairlea and Tarrengower women's prisons in Victoria there is provision for mothers to share a room with their child, from infancy to preschool age.

Do they work?

Mother and baby (nursery) units have been the subject of some controversy. Some argue that they should not exist because women with very young children should only be imprisoned as a last resort (Howard League, 1999a; Seear & Player, 1986). Others take the view that, since there will always be a need for some women with babies to be imprisoned, this option is the lesser of two evils; the alternative being the separation of mother and child (Catan, 1988a, 1988b).

Arguments in favour of mother and baby units invariably relate to the development of infant attachment and maternal bonding and there is evidence to show that they are at least effective in this sense (Gabel & Girard, 1995). A study carried out by Grossman and MacDonald (1984) showed that, of 28 women who had babies in the Bedford Hills Nursery Program, the majority (64%) still retained custody of these children two years later.

Moreover, it has been proposed that the impact of the presence of children on prison life is positive, ameliorating some of the more debilitating effects of institutionalization (Baunach, 1985; Hartz-Karp, 1983). In contrast, it could be argued that the restrictive regimes of prison nursery units fail to allow the mothers autonomy to develop their own methods of baby care and, as a consequence, reduce what little confidence some may have in their ability to cope with their babies on release from prison, as well as failing to provide a stimulating environment for the rearing of the infants (Carlen, 1990).

A study commissioned by the Home Office monitored the physical and psychological development of babies between one and 18 months old who accompanied their mothers into Mother and Baby Units at three different English prisons (Catan, 1988a). Their development was compared with that of babies of similar age who were separated from their mothers and cared for by relatives or others while the mother was in prison. Little difference was found between the two groups in babies' development over a short period. However, Catan (1988a) added that there was evidence of a gradual decline over time in the cognitive and locomotor development of infants who stayed in the prison facilities for four or more months. She attributed these effects to the lack of educational toys and playground facilities in the units. This developmental decline was not permanent, however, and was remedied in all the infants within a few months of the mother's release from prison.

---

[292]   Applications are usually made to the Director-General of the individual State Office of Corrections.

In contrast, a recent multi-disciplinary inspection of the Mother and Baby Units in England carried out during 1990[293] found the quality of interaction between the mothers and their babies to be poor. This was attributed to a combination of factors including: the tiredness of the mothers exacerbated by the effects of prison life, the lack of mothering skills in some women and little sense of direction and purpose in relation to childcare within the units (Department of Health, 1992). In addition, in the manner of Catan (1988a), the team noted the lack of attention paid to the infants' developmental needs. Moreover, another multi-disciplinary inspection carried out in 1992 revealed that there was no systematic collection of information on mothers' applications which had been refused (Department of Health, 1994). Therefore, data were not available on how many mothers and babies were, in effect, forcibly separated from each other in any given period.[294]

During 1999, the English Prison Service brought together a working group to conduct a review of principles, policies and procedures on mothers and babies/children in prison. The final report recommended that the overriding principle guiding the provision and allocation of places in mother and baby units should be the best interests of the child (HM Prison Service, 1999). Other recommendations included that the ethos and management of mother and baby units should encourage women to take a greater part in decision making about their children and that each child who is resident in prison should have a care plan. More, mother and baby units should prioritise the provision of crèche facilities organised and run by nursery nurses to enable mothers to work, study or attend programmes aimed at addressing offending related behaviours. The working group also noted the importance of continued monitoring of mother and baby units and commended the three multi-disciplinary inspections conducted by the Department of Health (HM Prison Service, 1999).

Whatever the pros and cons of prison nursery units, it is immediately obvious that the small number of such facilities will create problems in that, if a woman elects to keep her youngest child with her, she may not necessarily be detained at the prison closest to her home. This may lead to difficulties in maintaining contact with other children and family members (Hayman, 1996). Moreover, the allocation of places in mother and baby units is discretionary and the few places available do not adequately cater for all the imprisoned mothers who are eligible to apply, or for all the pregnant women who will give birth whilst in prison and who desire to keep their babies with them in such a unit (Caddle & Crisp, 1997). However, the demand for places is unpredictable. Although at no time has a mother's application been refused due to the unavailability of a place (HM Prison Service, 1999). Caddle and Crisp (1997) noted that women who were potentially eligible were often not given information about the units.

The implementation of mother and baby units does not necessarily ameliorate the plight of women with babies, especially those with more than one child. There are few such units due to limited resources and this results in placing an even greater geographical distance between women and their families. Therefore, obtaining a place for themselves and their babies would inevitably exacerbate the problems women already have in maintaining contact with their

---

[293] This was the first of three inspections of mother and baby units which were commissioned by the Home Secretary in 1989 (Howard League, 1995). The inspection team for each was drawn from the Social Services Inspectorate and the Nursing and Medical Divisions of the Department of Health. The second and third inspections were carried out in 1992 and 1995/96 respectively. These inspections were introduced to provide an independent assessment mechanism and to ensure that the safeguards for babies on the units were comparable to those provided for children in day care in the community.

[294] The Prison Service has subsequently begun to collect these data (Howard League, 1995).

families and other children. Furthermore, a woman may not want to have her baby living with her in a prison environment and may be content with the childcare arrangements she already has in place.

Regional/mixed prisons

The bulk of the information available on mixed prisons relates to the
In recent years, the English Prison Service has developed the concept of "community prisons", where prisoners are held in establishments in, or near to, their home areas as a way of helping them to maintain family ties and community links (Caddle & Crisp, 1997; Hayman, 1996). However, in the case of women, due to the small numbers involved, the most feasible option would be to have completely separate units for women attached to or within male prisons. There are already four English prisons (Durham, Low Newton, Risley and Winchester) where women are held on the same site as men but in separate accommodation. Furthermore, shared-site facilities such as these exist at five Dutch prisons (Hayman, 1996). Co-ed prisons are also to be found in those jurisdictions in the United States and Canada where there are too few women to justify the construction of separate female only prisons (Faith, 1993).

Do they work?

It has been argued that mixed prisons are a step backwards when we consider the campaigning of early prison reformers such as Elizabeth Fry, who campaigned for separate prisons for women (O'Dwyer et al, 1987). Apart from this, there are two main arguments against shared-site or co-ed prisons. First, women in prison have enough problems without adding men to them! Many imprisoned women have been subjected to abuse, both physical and mental, from the men in their lives and ironically, for many, prison presents a safe haven from such abuse (O'Dwyer et al, 1987; Tchaikovsky, 1994). To place them in close proximity to male prisoners will inevitably place unnecessary psychological stress upon them which would outweigh any benefits gained from such an arrangement and could cause more problems for those women with jealous partners on the outside. Second, and on a more practical level, it is argued that given the numbers of male prisoners women will be marginalised and have even fewer resources and access to programming than they would in a female only prison. If resources are to be allocated the men's needs will prevail (Coyle, 1994).

However, despite the damning arguments of academics and researchers, when the women themselves are asked how they feel about shared-site facilities many are not adverse to such an arrangement. For example, Caddle & Crisp (1997) had hypothesised that if mothers could be housed in shared-site facilities closer to their children and families more would be in favour of this. However, they found that there was little difference between mothers (40%) and non-mothers (38%) who opted for women only prisons. Interestingly, they also found that women who had experience of shared-site facilities were no more against the idea of sharing than women elsewhere. In fact the percentage preferring women only prisons was slightly less (26% compared with 36% of women generally). Moreover, when asked whether they were in favour of mixed activities rather than the prevailing separatism, women in shared-site facilities in Holland and England agreed that they would not personally have any difficulties with this. This was even stated by those women who were known to have been victims of violence.(Hayman, 1996).

What has been noted by researchers is that, despite what advocates of mixed prisons term the 'civilizing' effect on male prisoners of the presence of women, the fear of sexual contact between male and female prisoners frequently leads to tighter restrictions and controls being placed on the women (Feinman, 1985). Also the level of security imposed on the whole prison is unnecessary for women and they are disadvantaged by it. In recognition of this last factor the Dutch are moving again towards the housing of women in separate self-contained prisons (Hayman, 1996).

Community based programmes

Community based alternatives to prison which house women and their children are to be found in the United States. Programmes such as Summit House in North Carolina, The Program Center/The Program for Female Offenders in Pennsylvania and ARC House in Wisconsin (Bloom & Steinhart, 1993, Austin et al, 1992). All address life issues for the women. These include parenting, health, addictions, family relationships, employment and social skills and invariably include substance abuse counselling.

In addition, there are residential programmes which cater specifically for the needs of pregnant women prisoners and mothers and babies. For instance, Neil J Houston House provides substance abuse services for pregnant women who are within 18 months of parole from the Massachusetts Correctional Institution (Bloom & Steinhart, 1993, Austin et al, 1992). The programme includes a 10 month residential and 12 month outpatient aftercare component. Women learn parenting skills and prepare for successful transition to their home communities with their babies. By the time they leave the residential pre-release programme, women have secured safe, affordable housing, have obtained employment or enrolled in training, and they have accessed ongoing community treatment services.

The Elizabeth Fry Centre in San Francisco is one example of the several residential pre-release centres in the State of California which cater for low-risk women offenders with children up to the age of 6 years. The California Department of Corrections contracts with public or private agencies to provide these services. Women referred from state prisons and their children participate in a range of services in a homelike and secure residential setting. Services promote economic and emotional independence and include parenting education, substance abuse counselling, budgeting skills and employment workshops (Austin et al, 1992; Bloom & Steinhart, 1993; Immarigeon & Chesney-Lind, 1992).

In contrast to residential programmes, community based day treatment programmes deal with women offenders in a way which enables them to remain at home with their children. One example is Genesis II for Women in Minneapolis. Its core services include individual and group therapy, life-skills training and parenting education. The women's case management plans focus on the family unit in addition to the women's individual needs (Austin et al, 1992). This approach results in issues such as domestic violence, sexual abuse, addictions and relationships being addressed.

Do they work?

Austin and colleagues (1992) noted that the programmes that appeared to be the most effective were highly structured and linked emotional support for the women with the development of their practical skills to prepare them for employment. Co-ordinated supervision measures formed an integral part of these programmes in order to maintain women offenders in the least restrictive settings, but keeping in mind the need for public safety. The provision of aftercare or ongoing assistance to the women was also deemed to be crucial. Without emotional support and practical assistance, many women are not able to maintain the treatment gains achieved in community programmes.

Evidence from the Elizabeth Fry Center in San Francisco indicates that this type of residential pre-release facility for women and their children is effective in easing women back into the community and in combating recidivism (Acorn, 1992). Data collected indicate that 84% of residents stay crime-free after their release.

Community based programmes, either residential or non-residential, for women and their children would appear to make the most sense in terms of dealing with the women's problems in a realistic environment whilst enabling them to maintain their parenting responsibilities and deal with their offending. The State is also saved the cost of financially supporting substitute care for these children. However, it is crucial that these programmes, especially residential ones, are utilised only for mothers who would normally receive a custodial sentence rather than as an alternative for another type of non-custodial sanction, thus exposing women to higher levels of surveillance and control than would otherwise be the case.

Post-release support/assistance

Some countries, for example England, provide aftercare through the probation service if an offender has served a sentence of more than 12 months. The probation service is also available for voluntary post-release assistance for all prisoners. However, this element of probation work tends to be given lower priority and thus few resources than statutorily required supervision (Penal Affairs Consortium, 1997).

Practical post-release assistance for women ex-prisoners such as assistance with obtaining welfare benefits and housing and assisting in family reunification is offered by organisations such as The National Women's Law Centre Women in Prison Project based in Washington DC. Other programmes offer support for women ex-prisoners. For example, Womencare is an advocacy/mentorship programme for mothers released from New York State Prisons. Volunteer mentors provide encouragement and a support system for mothers and children. Womencare contacts mothers in prison 90 days prior to their release, through classes on the programme. As with the Womencare programme, post-release support groups such as Women in Prison and Creative and Supportive Trust in the United Kingdom have often been founded by and are frequently staffed by ex-prisoners (Eaton, 1993). Some of these programmes which provide assistance for ex-prisoners (e.g. Chicago Legal Aid to Mothers Inc) also provide imprisoned mothers with information regarding issues such as parental rights, child custody, legal guardianship, foster care and visitation.

Does it work and is it needed?

Post-release supervision can play a crucial role in reducing re-offending. Two studies carried out by the Home Office in England indicate that the re-offending rates of offenders who had successfully completed a period of parole or supervision were well below those expected even when taking into account previous offending and personal characteristics of offenders (Penal Affairs Consortium, 1997). However, in terms of providing support and assistance specifically to women released, as Morris and her colleagues (1995) noted almost two-fifths of the women in their sample who had been released from prison subject to statutory supervision, stated that they had not found their contact with their probation officer helpful.

These women said that visits to their probation officer consisted of either impersonal routine reporting or being questioned about personal issues rather than being offered practical assistance. Morris et al (1995) also commented that other women ex-prisoners although clearly in need of help, were not aware that they could seek assistance from their local probation office even though they were not subject to statutory supervision. Moreover, women are often reluctant to approach probation officers for post-release assistance (Wilkinson, 1988). Reporting to a probation officer is regarded for most as a condition of release from prison rather than a support system.

Post-release support is crucial to women after they leave prison, especially women who are attempting to regain custody of their children and women who are, or who have been, addicted. It is not unusual for women to face post-release problems such as homelessness, debts and damaged relationships with families, partners and/or children In addition, many women leave prison with the best of intentions, determined not to return to crime, to be perfect mothers and to beat addictions and are often devastated when they are unable to achieve these goals. Such women need access to support and advocacy networks, possibly with the involvement of other ex-prisoners, if they are to successfully care for their children and not get caught up in a cycle of re-offending and addictions. It would seem that the best method for providing women with such support would be the establishment of resource centres in the community, as suggested by Morris et al (1995), under the auspices of the probation service, yet staffed by volunteers or ex-prisoners who have some idea of the problems that the women are facing and in that respect may be able to be more pro-active in the advice offered.

Advocacy, support and services for children of imprisoned women and their caregivers

Pre- or post-release advocacy and support services for children of imprisoned mothers and their caregivers are available in a number of countries including the United States (Bloom & Steinhart, 1993; Poe, 1995; Weilerstein, 1995), the United Kingdom (Light, 1992), Australia (Larman & Aungles, 1993) and France (Ayre, 1996). The information available on these is largely descriptive in nature rather than evaluative. Services provided by such groups include:

- Support groups for children of imprisoned parents and caregivers
- Providing caregivers with information on public benefits and social services
- Providing caregivers with resources (e.g. clothing and food) and respite care
- Mediation services between imprisoned parents and caregivers
- Taking children to visit parents in prison/providing free transport to prisons for families
- Self-help booklets by and for children of imprisoned parents
- Visitors' centres: these have been established in some prisons in the United Kingdom with the help of the voluntary sector, social services and the Probation Service, where families can refresh themselves after their journey to the prison (Caddle & Crisp, 1997). Similar facilities exist at Western Australia's Bandyup Women's Prison (Barnao, 1996) and at Californian State prisons (Boudoris, 1996). Standards of accommodation and services provided vary, but basically these offer a shelter where visitors can rest and relax before a prison visit, this has obviously benefits for staff, prisoners and families (Dunbar, 1992).

166

Conclusion and Recommendations

The results of this study have shown that women prisoners need (and in fact desire) services that empower them as parents and increase their parental decision making capabilities. Thus parent education programmes, services supporting parent-child relationships and continued parent-child contact during incarceration are required along with post-release support for both mothers and children. What has also emerged from this study is that the caregivers of the children of imprisoned women are primarily an under-resourced, unsupported group who are often single female members of the women's own families. Therefore, these findings, along with those discussed from other studies carried out in New Zealand and overseas, highlight the importance of addressing the needs of these groups if we are to prevent the sons and daughters of imprisoned women becoming the casualties of their mothers' offending and imprisonment.

The implications of the lack of specific policies for women in prison, children, and caregivers are that practice tends to be ad hoc - women and children do not have any rights per se. This lack should be viewed against New Zealand's 1993 ratification of the United Nations Convention on the Rights of the Child, in particular against Article 3 (1) (United Nations Children's Fund, 1992) which states:

> *In all actions concerning children, whether undertaken by public or private social welfare institutions, courts of law, administrative authorities or legislative bodies, the best interest of the child shall be a primary consideration.*

Article 9 (3) is also relevant (United Nations Children's Fund, 1992) and states:

> *States Parties shall respect the right of the child who is separated from one or both parents to maintain personal relations and direct contact with both parents on a regular basis, except if it is contrary to the child's best interests.*

These Articles place an obligation on the Department of Corrections and the Department of Social Welfare to develop polices and practices which promote and facilitate contact between women in prison and their children, including those in State care.

However, recommendations which place an onus on the State to aid imprisoned women in maintaining meaningful relationships with there children do not always take into account the fact that the needs of the mother do not always equate with the needs of the child. It is crucial to remember that the best interests of the child/ren are the ultimate goal. Not every separation between mother and child is damaging to the child especially if the substitute care provided yields stability and safety in a caring environment. Where mothers are addicted or have been abusing their children, clear guidelines need to be set in place for any contact between a mother and her children, utilising supervised visits if necessary if the child has expressed a wish to see his/her mother. It is not always easy, or political, to admit that sometimes serving the best interests of the child does not always serve the best interests of the mother, no matter how much she expresses her concern for their welfare.

The way forward

There is some indication that there may be a move within the Department of Corrections towards considering in more depth the needs of women in prison especially those who have children. In May of 1998, a project was set up to investigate the concept of allowing mothers to have their babies with them in prison. However, this is in some way "re-inventing the wheel" as a 1981 Department of Justice paper examined the use of mother and child units in overseas prisons and presented a proposal for the establishment of similar units in New Zealand women's prisons as an alternative to the practice of separating children from their primary caregivers (Saphira, 1981).

Pilot parenting programmes were also initiated in 1997 in three New Zealand prisons, two male and one female,[295] with a view to addressing issues related to the perpetuation of cycles of violence, abuse and offending within families. Ironically though, the Manager of Christchurch Women's Prison[296] indicated that criteria for the programme meant that it was restricted to longer term prisoners whereas she saw the mothers who were serving shorter terms, then re-offending and returning to prison, as being the ones with the greater need. And, indeed, these women make up the majority of the prison muster.

Furthermore, a recent Department of Corrections report to senior management on women offenders in the corrections system (Department of Corrections, 1998) has highlighted the dearth of policies which are specific to the maintenance of bonds between mothers and their children and the importance of this in the light the of specific difficulties faced by imprisoned mothers and of New Zealand's ratification of the United Nations Convention on the Rights of the Child. In addition to the lack of specific policies to ensure the maintenance of mother-child relationships, crowded visiting facilities and the geographical distance between imprisoned mothers and children work against the likelihood that meaningful relationships between mothers and their children can either be developed or maintained. The report states that such factors may influence the successful reunification of mothers and children and refers to the importance of identify the gender specific needs of sentenced female offenders including, addictions, physical and mental health and parental responsibilities.[297]

Recommendations

The following recommendations for policy or operational change are based on areas of concern which were frequently mentioned by women and caregivers, on examinations of practice overseas and on my observations. Inter-agency co-operation between the Department of Corrections and the Department of Social Welfare[298] is essential if the needs of the women, their children and the children's caregivers are to be effectively met.

---

[295] These were Christchurch Women's Prison, Rimutaka Prison and New Plymouth Prison.

[296] Personal communication with Ces Lashlie November 1997.

[297] However, this change of attitude has not extended, so far, to the funding of community based alternatives to prison for women with children. In 1996, The Puriri Foundation for Women and Children presented an application to the Department of Corrections for funding to establish a pilot residential rehabilitation programme for women offenders with their children as an alternative to prison (Williamson, 1996). The envisaged programme was to provide accommodation and services for up to seven mothers and their children provisionally up to the age of 10 years. This application was unsuccessful (Harris-Isles, 1997).

[298] On October 1 1999 the Children, Young Persons and Their Families Agency (CYPFA) became the Department of Child, Youth and Family Services. The remaining Department of Social Welfare business and policy units integrated to form the Ministry of Social Policy. Therefore, at the time of writing it is unclear which of these two Government agencies will have responsibility for the areas of change that I have recommended to be addressed by the Department of Social Welfare.

1. It is recommended that the Department of Corrections provide information and booklets or leaflets for the women and their families about how the prison system works and their entitlements.

2. It is recommended the Department of Corrections and/or the Department of Social Welfare provide resources committed to maintaining family contact.

3. It is recommended that the Department of Corrections implement and fund extended visiting programmes for the women and their children.

4. It is recommended that prisons provide prison visiting facilities for women and their families where the children can play safely and where the women are able to interact with their children, including facilities for changing and feeding babies.

5. It is recommended that the Department of Social Welfare provide regular information to mothers who have children in foster care.

6. It is recommended that the Department of Social Welfare provide mothers who have children in the care of the State with information on their legal rights and obligations regarding their children, including information on how to regain custody of their children, keeping in mind that the best interest of the children are paramount.

7. It is recommended that the prison system acknowledge the unique needs of women in their role as primary caregivers by providing programmes which address the women's needs as mothers and as single parents if applicable and programmes for all women which address issues such as addictions, abuse, cognitive skills, education and employment skills.

8. It is recommended that adequate financial and emotional support be provided for the caregivers and the children of imprisoned women.

9. It is recommended that the Department of Corrections and the voluntary sector in collaboration provide post-release support and advocacy systems for women and their children to ameliorate the effects of the women's imprisonment and to help with family reunification.

10. It is recommended that the Department of Corrections explore the possibility of setting up pilot residential and/or non-residential community-based programmes for women with dependent children, taking care that net-widening does not occur.

11. It is recommended that prison managers us and fund home leave more creatively to enable women to maintain family ties and relationships with their children.

12. It is recommended that research should be carried out into the viability of regional prisons for women and/or shared-site prisons for men and women to enable those women who are in favour of such initiatives to be able to be contained closer to their children and families.

13. It is recommended that research should be carried out to assess more fully the needs of the children of imprisoned women and their caregivers and, in order to facilitate this, that

statistical information on imprisoned mothers and their children should be collected on a routine basis.

14. It is recommended that all programmes and services are culturally appropriate and in particular that the needs of Māori an Pacific Island women and their families/whānau are addressed accordingly.

Finally

None of the findings from this research are new: these issues and concerns have been documented in virtually every study that has been carried on imprisoned mothers and their children both in New Zealand and overseas. Yet, despite the small number of women in prison which would theoretically enable these problems that these women have in maintaining relationships with their children to be addressed in an effective manner, government policies and practices still continue to ignore the needs of imprisoned mothers and their families:[299] providing more places for women in prison will not address the problems of mothers who break the law! Imprisoned women come from our communities and return to live there on their release with their children and families. In terms of human costs to mothers and children, alternatives to imprisonment are by far the most progressive options within existing criminal justice systems. However, some mothers will always need to be imprisoned due to the seriousness of their offending. This population is sufficiently small for well-planned and co-ordinated initiatives to produce meaningful results. In the process, it would be possible to also learn more about how to develop cost-effective and humane methods of reducing society's reliance on imprisonment as a sanction for both mothers and fathers and subsequently how to strengthen at-risk families instead of fragmenting them. In so doing, re-offending may be reduced and intergenerational cycles of abuse, addiction, crime and imprisonment may be broken.

---

[299] Although one of the key areas of the New Zealand Crime Prevention Strategy is to support 'at risk' families, imprisoned women and their children have not been a specific target of this strategy (Crime Prevention Unit, 1994).

REFERENCES

Acorn, L. (1992). California Program Helps Women Offenders Make Smooth Transition. **Corrections Today, June,** 102.

Aikman, H. (1981). **Victims of our Institutions: The Children of Women Prisoners.** Unpublished LLM Research Paper. Wellington: Victoria University of Wellington.

Alliance of Non-Governmental Organizations on Crime Prevention and Criminal Justice. (1987). **Children in Prison with Their Mothers: A Report of the Alliance of NGOs Working Party.** New York: Alliance of Non-Governmental Organizations on Crime Prevention and Criminal Justice.

Arias-Klein, M. (1984). **The Children of Incarcerated Female Offenders: The Forgotten Victims of Crime.** Paper presented at the American Society of Criminology Annual Conference, Cincinnati, November 7-11.

Austin, J., Bloom, B. & Donahue, T. (1992). **Female Offenders in the Community: An Analysis of Innovative Strategies and Programs.** Washington, D.C.: National Institute of Corrections.

Ayre, E. (1996). **They Won't Take No For An Answer: The Relais Enfants-Parents.** Early Childhood Development: Practice and Reflections Number 11. The Hague: Bernard van Leer Foundation.

Bardsley, B. (1987). **Flowers in Hell: An Investigation into Women and Crime.** London: Routledge & Kegan Paul Ltd.

Barnao, A. (1996). **Assisting a Future Generation: The Children of Imprisoned Women.** Unpublished Master of Public Policy Research Paper. Wellington: Victoria University of Wellington.

Barry, E. (1985). Reunification Difficulties for Incarcerated Parents and Their Children.. **Youth Law News, July-August,** 14-16.

Baunach, P.J. (1979). **The Separation of Inmate-Mothers From Their Children.** College Park, Maryland: National Institute of Law Enforcement and Criminal Justice and University of Maryland.

Baunach, P.J. (1984). You Can't Be a Mother and Be in Prison ... Can You? Impacts of the Mother-Child Separation. In B. Price & N. Sokolof (Eds), **The Criminal Justice System and Women (3rd Ed).** New York: Clark Boardman.

Baunach, P.J. (1985). **Mothers in Prison.** New Brunswick: Transaction Books. Bayse, D., Allgood, S. & Van Wyk, P. (1991). Family Life Education: An Effective Tool for Prisoner Rehabilitation. **Family Relations, 40,** 254-257.

Beckerman, A. (1989). Incarcerated Mothers and Their Children in Foster Care:: The Dilemma of Visitation. **Children and Youth Services Review, 11,** 175-183.

Beckerman, A. (1991). Women in Prison: The Conflict Between Confinement and Parental Rights. **Social Justice, 18** (3), 1171-1183.

Beckerman, A. (1994). Mothers in Prison: Meeting the Prerequisite Conditions for Permanency Planning. **Social Work, 39** (1), 9-14.

Bekir, P., McLellan, T., Childress, A. & Gariti, P. (1993). Role Reversals in Families of Substance Misuers: A Transgenerational Phenomenon. **The International Journal of the Addictions, 28** (7), 613-630.

Bloom, B. (1993). Incarcerated Mothers and Their Children: Maintaining Family Ties. In American Correctional Association (Ed), **Female Offenders: Meeting Needs of a Neglected Population.** Laurel, MD: American Correctional Association.

Bloom, B. (1995). Imprisoned Mothers. In K. Gabel & D. Johnston (Eds), **Children of Incarcerated Parents.** New York: Lexington Books.

Bloom, B. & Steinhart, D. (1993). **Why Punish the Children? A Reappraisal of the Children of Incarcerated Mothers in America.** San Francisco: National Council on Crime and Delinquency.

Bonta, J., Pang, B. & Wallace-Carpetta, S. (1995). Predictors of Recidivism Among Incarcerated Female Offenders. **The Prison Journal, 75** (3), 277-294.

Boudouris, J. (1985). **Prisons and Kids.** College Park MD: American Correctional Association.

Boudouris, J. (1996). **Parents in Prison: Addressing the Needs of Families.** College Park MD: American Correctional Association.

Braybrook, B. & O'Neill, R. (1988). **A Census of Prison Inmates.** Wellington: Policy & Research Division, Department of Justice.

Bremner, J.G. (1994). **Infancy (2nd Ed).** Oxford: Basil Blackwell Ltd.

Bresler, L. & Lewis, D. (1983). Black and White Women Prisoners: Differences in Family Ties and Their Programmatic Implications. **The Prison Journal, 62** (2), 116-123.

Brodsky, S.L. (1975). **Families and Friends of Men in Prison: The Uncertain Relationship.** Lexington: D.C. Heath and Company.

Browne, D. (1989). Incarcerated Mothers and Parenting. **Journal of Family Violence, 4** (2), 211-221.

Butler, J. (1994). **Mending the Broken Bond: The Post-Release Experience of Imprisoned Mothers.** Report to the Criminology Research Council. Canberra: Criminology Research Council.

Caddle, D. (1991). **Parenthood Training for Young Offenders: An Evaluation of Courses in Young Offender Institutions.** Research and Planning Unit Paper 63. London: Home Office.

Caddle, D. & Crisp, D. (1997). **Imprisoned Women and Mothers.** Home Office Research Study 162. London: Home Office.

Cannings, K.L. (1990). **Bridging the Gap: Programs and Services to Facilitate Contact Between Inmate Parents and Their Children.** Canada: Ministry of the Solicitor General.

Caramouche, J. & Jones, J. (1989). Her Children, Their Future: Learning to Parent in Federal Prison. **Federal Prison Journal, Fall,** 23-27.

Carlen, P. (1983). **Women's Imprisonment: A Study in Social Control.** London: Routledge & Kegan Paul.

Carlen, P. (1985). **Criminal Women.** Cambridge: Polity Press.

Carlen, P. (1988). Women's Imprisonment: Current Issues. **Prison Service Journal, April,** 7-12.

Carlen, P. (1990). **Alternatives to Women's Imprisonment.** Buckingham: Open University Press.

Catan, L. (1988a). **The Development of Young Children in HMP Mother and Baby Units.** Occasional Papers in the Social Sciences, 1. University of Sussex: School of Social Sciences.

Catan, L. (1988b). The Children of Women Prisoners: What are the Issues? In A. Morris & C. Wilkinson (Eds), **Women and the Penal System: Cropwood Conference Series No. 19.** Cambridge: Institute of Criminology.

Catan, L. (1989). **Young Families of Female Prisoners.** Unpublished Paper. University of Sussex: School of Social Sciences.

Catan, L. (1992). Infants with Mothers in Prison. In R. Shaw (Ed), **Prisoners' Children: What are the Issues?** London: Routledge.

Chesney-Lind, M. (1997). **The Female Offender: Girls, Women and Crime.** Thousand Oaks, California: Sage Publications.

Clark, J. (1995). **The Impact of the Prison Environment on Mothers.** The Prison Journal, 22 (3), 306-329.

Clark, S.R. (1979). Women in Prison. **Auckland University Law Review, 3** (4), 401-428.

Clement, M. (1993). Parenting in Prison: A National Survey of Programs for Incarcerated Women. **Journal of Offender Rehabilitation, 19** (1/2), 89-100.

Cobean, S. & Power, P. (1978). The Role of the Family in the Rehabilitation of the Offender. **International Journal of Offender Therapy and Comparative Criminology, 22** (1), 29-38.

Comack, E. (1996). **Women in Trouble.** Halifax: Fernwood Publishing.

Coyle, A. (1994). **The Prisons We Deserve.** London: Harper Collins.

Crime Prevention Unit. (1994). **The New Zealand Crime Prevention Strategy.** Wellington: Crime Prevention Unit, Department of the Prime Minister and Cabinet.

Crites, L. (1976). Women Offenders: Myth vs. Reality. In L. Crites (Ed), **The Female Offender.** Lexington: D.C Heath and Company.

D'Arcy, M. (1994). **Women in Prison: Women's Explanations of Offending Behaviour and Implications for Policy.** Unpublished Masters Thesis. Victoria: La Trobe University.

Datesman, S. & Cales, G. (1983). "I'm Still the Same Mommy": Maintaining the Mother/Child Relationship in Prison. **The Prison Journal, 63** (2), 142-154.

Deane, H. (1988). **The Social Effects of Imprisonment on Male Prisoners and Their Families.** Study Series 2, Institute of Criminology. Wellington: Victoria University.

Department of Health. (1992). **Inspection of Facilities for Mothers and Babies in Prison: A Multi-Disciplinary Inspection.** London: Department of Health.

Department of Health. (1994). **Inspection of Facilities for Mothers and Babies in Prison: A Multi-Disciplinary Inspection.** London: Department of Health.

Department of Justice. (1988). **Prisons in Change.** Submission of the Department of Justice to the Ministerial Committee of Inquiry into the New Zealand Prison System. Wellington: Department of Justice.

Department of Justice Working Party on Women in Prison. (1990). **Women in Prison.** Report of the Department of Justice Working Party on Women in Prison. Unpublished report. Wellington: Department of Justice.

Department of Corrections. (1998). **Women Offenders in the Corrections System.** Unpublished report. Wellington: Department of Corrections.

Dobash, R.P., Dobash, R.E. & Gutteridge, S. (1986). **The Imprisonment of Women.** Oxford: Basil Blackwell.

Du Bois, B. (1983). Passionate Scholarship: Notes on Values, Knowing and Method in Feminist Social Science. In G. Bowles & R. Duelli Klein (Eds), **Theories of Women's Studies.** London: Routledge and Kegan Paul.

Dunbar, I. (1992). Prison Department Perspective. In R. Light (Ed), **Prisoners' Families: Keeping in Touch.** Bristol: Bristol Centre for Criminal Justice.

Dutton. D. & Hart, S. (1992). Risk Markers for Family Violence in a Federally Incarcerated Population. **International Journal of Law and Psychiatry, 15,** 101-112.

Eaton, M. (1993). **Women after Prison.** Buckingham: Open University Press.

Fabb, B. (1995). Post Release Female Prisoners' Experience. In Women and Imprisonment Group (Eds), **Women and Imprisonment.** Melbourne: Fitzroy Legal Service.

Faith, K. (1993). **Unruly Women: The Politics of Confinement & Resistance.** Vancouver: Press Gang.

Farrell, A. (1996). **A Comparative Policy Study of Incarcerated Mothers and their Young Children in Queensland, New South Wales, Victoria and England.** Unpublished Ph.D Thesis. St Lucia: University of Queensland.

Farrell, A. (1998). Policies for Incarcerated Mothers and their Families in Australian Corrections. **The Australian and New Zealand Journal of Criminology, 31** (2), 101-118.

Farrington, D. (1988). Studying Changes within Individuals: The Causes of Offending. In M. Rutter (Ed), **Studies of Psychosocial Risk: The Power of Longitudinal Data.** Cambridge: Cambridge University Press.

Farrington, D. (1989). The Origins of Crime: The Cambridge Study of Delinquent Development. **Home Office Research and Planning Unit Research Bulletin, 27,** 29-32.

Farrington, D. (1995). The Development of Offending and Antisocial Behaviour from Childhood: Key Findings from the Cambridge Study in Delinquent Development. **Journal of Child Psychology and Psychiatry, 36** (6), 929-964.

Feinman, C. (1985). A Statement on the Issues: United States View. In S. Hatty (Ed), **Women in the Prison System.** Canberra: Australian Institute of Criminology.

Feinman, C. (1986). **Women in the Criminal Justice System (2nd Ed).** New York: Praegar Publishers.

Fergusson, D.M., Horwood L.J. & Lynskey, M. (1992). Family Change, Parental Discord and Early Offending. **Journal of Child Psychology and Psychiatry, 33** (6), 1059-1075.

Fergusson, D.M., Horwood, L.J. & Lynskey, M. (1993). Ethnicity, Social Background and Young Offending: A 14-year Longitudinal Study. **Australian and New Zealand Journal of Criminology, 26,** 155-170.

Fergusson, D.M., Horwood, L.J., & Lynskey, M. (1994). The Childhoods of Multiple Problem Adolescents: A 15-Year Longitudinal Study. **Journal of Child Psychology and Psychiatry, 35** (6), 1123-1140.

Fishman, L.T. (1990). **Women at the Wall: A Study of Prisoners' Wives Doing Time on the Outside.** Albany: State University of New York Press.

Fritsch, T. & Burkhead, J. (1981). Behavioral Reactions of Children to Parental Absence Due to Imprisonment. **Family Relations, 30,** 83-88.

Fuller, L. (1993). Visitors to Women's Prisons in California: An Exploratory Study. **Federal Probation, 57** (4), 41-47.

Gabel, K. & Girard, K. (1995). Long-Term Care Nurseries in Prisons: A Descriptive Study. In K. Gabel & D. Johnston (Eds), **Children of Incarcerated Parents.** New York: Lexington Books.

Gaudin, J. & Sutphen, R. (1993). Foster Care vs. Extended Family Care for Children of Incarcerated Mothers. **Journal of Offender Rehabilitation, 19** (3/4), 129-147.

Gelsthorpe, L. (1990). Feminist Methodologies in Criminology: A New Approach or Old Wine in New Bottles? In L. Gelsthorpe & A. Morris (Eds), **Feminist Perspectives in Criminology.** Buckingham: Open University

Gelsthorpe, L. & Morris, A. (1990). Introduction: Transforming and Transgressing Criminology. In L. Gelsthorpe & A. Morris (Eds), **Feminist Perspectives in Criminology.** Buckingham: Open University Press.

Genders, E. & Player, E. (1988). Women Lifers: Assessing the Experience. In A. Morris & C. Wilkinson (Eds), **Women and the Penal System: Cropwood Conference Series No. 19.** Cambridge: Institute of Criminology.

Gibbs, C. (1971). The Effect of the Imprisonment of Women Upon Their Children. **British Journal of Criminology, 11** (2), 113-130.

Gilbert, N. (Ed) (1993). **Researching Social Life.** London: Sage Publications.

Giles, S. (1995). **Services in Prisons and Jails that Help Incarcerated Mothers with Parenting Needs.** Unpublished Thesis presented in partial fulfillment of the Requirements for the Degree of Master of Science. Bloomsburg, Pennsylvania: Bloomsburg University.

Glaser, B. & Strauss, A. (1967). **The Discovery of Grounded Theory: Strategies for Qualitative Research.** Chicago: Aldine.

Grace, S. (1990). The Needs of Women Prisoners. **Home Office Research and Planning Unit Research Bulletin, 29,** 42-46.

Gray, T., Mays, G. & Stohr, M. (1995). Inmate Needs and Programming in Exclusively Women's Jails. **The Prison Journal, 75** (2), 186-202.

Gray Matter Research Ltd. (1996). **Male Inmates Who Were Their Children's Primary Care Givers.** Wellington: Ministry of Justice.

Grossman, J. & MacDonald, D. (1984). **Bedford Hills Nursery Mothers Follow-up.** Unpublished report. Albany, New York: Division of Program Planning, Research and Evaluation, State of New York Department of Correctional Services.

Hadley, J. (1981). **Georgia Women Prison Inmates and Their Families.** Unpublished Masters Thesis. Atlanta: Emory University.

Hairston, C. (1988). Family Ties During Imprisonment: Do They Influence Future Criminal Activity? **Federal Probation, 52** (1), 48-52.

Hairston, C. (1989). Men in Prison: Family Characteristics and Parenting Views. **Journal of Offender Counseling, Services & Rehabilitation, 14** (1), 23-30.

Hairston, C. (1990). Parenting Programs in Prison: A Program Development and Research Agenda. In The **State of Corrections: Proceedings ACA Annual Conferences.** Laurel MD: American Correctional Association.

Hairston, C. (1991a). Family Ties During Imprisonment: Important to Whom and For What? **Journal of Sociology and Social Welfare, 18** (1), 87-104.

Hairston, C. (1991b). Mothers in Jail: Parent-Child Separation and Jail Visitation. **Affilia, 6** (2), 9-27.

Hairston, C. (1995). Fathers in Prison. In K. Gabel & D. Johnston (Eds), **Children of Incarcerated Parents.** New York: Lexington Books.

Hairston, C. & Lockett, P. (1987). Parents in Prison: New Directions for Social Services. **Social Work, 32** (2), 162-164.

Hall, G. (1987). **Hall on Sentencing in New Zealand**. Wellington: Butterworths.

Hampton, B. (1993). **Prisons and Women.** Kensington: New South Wales University Press.

Harris, Z. (1996). How to Help the Children When Mothers go to Jail. **American Jails, Jan/Feb,** 31-36.

Harris-Isles, R. (1997). Puriri Foundation Gets the Run-around. **Movement for Alternatives to Prison Newsletter, 69** (September), 2.

Hartz-Karp, J. (1983). The Impact of Infants in Prison on Institutional Life: A Study of the Mother/Infant Prison Programme in Western Australia. **Australian and New Zealand Journal of Criminology, 16,** 172-188.

Hatty, S. (1983). The Impact of Infants in Prison on Institutional Life: A study of the Mother/Infant Prison Programme in Western Australia. **Australian & New Zealand Journal of Criminology, 16** (3), 172-188.

Hayman, S. (1996). **Community Prisons for Women: A Comparative Study of Practice in England and the Netherlands.** London: Prison Reform Trust.
Heidensohn, F. (1996). **Women & Crime (2nd Ed).** London: Macmillan Press Ltd.

Henriques, Z. (1982). **Imprisoned Mothers and Their Children.** Washington: University Press of America, Inc.

Henriques, Z. (1996). Imprisoned Mothers and Their Children: Separation-Reunion Syndrome Dual Impact. **Women & Criminal Justice, 8** (1), 77-95.

Henry, B., Moffitt, T., Robins, L., Earls, L. & Silva, P. (1993). Early Family Predictors of Child and Adolescent Antisocial Behaviour: Who are the Mothers of Delinquents? **Criminal Behaviour and Mental Health, 3,** 97-118.

Hesketh, B. & Young, W. (1994). **Sentencing and Plea Making.** New Zealand Law Society Seminar: July 1994. Wellington: Continuing Legal Education Department of the New Zealand Law Society.

Hinson-Smith, V. (1990). Where the Boys Aren't: Women behind bars present an entirely different world from that of male prisons. **Police, October,** 50-54.

HM Prison Service. (1995). **Admission to Mother and Baby Units.** London: HM Prison Service.

HM Prison Service. (1999). **Report of a Review of Principles, Policies and Procedures on Mothers and Babies/Children in Prison.** London: HM Prison Service.

Holt, N. & Miller, D. (1972). **Explorations in Inmate-Family Relationships.** Sacramento, CA: California Department of Corrections.

Howard League for Penal Reform. (1993a). **The Voice of a Child: The impact on children of their mother's imprisonment.** London: Howard League for Penal Reform.

Howard League for Penal Reform. (1993b). **Families Matter.** London: Howard League for Penal Reform.

Howard League for Penal Reform. (1995). **Prison Mother and Baby Units.** London: Howard League for Penal Reform.

Howard League for Penal Reform. (1999a). **In the Best Interests of Babies?** The Howard League Submission to the Prison Service Review of Mother and Babies in Prison. London: Howard League for Penal Reform.

Howard League for Penal Reform. (1999b). **Life in the Shadows: Women Lifers.** London: Howard League for Penal Reform.

Howser, J. & MacDonald, D. (1982). Maintaining Family Ties. **Corrections Today, 44** (4), 96-98.

Hungerford, G. P. (1993). **The Children of Inmate Mothers: An Exploratory Study of Children, Caretakers and Inmate Mothers in Ohio.** Unpublished PhD Thesis. Ohio: Ohio State University.

Immarigeon, R. & Chesney-Lind, M. (1992). **Women's Prisons: Overcrowded and Overused.** San Francisco: NCCD.

Johnston, D. (1995a). Child Custody Issues of Women Prisoners: A Preliminary Report From the CHICAS Project. **The Prison Journal, 75** (2), 222-239.

Johnston, D. (1995b). Intervention. In K. Gabel & D. Johnston (Eds), **Children of Incarcerated Parents.** New York: Lexington Books.

Johnston, D. (1995c). Jailed Mothers. In K. Gabel & D. Johnston (Eds), **Children of Incarcerated Parents.** New York: Lexington Books.

Johnston, D. (1995d). Parent-Child Visitation in the Jail or Prison. In K. Gabel & D. Johnston (Eds), **Children of Incarcerated Parents.** New York: Lexington Books.

Johnston, D. (1995e). The Care and Placement of Prisoners' Children. In K. Gabel & D. Johnston (Eds), **Children of Incarcerated Parents.** New York: Lexington Books.

Johnston, D. & Gabel, K. (1995). Incarcerated Parents. In K. Gabel & D. Johnston (Eds), **Children of Incarcerated Parents.** New York: Lexington Books.

Jose-Kampfner, C. (1991). Michigan Program Makes Children's Visits Meaningful. **Corrections Today, August,** 132-34.

Kampfner, C.J. (1995). Post-Traumatic Stress Reactions in Children of Imprisoned Mothers. In K. Gabel & D. Johnston (Eds), **Children of Incarcerated Parents.** New York: Lexington Books.

Kemper, K. & Rivara, F. (1993). Parents in Jail. **Pediatrics, 92** (2), 261-264.

Koban, L. (1983). Parents in Prison: A Comparative Analysis of the Effects of Incarceration on the Families of Men and Women. **Research in Law, Deviance and Social Control, 5,** 171-183.

Kolman, A. (1983). Support and Control Patterns of Inmate Mothers: A Pilot Study. **The Prison Journal, 63** (2), 155-166.

Kiser, G. (1991). Female Inmates and Their Families. **Federal Probation, September,** 56-63.

Kumpfer, K. (1995). **Impact of Maternal Characteristics and Parenting Processes on Children of Drug Abusers.** Paper presented at the American Society of Criminology Annual Conference, Boston, November 15.

Larman, G. & Aungles, A. (1993). Children of Prisoners and Their Outside Carers: The Invisible Population. In Eastel, P. & McKillop, S. (Eds), **AIC Conference Proceedings No. 16: Women and the Law.** Canberra: Australian Institute of Criminology.

Lash, B. (1996). **Census of Prison Inmates 1995.** Wellington: The Ministry of Justice.

Lash, B. (1998). **Census of Prison Inmates 1997.** Wellington: The Ministry of Justice

LeFlore, L. & Holston, M. (1989). Perceived Importance of Parenting Behaviors as Reported by Inmate Mothers: An Exploratory Study. **Journal of Offender Counseling, Services & Rehabilitation, 14** (1), 5-21.

Leibrich, J. (1993). **Straight to the Point: Angles on Giving Up Crime**. Dunedin: University of Otago Press, in association with the Department of Justice, Wellington.

Light, R. (1992). Introduction. In R. Light (Ed), **Prisoners' Families: Keeping in Touch**. Bristol: Bristol Centre for Criminal Justice.

Light, R. (1993). Why Support Prisoners' Family-tie Groups? **The Howard Journal, 32**, 322-329.

Lloyd, E. (1992). A Blueprint for the Future. **Children Visiting Holloway Prison**. London: Save the Children Fund.

Lord, E. (1995). A Prison Superintendent's Perspective on Women in Prison. **The Prison Journal, 75** (2), 257-269.

McCarthy, B. (1980). Inmate Mothers: The Problems of Separation and Reintegration. **Journal of Offender Counselling Services & Rehabilitation, 4** (3), 199-212.

McGowan, B. & Blumenthal, K. (1976). Children of Women Prisoners: A Forgotten Minority. In L. Crites (Ed), **The Female Offender**. Lexington: D.C Heath and Company.

McGowan, B. & Blumenthal, K. (1978). **Why Punish the Children? A Study of Children of Women Prisoners**. Hackensack: National Council on Crime and Delinquency.

Mandaraka-Sheppard, A. (1986). **The Dynamics of Aggression in Women's Prisons in England.** Aldershot: Gower Publishing Company Limited.

May, T. (1993). **Social Research: Issues, Methods and Process**. Buckingham: Open University Press.

Marsh, R. (1983). Services for Families: A Model Project to Provide Services for Families of Prisoners. **International Journal of Offender Therapy and Comparative Criminology, 27** (2), 156-162.

Maxwell, G. & Robertson, J. (1995). **Child Offenders: A Report to the Minister of Justice, Police and Social Welfare**. Wellington: Office of the Commissioner for Children.

Michigan Women's Commission. (1993). **Unheard Voices: A Report on Women in Michigan County Jails**. Lansing, Michigan: Michigan Women's Commission.

Minichiello, V., Aroni, R., Timewell, E. & Alexander, L. (1990). In-Depth Interviewing: Researching People. Melbourne: Longman Cheshire Pty Limited.

Ministerial Committee of Inquiry into the Prisons System. (1989). **Prison Review: Te Ara Hou: The New Way.** Wellington: The Crown.

Moon, D., Thompson, R. & Bennett, R. (1993). Patterns of Substance Use Among Women in Prison. In B. Fletcher, L. Shaver & D. Moon (Eds), **Women Prisoners: A Forgotten Population.** Westport: Praegar.

Morris, A. (1988). Women in the Criminal Justice System. **Prison Service Journal, April,** 2-5.

Morris, A., Wilkinson, C., Tisi, A., Woodrow, J. & Rocklyn, A. (1995). **Managing The Needs of Female Prisoners.** London: Home Office.

Morris, P. (1965). **Prisoners and Their Families.** London: George Allen & Unwin Ltd.

Moses, M. (1995). **Keeping Incarcerated Mothers and Their Daughters Together: Girl Scouts Beyond Bars.** Washington DC: National Institute of Justice.

National Policy Committee on Resettlement. (1993). **Opening the Doors: Women Leaving Prison.** London: Nacro.

Neto, V. & Bainer, L. (1983). Mother and Wife Locked Up: A Day With the Family. **The Prison Journal, 63** (2), 124-141.

O'Connor, B. (1996). Creating Choices - Or Just Softening the Blow? The Contradictions of Reform: Inmate Mothers and Their Children. **Current Issues in Criminal Justice, 8** (2), 144-151.

O'Dwyer, J., Wilson, J. & Carlen, P. (1987). Women's Imprisonment in England, Wales and Scotland: Recurring Issues. In P. Carlen & A. Worrall (Eds), **Gender, Crime and Justice.** Milton Keynes: Open University Press.

O'Neill, R. (1989). **The Experience of Imprisonment for Women: A New Zealand Study.** Unpublished Masters Thesis. Hamilton: University of Waikato.

Owen, B. & Bloom, B. (1995a). **Profiling the Needs of California's Female Prisoners: A Needs Assessment.** Washington D.C.: U.S. Department of Justice, National Institute of Corrections.

Owen, B. & Bloom, B. (1995b). Profiling Women Prisoners: Findings from National Surveys and a California Sample. **The Prison Journal, 75** (2), 165-185.

Padel, U. & Stevenson, P. (1988). **Insiders: Women's Experience of Prison.** London: Virago Press.

Penal Affairs Consortium. (1997). **Reducing Reoffending.** London: Penal Affairs Consortium.

Phillips, C. (1992). Women in Prison. In C. Briar, R. Munford and M. Nash (Eds), **Superwoman Where Are You?.** Palmerston North: The Dunmore Press.

Poe, L. (1995). A Program for Grandparent Caregivers. In K. Gabel & D. Johnston (Eds), **Children of Incarcerated Parents.** New York: Lexington Books.

Pollock-Byrne, J. (1990). **Women, Prison, & Crime.** California: Brooks/Cole Publishing Company.

Pollock, J., Williams, S., Sartor, D. & Schroeder, S. (1996). **Women in Prison: A Texas Profile.** Report submitted to Texas Department of Criminal Justice. San Marcos, Texas: Southwest Texas State University.

Prison Reform Trust. (1996). **Women in Prison: Recent Trends and Developments.** London: Prison Reform Trust.

Public Prisons Service. (1998). **Policy and Procedures Manual.** Wellington: Public Prisons Service, Department of Corrections.

Rapoport, R. & Rapoport, R. (1976). **Dual Career Families Re-examined.** London: Martin Robertson.

Rickford, F. (1991). Scarred for Life. **Social Work Today, November, 12.**

Richards, M. (1992). The Separation of Children and Parents: some issues and problems. In R. Shaw (Ed), **Prisoners' Children: What are the issues?** London: Routledge.

Roberts, H. (Ed) (1981). **Doing Feminist Research.** London: Routledge and Kegan Paul.

Rosenkrantz, L. & Joshua, V. (1982). Children of Incarcerated Parents: A Hidden Population. **Children Today, 11,** 2-6.

Roulet, E. (1993). New York's Prison Nursery/Children's Center. **Corrections Compendium, December,** 4-6.

Rutter, M. (1972). **Maternal Deprivation Reassessed.** Harmondsworth: Penguin Books Ltd.

Rutter, M. (1981). **Maternal Deprivation Reassessed (2nd Ed).** Harmondsworth: Penguin Books.

Sack, W., Seidler, J. & Thomas, S. (1976). The Children of Imprisoned Parents: A Psychosocial Exploration. **American Journal of Orthopsychiatry, 46** (4), 618-628.

Saphira, M. (1981). Children in Prison: **An Alternative to Incarceration with Separation.** Unpublished report. Wellington: Department of Justice.

Seear, N. & Player, E. (1986). **Women in the Penal System.** London: Howard League for Penal Reform.

Shaw, M., Rodgers, K., Blanchette, J., Hattem, T., Seto Thomas, L. & Tamarack, L. (1990). **Survey of Federally Sentenced Women.** Final Report. Ottawa, Canada: Solicitor General, Canada.

Shaw, R. (1987). **Children of Imprisoned Fathers.** London: Hodder and Stoughton.

Showers, J. (1993). Assessing and Remedying Parenting Knowledge Among Women Inmates. **Journal of Offender Rehabilitation, 20** (1/2), 35-46.

Simon, R. (1975). **Women and Crime.** Lexington, Massachusetts: D.C. Heath & Company.

Smith, B., Elstein, S. Laszlo, A., Akimoto, M., Ayres, M. & Smith, J. (1994). **Children on Hold: Improving the Response to Children whose Parents are Arrested and Incarcerated.** Report submitted to The Children's Bureau. Washington, DC: Administration on Children, Youth and Families US Department of Health and Human Services.

Sommers, E. (1995). **Voices from Within: Women Who Have Broken the Law.** Toronto: University of Toronto Press.

Spier, P. (1997). **Conviction and Sentencing of Offenders in New Zealand: 1987 to 1996.** Wellington: Ministry of Justice.

Spier, P. (1998). **Conviction and Sentencing of Offenders in New Zealand: 1988 to 1997.** Wellington: Ministry of Justice.

Spier, P. & Norris, M. (1993). **Conviction and Sentencing of Offenders in New Zealand: 1983 to 1992.** Wellington: Ministry of Justice.

Stanley, L. & Wise, S. (1983). **Breaking Out: Feminist Consciousness and Feminist Research.** London: Routledge & Kegan Paul.

Stanley, L. & Wise, S. (1993) **Breaking Out Again: Feminist Ontology and Epistemology.** London: Routledge.

Stanton, A. (1980). **When Mothers Go to Jail.** Lexington: D.C. Heath and Company.

Statistics New Zealand. (1996). **New Zealand Now: Crime.** Wellington: Statistics New Zealand.

Statistics New Zealand. (1997). **1996 Census of Population and Dwellings: Ethnic Groups.** Wellington: Statistics New Zealand.

Stumbo, N. & Little, S. (1991). Campground Offers Relaxed Setting for Children's Visitation Program. **Corrections Today, August,** 136-144.

Sugar, F. & Fox, L. (1990). **Survey of Federally Sentenced Aboriginal Women in the Community.** Ottawa, Canada: Native Women's Association of Canada.

Task Force on the Female Offender. (1990). **The Female Offender: What Does the Future Hold?** Laurel, MD: American Correctional Association.

Tchaikovsky, C. (1991). Mixed Prisons: Misogynistic and Misguided. **Prison Report, 16,** 12-13.

Tilbor, K. (1993). **Prisoners as Parents: Building Parenting Skills on the Inside.** Portland, Maine: Edmund S. Muskie Institute of Public Affairs, University of Southern Maine.

Toner, P. (1984). Women Prisoners in Victoria. In S. Hatty (Ed), **Women in the Prison System.** Conference Proceedings 12-14 June. Canberra: Australian Institute of Criminology.

United Nations Children's Fund. (1992). **The United Nations Convention on the Rights of the Child (NZ Ed).** Wellington: Office of the Commissioner for Children.

Weilerstein, R. (1995). The Prison MATCH Program. In K. Gabel & D. Johnston (Eds), **Children of Incarcerated Parents.** New York: Lexington Books.

White, S. (1989). Mothers in Custody and the Punishment of Children. **Probation Journal,** 106-109.

Whitney, L. (1992). **Substance Abuse: A Survey of the Treatment Needs of Prison Inmates.** Wellington: Policy and Research Division, Department of Justice.

Widom, C. (1989). Child Abuse, Neglect, and Violent Criminal Behavior. **Criminology, 27** (2), 251-271.

Wilkinson, C. (1988). The Post-Release Experience of Female Prisoners. In A. Morris & C. Wilkinson (Eds), **Women and the Penal System: Cropwood Conference Series No. 19.** Cambridge: Institute of Criminology.

Williamson, P. (1996). The Puriri Foundation: A New Penal Alternative for Female Offenders and Their Children. **Auckland University Law Review, 8** (1), 143-162.

Wine, S. (1992). **A Motherhood Issue: The Impact of Criminal Justice System Involvement on Women and Their Children.** Canada: Ministry of the Solicitor General.

Woodrow, J. (1992a). Mothers Inside, Children Outside: what happens to the dependent children of female inmates? In R. Shaw (Ed), **Prisoners Children: What are the Issues?** London: Routledge.

Woodrow, J. (1992b). **Mothers in Prison: The Problem of Dependent Children.** Unpublished Ph.D. Thesis. Cambridge: University of Cambridge.

Young, P. (1993). **Mothers in Prison: The Experience of Being Separated From Their Children.** Unpublished Masters Thesis. Hamilton: Te Whare Wananga o Waikato.

Zalba, S. (1964). **Women Prisoners and Their Families.** Los Angeles: Delmar Publishing Company.

APPENDIX 1

**Performance Standards - Public Prisons Service National Policy: Family/Whanau
Relationship Maintenance & Enhancement (A.02, Public Prisons Service, 1998)**

a   When developing a case management plan family/whanau are identified in discussion
with the inmate.

b   Inmates are assisted to assess their needs in terms of maintaining and enhancing
family/whanau relationships.

c   Input from family/whanau and significant others is sought for the development of their
case management plan.

d   Family/whanau visits are encouraged and supported.

e   Culturally appropriate family/whanau visiting areas are provided which reflect the needs
of visitors including, access for differently-abled persons, access to toilets, storage for
visitors' belongings, adequate seating, a play area for child/parent interaction and a
suitable area to feed and change babies/toddlers.

f   Additional family/whanau visits are provided in special circumstances where negotiated
between the family/whanau member and the Regional/General Manager or their
representative.

g   Rooms where visitors may be observed but not heard are provided where appropriate.

h   Access to a telephone is available to maintain family/whanau relationships through the
inmates' telephone system..

i   As far as practicable and with consideration to an inmate's security rating inmates are
placed in institutions nearest to their families/whanau support.

j   Communication via incoming phone calls from family/whanau to inmates is relayed
promptly and sensitively.

k   Encouragement and support is given to inmate participation in family group conferences
run by the New Zealand Care and Protection Service.

l   Recognition and support for the cultural differences of all inmates and their families in
respect of food, language and observed celebrations is provided without compromising
safety and security.

m   On the recommendation of the case management team temporary releases and escorted
outings to assist with the maintenance and enhancement of family/whanau relationships
are considered.

n   Where practicable, and with the agreement of the inmate, programme provider and case
management team, family/whanau participate in programmes and services.

o   Where supported by case management teams, special visits are arranged between
inmates in different prisons who are members of the same family/whanau.

p   Family days are provided to enhance family/whanau relationships.

q   As far as practicable and with consideration to an inmate's security rating importance of
an inmate maintaining his or her family/whanau relationship is considered before a
transfer to another prison away from the family/whanau is arranged.

r   All inmates due to be transferred are given the opportunity to contact a family/whanau
member before transfer, and where practicable a visit is arranged.

APPENDIX 2

**Performance Standards - Public Prisons Service National Policy: Women Inmates
(D.15, Public Prisons Service, 1998)**

a   Women inmates are housed in separate secure facilities and managed independently of male inmates.

b   The design and furnishing of new women's prisons takes into account the particular needs of women which are identified through consultation with a wide group of people, including women inmates, prison staff and community members.

c   The gender and cultural mix of staff working in women's prisons reflects the need to provide positive role models of both genders for women inmates.

d   Nurses appointed to women's prisons have training specific to women's health issues.

e   Contraceptive services are provided on request from the inmate for temporary releases and/or final release.

f   All women inmates are offered access to, and support in participating in, programmes aimed at reducing or stopping smoking.

g   Programmes offered to women inmates take into account issues impacting on women in New Zealand society which are identified through consultation with women's groups.

h   Employment, industry and vocational training provided to women inmates reflects the variety of skills which will be of value to them upon their return to the community including surviving without paid employment.

i   The prevalence of sexual abuse histories among women inmates is taken into account in both the development of programmes for them and day to day management.

j   Access for women inmates to information and counselling on abuse related issues is facilitated by prison management.

k   Women inmates have access to the national cervical screening programme.

l   Women inmates over the age of 50 years and/or identified as being at risk, have access to a mammography screening programme.

APPENDIX 3

Performance Standards - Public Prisons Service National Policy: Pregnant Inmates and Women Inmates with Babies (D.16, Public Prisons Service, 1998).

a   All pregnant inmates including those on remand are given a full ante natal assessment by a registered midwife or medical officer with obstetric qualifications as soon as is practical or immediately if there is any concern for the welfare of the inmate or her unborn child.

b   Each women's prison has 24 hour access to, and liaison with, appropriate hospital and community based obstetric and midwifery services.

c   Pregnant women who are known substance users are referred to a medical practitioner with obstetric qualifications with 24 hours of reception.

d   Pregnant inmates on a recognised substance abuse maintenance/withdrawal programme are continued on that programme without interruption, under the direction of the Medical Practitioner.

e   An individual health care plan is developed and incorporated into health care management, and the inmate's case management plan.

f   Pregnant women are placed in accommodation which provides unrestricted access to a flush toilet and hand washing facilities.

g   Where necessary the prison provides suitable maternity attire for the inmate.

h   Where necessary the prison provides a layette for a child born to a female inmate including a nightgown, a singlet, a pair of booties, a helmet/bonnet, two nappies, safety pins where necessary, and a shawl or blanket.

i   Pregnant inmates are offered information and counselling by qualified counsellors regarding pregnancy including advice on adoption, guardianship, early and temporary release community support options and/or termination in order to make an informed choice.

j   Counselling and support is available to women who are separated from their babies, or who have a miscarriage or a termination of pregnancy, or whose baby dies.

k   Maternity care is selected in consultation with the inmate and managed in a way that takes into account the particular risks and needs of the individual pregnant woman including cultural and ethnic values.

l   Where practicable, there is continuity of obstetric staff and/or midwife providing care before, during and after birth.

m   Pregnant women are encouraged to participate in ante natal and parenting programmes at the appropriate time and supported through their case management plan.

n   A sterile pack for the emergency delivery of a baby, which includes instructions on use, is available in the health centre.

o   Women are enabled to meet their religious, cultural and spiritual customs and beliefs relating to pregnancy, birthing and babies without compromising safety and security.

p   Women assessed as being at risk of, or having, post natal depression are monitored by staff and given appropriate support and counselling.

q   Pregnant women are provided with suitable employment and recreation which ensures a balance of rest and participation in constructive activities.

r   Women who are pregnant or have babies up to the age of six months are offered access to, and support in participating in, programmes aimed at reducing or stopping smoking.

s   If she wishes a pregnant inmate is supported to involve her partner/support person(s) in decisions and activities relating to the pregnancy, and have them attend the birth.

t   Women inmates with babies up to six months of age are offered information on release options which may be applicable to them and their right to seek legal advice on such options.

u   Visits between an inmate and her baby will be permitted daily for the purpose of creating a bond between them.

v   To facilitate bonding, suitable safe, secure and private facilities and equipment are available for an inmate with a baby up to six months of age to breast feed her baby each day and to express milk for the baby as necessary.

w   The necessity for bonding between the inmate, the inmate's partner, and their child, whanau or the nominated care giver is recognised and facilitated.

x   Any woman inmate who gives birth to a child, or who on admission has a child less than six months old, may keep the child with her until proper provision is made for the child's care.

y   Following a miscarriage within 20 weeks of gestation or an unscheduled birth, the inmate is advised of the options appropriate to the inmate's cultural or religious beliefs for the disposal of the foetus or after birth.

z   The inmate is assisted to select the most appropriate option for the disposal of the foetus or afterbirth and every facility is made available to the inmate to achieve the option chosen in a sensitive, culturally appropriate and hygienically safe manner.

aa   Where after 20 weeks of gestation an inmate delivers a dead baby within the prison every opportunity is made for the inmate to obtain appropriate funeral services and the support and advice of her family/whanau.

ab   Gender specific professional support is provided on request and where practicable.

APPENDIX 4

New Zealand Police - General Instruction section Arrest and Custody - Caregivers of Children: Ref: PG 89/463

A201 Sole Garegiver of a Young Child

(1)   The arrest of a person who is the sole caregiver of a child shall be undertaken only where there is no practical alternative and suitable temporary arrangements can be made for the care of the child.

(2)   Where there is no suitable substitute caregiver available to care for a child, an appropriate community organisation should be requested to assist. Suitable community organisations include:

- Prisoners Aid and Rehabilitation Society;
- Prison Fellowship;
- Māori Women's Welfare League;
- Maatua Whangai;
- Iwi Authorities;
- Church Groups;
- Cultural Authorities;
- Child and Family Support Service.

(3)   Where a sole caregiver of a young child is arrested, the circumstances are to be immediately referred to a commissioned officer. In appropriate cases, an early court hearing should be arranged or the caregiver is to be granted police bail.

A202 Detention of Breast Feeding Mothers

(1)   The necessity to detain a breast feeding mother in police custody shall be reviewed by a commissioned officer as soon as practicable.

(2)   Breast feeding mothers shall not be lodged in police cells without the approval of a commissioned officer.

(3)   Without good reason, such as the safety of the child or medical grounds, a suckling infant should not be separated from its mother. Where such a separation is on medical grounds, a certificate from a doctor shall be obtained.

(4)   Where detention is essential, alternative arrangements should be made to enable the mother and child to be together in a place that is more suitable than a police cell. If necessary, the assistance of the Department of Social Welfare or other welfare agency should be sought for this purpose.

A203 Administration

(1)   The O/C : Operations Support Group, Police National Headquarters, has administrative responsibility for the General Instruction section entitled "Arrest and Custody - Caregivers of Children".

APPENDIX 5

HM PRISON SERVICE CRITERIA FOR ADMISSION TO A MOTHER AND BABY UNIT (MBU)

- the age of the child
- the expectation that the child will be cared for by the mother after her release from prison
- the mother's ability to care for the child is not *seriously impaired* by physical or mental disorder (this usually excludes forms of post natal depression)
- there are no concerns held by social services or a court order governing custody of the baby
- the suitability of alternative care arrangements
- the mother has not shown herself to be disruptive during her time in custody and therefore not likely to disrupt the regime on the unit
- the mother must express a willingness to be responsible for her child in line with the regime
- the mother consents to her baby being searched from time to time
- the mother is aware that the MBU is drug free, with random testing. A positive drug result could lead to removal from the MBU
- whether admission to the MBU is in the best interests of the child (HM Prison Service, 1995).

VDM publishing house ltd.

Scientific Publishing House

offers

free of charge publication

of current academic research papers, Bachelor´s Theses, Master's Theses, Dissertations or Scientific Monographs

If you have written a thesis which satisfies high content as well as formal demands, and you are interested in a remune- rated publication of your work, please send an e-mail with some initial information about yourself and your work to *info@vdm-publishing-house.com.*

Our editorial office will get in touch with you shortly.

VDM Publishing House Ltd.
Meldrum Court 17.
Beau Bassin
Mauritius
www.vdm-publishing-house.com